About Island Press

Since 1984, the nonprofit Island Press has been stimulating, shaping, and communicating the ideas that are essential for solving environmental problems worldwide. With more than 800 titles in print and some 40 new releases each year, we are the nation's leading publisher on environmental issues. We identify innovative thinkers and emerging trends in the environmental field. We work with world-renowned experts and authors to develop cross-disciplinary solutions to environmental challenges.

Island Press designs and implements coordinated book publication campaigns in order to communicate our critical messages in print, in person, and online using the latest technologies, programs, and the media. Our goal: to reach targeted audiences—scientists, policymakers, environmental advocates, the media, and concerned citizens—who can and will take action to protect the plants and animals that enrich our world, the ecosystems we need to survive, the water we drink, and the air we breathe.

Island Press gratefully acknowledges the support of its work by the Agua Fund, Inc., The Margaret A. Cargill Foundation, Betsy and Jesse Fink Foundation, The William and Flora Hewlett Foundation, The Kresge Foundation, The Forrest and Frances Lattner Foundation, The Andrew W. Mellon Foundation, The Curtis and Edith Munson Foundation, The Overbrook Foundation, The David and Lucile Packard Foundation, The Summit Foundation, Trust for Architectural Easements, The Winslow Foundation, and other generous donors.

Urban Ecological Design

A Process for Regenerative Places

Urban Ecological Design

A Process for Regenerative Places

Danilo Palazzo and Frederick Steiner

ISLANDPRESS

Washington | Covelo | London

Library of Congress Cataloging-in-Publication Data

Palazzo, Danilo, 1962–
Urban ecological design : a process for regenerative places / Danilo Palazzo and Frederick Steiner.
p. cm.
Includes bibliographical references and index.
ISBN-13: 978-1-59726-828-8 (cloth : alk. paper)
ISBN-10: 1-59726-828-3 (cloth : alk. paper)
ISBN-13: 978-1-59726-829-5 (pbk. : alk. paper)
ISBN-10: 1-59726-829-1 (pbk. : alk. paper) 1. City planning. 2. Urban ecology (Sociology)
3. Ecological landscape design. I. Steiner, Frederick R. II. Title.
HT166.P325 2011
307.1'216--dc23 2011026666

Typesetting by Blue Heron Typesetters, Inc.
Printed on recycled, acid-free paper

Manufactured in the United States of America
10 9 8 7 6 5 4 3 2 1

Keywords: architecture; Battery Park City; campus master plan; charrette; Chisinau, Moldova; ecological planning; Envision Central Texas; GIS; Ground Zero; High Point, Seattle; historical data; land use planning; landscape architecture; Leamouth Peninsula, London; Mantua, Italy; McHarg, Ian; Nolli maps; Orsenigo, Italy; Piano, Renzo; public participation; Regional Plan Association; Reykjavík, Iceland; Riverside, Illinois; transects; transportation; United Kingdom; University of Cincinnati; University of Texas at Austin, urban design; urban morphology

For

Michela, Giulia, and Anil

and

Anna, Halina, and Andrew

Contents

Illustrations

Figures

Tables

Plates

Acknowledgments

This is the second edition of a book initially written by Danilo Palazzo in Italian and English for primarily a European audience. He invited Frederick Steiner to join him in order to merge the competencies in urban design with those in urban ecology and ecological planning and to collaborate in writing this more North American focused edition. Although the focus has shifted, Palazzo and Steiner have continued to use both European and North American examples, with more emphasis on the latter.

We appreciate the valuable comments and suggestions made by Anita Stauber Ahmadi, Angela Colucci, Barbara Faga, Talia McCray, Steven Moore, Sandi Rosenbloom, and Ming Zhang. At Milan Polytechnic and the University of Texas at Austin, Ms. Ahmadi, Ramon Busi, Ms. Colucci, Sara Hammerschmidt, Christine Marcin, Pamela Peters, Michael Shane, and Jane Futrell Winslow provided important support in producing this book. The Henry M. Rockwell Chair in Architecture assisted in the production of the book as did a University of Texas at Austin Subvention Grant awarded by President William C. Powers.

Danielle Pieranunzi of the Lady Bird Johnson Wildflower Center and former Wildflower Center research director Steve Windhager were especially helpful with the Sustainable Sites Initiative information. Ms. Pieranunzi provided significant assistance with the High Point and Point Fraser case studies, and Sally Campbell supplied images from Envision Central Texas, as did Matthew Dugan and Gregory Claxton for the City of Austin. We appreciate Susannah Drake's contribution of the cover, which her firm, dlandstudio, produced with ARO.

We value the efforts of Island Press through the publication process, most notably our editor, Heather Boyer. We also appreciate others on the Island Press team, including Courtney Lix, Angela Osborn, and Sharis Simonian.

Finally, though it may be unusual, Danilo Palazzo would like to thank his coauthor and friend, Frederick Steiner, for believing in this project and for sharing his knowledge with warm enthusiasm from the very beginning.

Foreword

In 1998, I was fortunate to work on Parc Diagonal Mar in Barcelona in collaboration with the talented team of Enric Miralles and Benedetta Tagliabue and their EMBT design firm. To promote the design and satisfy the Barcelona town planners, Jay Wyper, our client with Hines, asked us to put together a sustainability plan, nothing too complicated, but still the very first such plan prepared for a public park in Spain. We needed experts. Circumstance was on our side as Dr. Fritz Steiner was residing in Europe for the summer as a winner of the Rome Prize. Together we created a concise sustainability plan for the park. We included discussion on landscape, water, soils, hardscape, signs, and site interpretation. I say collaborated—basically, Fritz told us what and how to approach the design, and we did exactly as he said.

The Parc Diagonal Mar Sustainability Plan was translated into Catalan and became the pattern and guide for design and construction of the twenty-acre park, the centerpiece of redevelopment on a former brownfield and train shed storage lot. To say the plan was helpful is a huge understatement. When the same town planners later value-engineered the natural lake into a concrete-lined pool, eliminating the edge landscape and treating the water with chemicals so as to kill anything indigenous in terms of water plants or inhabitants, we referred them right back to the sustainability plan. It clearly stated that no chemicals were to be used on the land, water, or site. And it was the law. Today, the park and lake are vibrant—an award-winning example of sustainable design. This is a very brief description of what in reality involved years of sweat and negotiation to design

Parc Diagonal Mar, Barcelona. Design by EMBT Architects and EDAW (now AECOM). (Photograph by Dixi Carrillo. Courtesy AECOM.)

and build. It exemplifies, as do many of the case studies in this book, the positive outcome of building with the ecology of place.

This is a fairly new concept. Over the last half century, few designers knew much about or devoted much attention to sustainability or ecology. Though seen as extensions of our art or aspects of design that might be nice to have, neither were considered to be entirely necessary to the success of the design, and certainly not as essential. Look around and note how much contrived landscape we have built since the 1950s. We have turned the artificial into a commonplace, putting lawn in deserts and water features in drought-prone areas. Those artificial designs are now considered failures and rather comical in their attempt to engage people. How many of those fountains have turned into planters? While the theory of sustainable design existed and was a portion of practice, retrofitting anything was out of vogue. Our culture was to simply start over on a green field site.

Fortunately, this didn't happen everywhere. Amid the building excesses, we can also look back on the most successful projects, those that have stood the test of time, and understand that their success was primarily due to incorporating natural processes just as McHarg and Eckbo espoused. Those historic buildings that remained untouched were fortunately passed over by the hyperdevelopment of the 1980s and 1990s. Those areas the developers did not take down are now emerging as charming historic districts in our cities—San Francisco, Miami, Charlotte, to name a few—that we visit in droves today.

Once, we did little for ecological systems other than design a retention pond or two when the local government required. Those ponds were often shunted off to the far end of the site and treated like the remnants that we thought they were. Retention ponds that still remain tell the story: stark, small, and out-of-place water bodies that rarely relate to the site's design. What we used to refer to as swamps we drained and filled. Now they are prized watersheds, and we treat them gently, not touching or moving a single tree or endangered plant. Now even the LEED (Leadership in Energy and Environmental Design) rating system, established in 1998, protects ecological sites. Yes, this is the same rating system that only a few years ago gave us exactly one valuable point for preserving and retrofitting an entire historic building—proving everything old can be new again.

If we could not justify our designs by preserving, maintaining, or beautifying anything, then what was design but an ego-enhancing exercise? Above all, designers want justification; they want to be right. If design is merely egocentric, how do we justify the damage we have accomplished on all those green fields?

I began to think about this in the last ten years, in the midst of highly emotional community meetings that resulted in attendees who came to learn about the project leaving openly and loudly despising the designers. Anyone who has had the experience of presenting design ideas to the public knows that such circumstances would compel even the most confident practitioner to search for a theory to guide their way out of the morass. Many times as designers, we did not have the design justification to protect ourselves. It looked good, we thought it suited the site, and we drew it up and tried to sell it. We did not know how to look for justification in the elements of the land itself.

After thirty-five years of practice, my late-in-life quest for a PhD has convinced me that a necessary and vibrant continuum exists between practice and theory. Designers are problem solvers. Our practice demands an assessment of the problem with detailed analysis, an array of alternatives, an agreed-upon solution, and a design for implementation. Theory offers process, knowledge, encouragement, and solace to designers; it conveys that there is depth of thought to the design issues that we encounter and that within that framework can be found ideas and solutions. Theory illustrates how design has evolved over time with its forms and materials, both the successes and the failures. Theorists do an immense service for practitioners as they quantify, qualify, record, organize, and interpret outcomes and ideas—necessary functions that, unfortunately, most practitioners are not inclined to accomplish because of time and cost. While practice has led the way with design, practice needs theory. Theory sets the goal and supports the issues that practitioners encounter.

Experienced practitioners recognize that design is not a linear process; what can go wrong will go wrong. The projects we have today and those in our future are more complicated than the projects of the past fifty years. Work will include more brownfield sites. We will be retrofitting and redeveloping our cities, researching emergent landscapes, turning land that was once densely populated and is now vacant into agricultural uses, and turning abandoned industrial plants into new city centers. Those easy-to-design green field sites, the new projects in wide open spaces that so many of us worked on for years—and thought would never end—are finished. Let's face it: our new reality is that the easy projects are done; only the tough projects are left. It doesn't matter if it is a park in Boston over the Big Dig, a park in Barcelona where rail cars were the former inhabitants, one in downtown Atlanta where auto body shops once stood, or parks and boulevards surrounded by new high-rise towers in Miami or Milan: when the going gets tough, as designers we need precedent.

Urban design and landscape ecology are combined in this authoritative book compiled by the experts. Steiner and Palazzo have long been respected as leaders in ecology, sustainability, and the design of cities. As theorists, they have the unique advantage of anticipating the latest trends based on their preeminent knowledge and historical base. As practitioners, they have the experience to know realistically what works and what doesn't.

I think back now and wish I had focused on what Sitte, Olmsted, Hillier, Habermas, Jacobs, or Lynch would have suggested to make our work easier. We are, however, fortunate to have Steiner and Palazzo's insight into design going forward. Schools are offering more urban design degrees. The University of Miami recently transformed its master's of suburb and town design into a master of urban design. Georgia Tech has done the same. Students are flocking to the degree programs that in the past they may have overlooked. They are headed to China, India, and Africa to espouse ecological solutions to urban design. Palazzo and Steiner, as theorists, identify the changes and offer real-time case studies of how to accomplish our end game: sustainable and ecologically sound design.

And not a moment too soon. The United Nations estimates that half of the world's people now live in cities. By 2050, fully 66 percent of us will be living in urban areas. We have a lot of planning to do. What will this twenty-first-century new development look like and how it will perform? We need to decide now. This great recession, while significantly slowing down our current work, has given us the opportunity and the time to consider our design mistakes and contemplate our future. For many of us, we currently have the luxury of time to spend considering how we make our design and our world better.

Urban designers do the outside. We are fortunate to concentrate on everything we see around us, all that is not enclosed and hidden by ceilings and walls. Design for us includes the facade, street, pathway, landscape, vista, and view—everything we see and a lot we do not, if we consider the entire infrastructure on which we base our design. We've managed to stake our claim to design outdoor environments. It's a powerful and heady vocation we have chosen.

Barbara Faga, Executive Vice President, AECOM
October 2010
Atlanta, Georgia

Introduction

> Urban design is far from a clear area of activity. . . . Despite its frequent appearance in educational and professional literature, urban design is still an ambiguous term.
>
> —*Ali Madanipour*

The term *urban design* was coined in the mid-1950s (Lang 2005) almost coincidentally with its first appearance in academic curricula in the United States. In spite of its long history and the recent increased attention to the field of urban design, the term still lacks clarity. We consider some current definitions and then clearly define our use of the term in this book, which is primarily intended for students, design and planning practitioners, developers, and public officials.

Francis Tibbalds, former president of the Royal Town Planning Institute, collected many perspectives on urban design. Some are undoubtedly questionable and vague, such as "lots of architecture," "space between buildings," "a thoughtful municipal policy," "everything that you can see out of the window," and "the coming together of business, government, planning, and architectural design." Other definitions are more detailed and plausible. Urban design is "the interface between architecture, town planning, and related professions," "the three dimensional design of places for people . . . and their subsequent care and management," "the creative activity by which the form and character of the urban environment at the local scale may be devised," and "the physical design of public realm" (Tibbalds 1988, quoted in Madanipour 1996, 93).

Prominent protagonists of urban design practice and theory have proposed additional interpretations. The insightful American scholar Kevin Lynch described urban design as dealing with "the form of possible urban environments" (Lynch and Hack 1984). In *Good City Form*, Lynch (1984, 290) offered a broader definition of urban design as "the art of creating possibilities for the use, management, and form of settlements or their significant parts." Clarence Stein, an American architect and planner who with Lewis Mumford and others in 1923 cofounded the Regional Planning Association of America, described urban design (which Mumford called "city design") as "the art of relating STRUCTURES to one another and to their NATURAL SETTING to serve contemporary living" (as quoted in Strong 1990, 141). Matthew Carmona and Steve Tiesdell define urban design "as *the process* of making *better* places for people *than would otherwise be produced*" (emphasis in original). They also added that "urban design is the process by which the urban environment comes about" (2007, 1).

British architectural theorist Jeremy Till has argued that "time, and not space, should be seen as the primary context in which architecture is conceived" (2009, 95). If not primary, then the consideration of time should be put on at least equal footing with space production in urban design.

Ali Madanipour, an urban design theorist and scholar at the University of Newcastle in England, proposes a synthesis that, with greater emphasis on ecological issues, may be the most appropriate for this book. He writes: "Urban design . . . can be defined as the multidisciplinary activity of shaping and managing urban environments, interested in both the process of this shaping and the space it helps shape. Combining technical, social and expressive concerns, urban designers use both visual and verbal means of communication, and engage in all scales of the urban socio-spatial continuum. Urban design is part of the process of the production of space" (1996, 117).

In this book, we advocate for including urban ecology as a basic component of urban design. Urban ecology is more than understanding nature in cities. It also involves the integration of humans and nonhumans in functional and just ecosystems. Understanding urban ecology can help address the twin challenge of climate change and energy use. Buildings contribute approximately 40 percent of the greenhouse gases produced in the United States and consume around 40 percent of the energy (up to around half when building construction is considered). Transportation systems add another 27 percent of the greenhouse gas production and energy consumption in the United States. Urban design can help to shape urban form in a way that requires less travel and the consumption of fewer resources. Natural elements can be added to help mitigate climate change and energy consumption. For instance, trees can both store carbon and shade buildings. Urban ecological research also increases our understanding of animal life in urban areas. Fragmentation of their habitat is a threat to many species. Urban designers can address this problem by providing connections between green spaces in cities. Some urban ecologists also address vulnerable people in vulnerable places.

Many parallels exist between urban design and urban ecology. Both involve making connections and revealing relationships. Both are fields of studies searching for an integrated approach between different disciplines. Urban ecology requires an integrated framework "to assess the environmental implications of alternative urban development patterns and to develop policies to manage urban areas in the face of change" (Alberti 2008, xi). Urban design is an integrated discipline traditionally allied with architecture and city planning (Lang 1994). Ecology involves the reciprocal relationships between all organisms with other organisms as well as with their environments. Marina Alberti (2008, xiv) argues that "cities are hybrid phenomena—driven simultaneously by human and biophysical processes." These phenomena cannot be fully understood just by studying their component parts separately; "thus urban ecology is the study of the ways that human and ecological systems evolve together in urbanizing regions" (Alberti 2008, xiv). Urban ecological studies synthesize the diverse dimensions of urban systems dynamics into a coherent theoretical framework. Within these frameworks, urban planners and designers can find tools and aids for analysis, policies, and designs. At a minimum, the designer may begin with the precautionary principle—that is, first do no harm to the environment or to people. Furthermore, the designer helps to mitigate human impacts on the natural environment. More ambitiously, the designer helps to orchestrate our relationships with other living organisms in the built environment.

The concept of viewing cities as ecosystems has been around for some time. It received a considerable boost when the U.S. National Science Foundation (NSF) established two urban Long Term Ecological Research (LTER) projects in 1997. Previously, LTERs had been located in remote places with little human settlement, from islands off the coast of Maine to the interiors of Alaska. Ecologists lobbied the NSF for two urban LTERs, which were established in Baltimore (http://www.beslter.org) and Phoenix (http://caplter.asu.edu). These two LTERs have stimulated urban ecological research in other regions, notably in the Puget Sound of the Pacific Northwest (Alberti 2008).

This research is yielding helpful knowledge for urban design. For instance, we now know that black asphalt contributes to the urban heat island in Phoenix (Baker et al. 2002). Black asphalt does not reflect light, and it stores heat. In addition, asphalt covering parking lots and streets contributes to rapid stormwater runoff and water quality degradation. The Phoenix LTER has helped to quantify the urban heat island over the metropolitan region. Researchers have also demonstrated how urban nighttime temperatures remain higher than surrounding natural deserts. Urban design offers many potential solutions, such as using light-colored asphalt, porous paving, and increased plantings.

Many jurisdictions require projects to undergo environmental impact analysis. Urban ecology can help inform such analysis. In addition, it can help designers understand the ecological footprints of their projects (see Chapter 3, Knowledge).

Ian McHarg was one of a long line of theorists and practitioners to ponder the relationships between the city and nature. He wrote: "In the history of human development, man has long been puny in the face of the overwhelmingly powerful nature" (McHarg 1963, quoted in Steiner 2006, 2). According to McHarg's protégée Anne Whiston Spirn (2011), an American landscape architecture and urban design scholar, the practice and theory of the ecology of human settlements—which she calls "ecological urbanism"—has a long history and deep traditions in Western culture. Hippocrates, in the fourth century B.C., described the effects of airs, waters, and places on the health of individuals. Vitruvius (first century B.C.) described, in chapter 5 of the first book of *On Architecture*, the ideal site of a city according to its orientation toward the sun, the winds, and the climate. Leon Battista Alberti (in his *Ten Books on Architecture*, published at the end of the fifteenth century) emphasized the disasters suffered by cities that disregarded the power of nature.

This long lineage of thinkers about the interdependence between human settlements and nature crossed the Atlantic from Europe to North America and back during the past several centuries. For instance, George Perkins Marsh, the author of *Man and Nature* (1864), proposed the role of human beings as "co-worker with nature in the reconstruction of the damaged fabric" (35). Along with Marsh's influential work, pioneer landscape architects, such as Frederick Law Olmsted and Charles Eliot, as well as regional planning theorists, such as Scottish biologist Patrick Geddes and Americans Lewis Mumford and Benton MacKaye, promoted and advocated the importance of understanding nature and the complex interaction it plays with human beings and their artifacts, whatever they are: buildings, landscapes, cities, or regions (Luccarelli 1995; Palazzo 1997; Ndubisi 2002).

McHarg's seminal work *Design with Nature* (1969) deepened the ways to understand the role of nature in the creations of people—that is, buildings, places, and spaces. To recognize the relationship between nature and design, McHarg asserted, it is "essential to understand the city as a form, derived in the first instance from geological and biological evolution, existing as a sum of natural processes and adapted by man. It is also necessary to perceive the historical development of the city as a sequence of cultural adaptations reflected in the plan of the city and its constituent buildings both individually and in groups . . . this enquiry is described as an investigation into the given form—the natural identity—and the made form—the created city" (175). The ecological view, according to McHarg, "shows the way for the man who would be the enzyme of the biosphere—its steward, enhancing the creative fit of man-environment, realizing man's design with nature" (197).

In *Good City Form*, Kevin Lynch (1984) described the city as part of nature, aiming to build a theory that considered the role of nature from a scientific point of view more than from a romantic one. Like McHarg, Lynch was especially influenced by Lewis Mumford. Together, they are part of the increasing environmental attention relating to design and planning that has flourished in the United States since the 1950s (see Udall 1988; Sale 1993; Shabecoff 2003; Barnett 2011; Calthorpe 2011; Beatley 2011).

In 1993, the Congress for the New Urbanism was established to "examine a redefinition of the urban 'project' that de-emphasizes the singular act of design and favors, instead, a more nuanced and complex series of related practices that affect urban structure" (Dutton 2000, 29). In subsequent years, this goal has been enriched by many books and projects (see Katz 1994; Hall and Porterfield 2001; Talen 2005, Grant 2006). Peter Calthorpe, a founder of the Congress for the New Urbanism, is an innovative thinker who pinpointed the need to combine the design of neighborhoods, suburbs, and city parts with ecology. In the preface of *The Next American Metropolis* (1993, 9), he wrote: "This book is about the ecology of communities. Not about the ecology of natural systems—but about how the ecological principles of diversity, interdependence, scale, and decentralization can play a role in our concept of suburb, city, and region."

The Congress for the New Urbanism adopted the *Canons of Sustainable Architecture and Urbanism* (Congress for the New Urbanism 2009), a companion to the *Charter of the New Urbanism* (Congress for the New Urbanism 1996). These canons provide the guiding principles for urban planning and design, emphasizing such topics as climate change, rural-to-urban relationships, the need to reduce carbon, and the production of greenhouse gases.

An integrated view encompassing both ecology and design in urbanism requires that the specific parts of the city be understood as forming a complex urban system. In 1979, urban planner Kenneth Schneider emphasized the need for planners and urbanists to deal with the entire system, not just with their parts: "Despite the statements of many urbanists and environmentalists to the contrary, the central issues are not clean air and water, endangered species or environments, more money for housing and urban renewal, or even energy; certainly not in their separate capacities. These issues are relevant, perhaps necessary, but not basic. What is basic is the structure of the human environment, the city. Building a good city—a framework for all separate things to work harmoniously—is essential in order to alleviate each of the separate issues of development" (Schneider 2003, 34).

An interest in urban challenges, such as growth, environmental quality, and livability, has grown since the 1990s and into the twenty-first century. Ecocities (Register 2006), sustainable cities (Jenks and Jones 2010), and green cities (Low et al. 2005) are a few of the catchphrases used to combine "traditional" city design and an attention to landscapes and ecological systems. Jonathan Barnett (2011) provides an eloquent synthesis of different approaches, noting: "In green city design the landscape is dominant and the building arrangements are informal and in accord with the land contours, while in systems city design building and open space become integral parts of the same system, which means that open space may be included within a structural framework that also encloses buildings" (204–5). We seek to combine ecological planning heritage with that of city design.

How might urban design become more ecological? Because ecology addresses how all organisms, including humans, interact with one another and the built and natural environments, the design of our urban habitat may be our most fundamental ecological activity. Increasingly, we seek to create urban places that are at a minimum sustainable and we hope even regenerative. Peter Calthorpe (2011) makes an especially compelling case for urbanism in this age of climate change. Both Calthorpe and Timothy Beatley (2011) illustrate how more compact and dense urban places can be more livable as well as better for the planet. The Museum of Modern Art's Rising Currents exhibit illustrated how design could be used to mitigate the impact of climate change on New York City's waterfront (Nordenson, Seavitt, and Yarinsky 2010). In making design more ecological, such urban design concerns as density, walkability, and connectivity become important to consider. In *Green Metropolis*, David Owen (2009) makes a strong case for New York City as a sustainability leader. For instance, he notes that 82 percent of Manhattan residents travel to work by public transit, bicycle, or foot. Because New York is densely populated, green spaces have been designed for refuge, relaxation, and recreation, from large parks like Central and Prospect to the pocket parks that blanket the city to such innovative new parks as the popular High Line Project in Lower Manhattan.

Drawing on the works of the many individuals and theories noted above, we have gathered the following seven characteristics of urban design:

- It is interested in the process of making the built form and in managing what has been made.
- It applies to different scales and different parts of urban environments.
- It combines elements of urban planning and the design of buildings and of open and green spaces.
- It involves different skills and technical knowledge for analysis, design, representation, and communication.
- It favors an objective-rational process ("scientific") rather than an expressive-subjective one ("artistic") but does not reject the latter.
- It responds to the ecology of the region and of the urban environment in the project location.
- It is flexible enough to adjust to changes through time.

The Development of Urban Design as a Discipline

Urban design, despite its many applications and the interest in the literature, is usually not considered a discipline in and of itself. Rather, it is more often viewed as an interface between different disciplines. Urban design in continental Europe tends to be recognized as a specialty in both architecture and urban planning, which compete for urban design tasks and activities. The application of urban design can range from the *architectural project* that considers a broader physical context to a *town planning project* where a land-use regulation tends to extend its authority on the shapes, volumes, distances, and functions of the urban environment. In the United Kingdom, urban design has been recognized by the central and local governments and is incorporated into the planning remit (Carmona et al. 2003). In other countries, including the United States and Canada, conflicts occur when other disciplines, such as landscape architecture or landscape urbanism (Waldheim 2006; Almy 2007), compete with architecture and planning, and perhaps with urban design itself, for the task of shaping urban environments. In fact, many leading landscape architecture studios in North America present themselves as urban designers also, and many urban design practitioners have an academic background in landscape architecture. A positive role of urban design is to transcend the boundaries of the disciplines from which it draws.

Urban design is both holistic and interdisciplinary. Those disciplines include architecture, community and regional planning, engineering, landscape architecture, ecology, law, real estate development, economics, and other specialties that feed its capacity to analyze, understand, interpret, and intervene in the city. Knowledge from these disciplines is used to create public spaces that should benefit both people and their environments.

The development of urban design as a separate technical specialty is relatively recent even in Anglo-American countries, although it has swiftly developed within the academy, where it "is offered at dozens of universities either as a degree program or as an area of concentration within architecture and city planning" (Barnett 1982, 12–13; Palazzo 2011). It is also being recognized more and more by professional associations and organizations (including the Urban Design Group, and Resources for Urban Design Information, better known as RUDI, in the United Kingdom, and the Forum for Urban Design, the Van Alen Institute, and the Institute for Urban Design in the United States).

The first academic program in urban design in the United States was the University of Pennsylvania's Civic Design Program, started in 1956 (Barnett 1982; Strong 1990), followed by Harvard's Urban Design Program in 1960. Thereafter, the term was imported into the United Kingdom, even though it was in Great Britain where the first course and the first department of "Civic Design" began in 1909, at Liverpool University. The Liverpool University course was intended to train planners (Cullingworth and Nadin 2006), with a "close connotation to municipal government and functions such as 'Civic Centre'" (Cuthbert 2007, 180) and town planning (The Builder 1908), and thus it cannot claim the progenitorship of today's urban design curriculum.

Urban design can play two possible roles in the governance and planning of urban areas: evaluative and imaginative. Jonathan Barnett (1995) places particular emphasis on the advantages produced by the *evaluative* role of urban design on the physical consequences of urban planning. He writes: "One of the most important changes [in the philosophy of planning and design] has been the addition of design methods to the practice of planning. Design is a way of making a complex decision where a series of potential actions are interrelated and choices on one issue affect choices about others" (179). Urban design applied to public policy, states Barnett, suggests an "understanding, and planning, the interaction between a highway and surrounding neighborhoods; it means understanding that zoning regulations inevitably shape buildings and that these design consequences should be anticipated and intended" (179–80).

Urban design should be viewed as a powerful partner with urban planning in the physical transformation of the city. A well-known example is the evaluation of the choices in the Greater London Plan that Patrick Abercrombie delivered to the British government in 1944 (and which was subsequently published in 1945). Abercrombie suggested urban expansion designs that were possible through alternative forms of settlements. The London plan is an extraordinary example of the virtuous and possible relationship between urban planning and urban design, where the latter acts as a means to assess the assumptions to guide the transformation and to support the decision-making processes (Figures 0.1, 0.2, and 0.3). A more recent example is the Ballymun Master Plan (Ballymun Regeneration Limited 2004), in which the regeneration of this "satellite dormitory of Dublin" into a town with its own identity and a series of new opportunities for the twenty thousand inhabitants was conceived through the collaboration between a flexible urban plan and urban design guidelines, defined by professionals and the community, with the ambition to make "places" rather than "spaces." Urban planning, when integrated with urban design, should be able to show the expected outcomes of plans by producing visual and imaginative representations.

In the United States, several activist mayors, notably Richard M. Daley in Chicago and Michael Bloomberg in New York City, have taken on the physical transformations of their cities through urban design. For instance, Millennium Park (Figure 0.4/Plate #1) and the renewal of the Magnificent Mile (Michigan Avenue) have done much to reinvigorate Chicago, while projects like the High Line (Figure 0.5) and Brooklyn Bridge Park have had similar consequences for New York City. In Canada, a series of design competitions is setting the framework for the transformation of the Toronto waterfront along Lake Ontario (Figure 0.6).

Emily Talen (2009) urges planners to "reclaim urban design." We suggest that by embracing urban design, planners can reclaim planning. Since its appearance as a discipline with its own methods (in the second half of the 1800s with Ildefonso Cerdà and his "general theory of urbanization" in Europe, and with Frederick Law Olmsted in North America), urban planning has produced relevant visualizations of the physical city. Extraordinary examples are found in the planning experiences in Europe with Tony Garnier and his Cité Industrielle (Industrial City) in Lyon, France; Arturo Soria y Mata and his Ciudad Lineal (Linear City) in Spain; Ludwig Karl Hilberseimer's Ideal City; Le Corbusier's Algiers Plan; Adriano Olivetti's Val d'Aosta Plan; and the British garden cities and new towns; as well as in the United

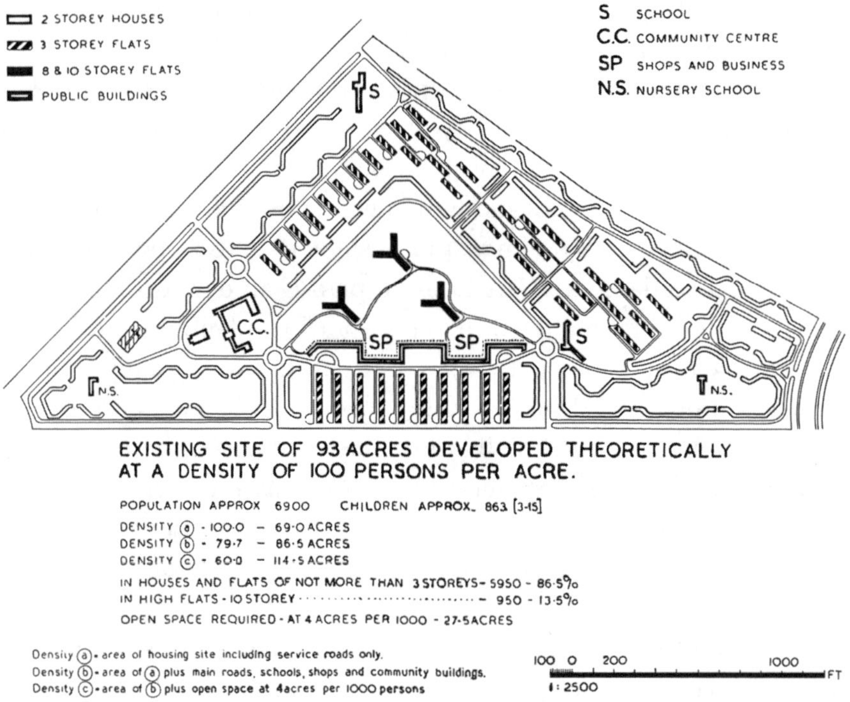

Figure 0.1 Greater London Plan by Sir Patrick Abercrombie. An existing site of 93 acres (37.7 hectares) in Bermondsey, London, theoretically developed at different densities: 100 persons per acre (Figure 0.1), 136 persons per acre (Figure 0.2), and 200 persons per acre (Figure 0.3). (From Abercrombie 1945, 80–82.)

States, with the 1907 Chicago Plan by Daniel H. Burnham and Edward P. Bennett, John Nolen's 1922 Mariemont Plan, Frank Lloyd Wright's Broadacre City, and the more recent contributions by David Wallace (2004) and his Wallace Roberts & Todd colleagues.

Beginning in the 1960s, this design-based practice of urban planning was abandoned in favor of a bi-dimensional, regulative, and "policy-oriented" system, which has become increasingly uncommunicative with the public. This orientation perhaps helped to distance the planning community from the physical design of the city and its construction. Meanwhile, others, such as the New Urbanists, have tried to seize control of planning. In the process, many planning practitioners have embraced the commonsense tenets of New Urbanists, whereas others,

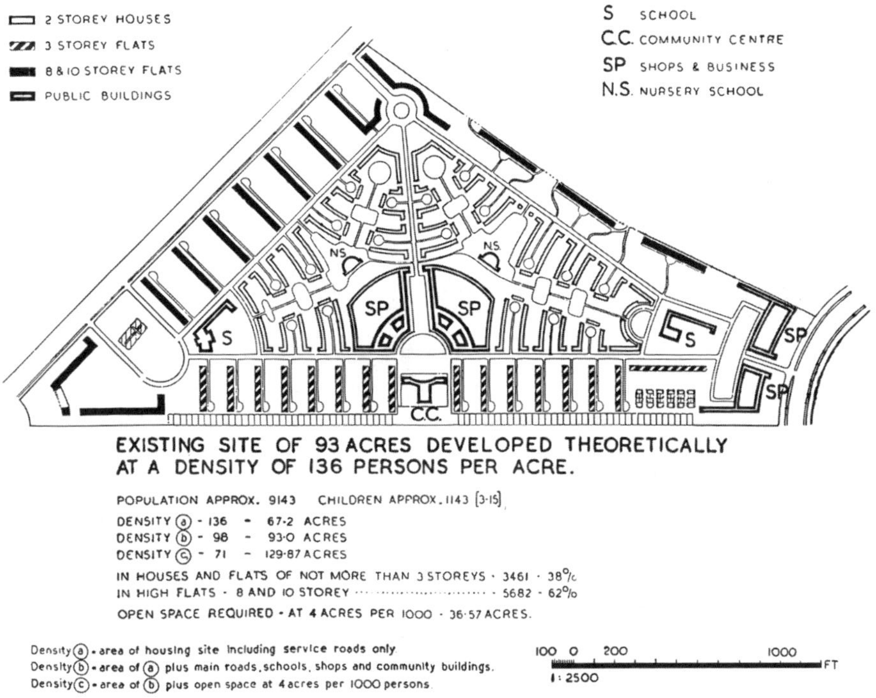

Figure 0.2

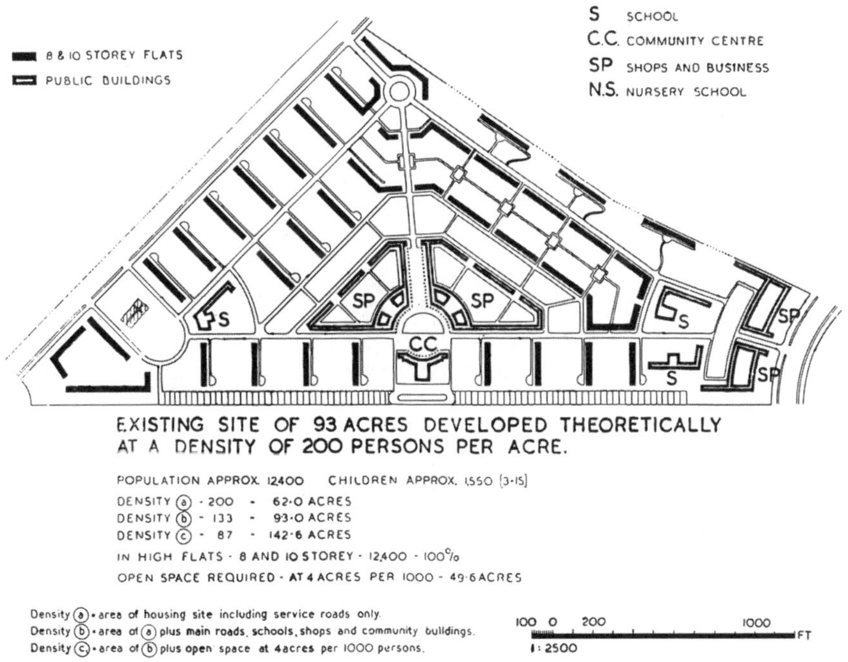

Figure 0.3

Figure 0.4 (also Plate #1) Millennium Park, Chicago. This 24.5-acre (9.9-hectare) park transformed an area of rail yards and parking lots into a prominent civic center near the Lake Michigan shoreline. The park features the work of prominent artists, architects, and landscape architects, including Frank Gehry, Anish Kapoor, Kathryn Gustafson, Piet Oudolf, and Jaume Plensa. (Photograph by Terry Guen.)

Figure 0.5 The High Line, New York City. James Corner Field Operations and Diller Scofidio + Renfro designed this 1.45-mile (2.33-kilometer) park on a former elevated railroad spur on the lower west side of Manhattan. (Photograph by Frederick Steiner.)

Figure 0.6 Lower Don Lands Proposal, Toronto, Canada. The Lower Don Lands is part of a series of projects intended to transform Toronto's lakefront. This StossLU finalist proposal suggests a hybridized river and river marsh, carefully structured with a full range of armored to porous surfaces to create a new habitat for fish and wildlife and to create a new type of green city. (©StossLU.)

especially architecture academics, have rejected New Urbanism because of its perceived embrace of nostalgic styles.

The Granite Garden, by Anne Whiston Spirn (1984), puts urban design in a new light by adding a role related to planning: "If cities are to become more livable, it will be by design: not just through the design of built project—homes and workplaces, gardens and parks, streets and sewer systems—but also through vision that may never be realized. Urban design is a process of envisioning and describing the shape of the future, of posing alternatives from which to choose. Without visions to guide their development, cities will be shaped by the politics of expedience" (Spirn 2000, 297). Elsewhere, she emphasizes the potential contributions of urban ecology to urban design and urban planning (Spirn 1998).

The collaboration between urban design and architecture is more fluid and difficult to define. The border between architecture and urban design is often blurred. Where does an architectural project end and an urban design project begin? Is a neighborhood design, for example, a matter of architecture or of urban design? Do urban designers draw only the void and architects only the solid? Questions like these do not have simple answers. Spirn (2000, 297) defines urban design as "a process of envisioning and describing the shape of the future, of posing alternatives from which to choose." This is what specifically distinguishes urban design from architecture and establishes the space for collaboration. Architecture is able to provide vision and shape possible futures, but on a smaller range. Through master plans, urban design describes and envisions the future, or alternatives for the future, often as a result of a process that involves, directly or indirectly, human expectations and values. Architecture transforms images of solids and voids into real places for people. Building representations in an urban design master plan evolve from a complex evaluation of the site, urban planning rules, and client and public expectations that, rather than dampen architectural creativity, elevate the prospects for architecture.

Meanwhile, urban design can encourage new building opportunities for architects. Urban design provides a link between urban plans and architecture by expanding the scope of architecture, which has traditionally been focused on the building level, and works as a partner of both. These reciprocal relationships can be extended to planning and landscape architecture. A city plan can mandate that an urban design be undertaken. The realization of an urban design can advance the implementation of the plan. Landscape architecture can help elaborate the relationships between culture and nature in a plan that may be utilized to undertake landscape architecture projects as part of an urban design or as a result of it.

Purposes of the Book

In this book, we seek not to define the field of urban design but, rather, to present an interdisciplinary process. Our goal is not to explain how to design a specific city precinct or public space but to describe steps to help transform these spaces into inviting and sustainable urban places. We propose a process for urban design called the not-only-one-solution process.

The Not-Only-One-Solution Process

In many cases, the planning and urban design processes are not explicit but work as an underlying current or an invisible force that drives the design or the planning task from its very first inception to the final step. Skilled and experienced practitioners use their mental design process to go from A to Z, but in many cases they would be unable to describe the path they followed. They could not tell whether they passed through B and C to go to D, or if they arrived at D by passing through J and P.

In this book, we present the *not-only-one-solution process*, reiterating that urban design, like other design and planning activities, not only permits but demands that different answers and different solutions are considered for a given problem. The design process should not be organized to produce only one output. A process employs a structure, a route strategy, which helps the designer to move toward the target, but not necessarily to arrive there prematurely.

The phases of the not-only-one-solution process will be described in more detail in subsequent chapters. They reflect the progression of thought in the different fields of planning and design. The not-only-one-solution process is systematic, precisely linear, and highly optimistic. It assumes, for the sake of descriptive convenience and the necessary simplification, a relative lack of conflict among the participants involved, a high level of honesty, and competence by every party involved in the process and its application to situations with a "moderate" complexity.

Although the process described is linear and systematic, anyone who has been involved in a land transformation process, at any scale, can state that even a precise and ad hoc program prepared in advance by designers, together with the clients, is rarely followed in full.

The not-only-one-solution process should be considered a guide for managing an urban design project. The challenge to the designer will be to adapt the process to the particular situation, task, and mission. Urban design processes are certainly not a magic wand for problem solving, but they are guides that seek to improve the outcomes for people in this first urban century.

The acronym for our approach, *Noos*, is also an ancient Greek word (νόος) that means reason, mind, intelligence, and wisdom but also project and plan, in the meaning of intention (Rocci 1968), and resolve, purpose, to have the mind directed to something (Liddell and Scott 1940). Reason, in urban design, helps to direct the designer's approach to respond to the project's complexities. Reason prompts us to take all the steps to reach an ideal solution, in the platonic sense, or, as Aristotle would have preferred, one that is *phronetic*, or practical, and in the interests of all sectors of the community.

The not-only-one-solution process consists of ten phases, which have been graphically reproduced in a scheme (see Figure 0.7) and which form the bases for the chapters that follow. The scheme consists of two parts. A central column with progressively darker shades of gray from top to bottom highlights the different phases, also contained in initials, which will serve as a navigator, through the text, to mark the different steps. At the left of the scheme, five thin columns, also in graduated colors, offer an interpretation of the phases in clusters of actions: analysis-preproject-project-execution-involvement, bringing together and even overlapping some of the nine stages. Of these five columns, the one on the far left shows the involvement of the population or of the client, or both, that permeates the whole process.

Step 1. Processes

Even before receiving a commission, the designer may be expected to propose how the project will be approached. This step requires a game plan for the project: what steps and activities are required and what will be produced as a result. The products of the process are commonly called "deliverables." In some cases, each step results in a deliverable. As there is no one end solution, there is also no single process. As a result, the designer prepares the process that is appropriate for the situation, then adjusts and calibrates the approach with each step.

Step 2. Prerequisites

Traditionally, to start a project or plan, three elements are needed: a client, a designer, and a mission. The client provides the mission to the designer. This mission, usually written in a contract or specified in a brief, directs the designer to accomplish something in a specific time and for a specific budget. Aside from the mission, the designer needs to know what demands the client has in mind and the environmental conditions to be considered. Environmental conditions represent those components of the site and context, and their actual and dynamic characteristics, that could direct or limit the development of a project. In situ requirements and assumptions are summarized here by the word *prerequisites*.

Sometimes client requirements can be very precise and strict; other times, loose and flexible. In some cases, the client can provide conditions together with strategies, visions, and values to be considered. Project requirements can be summarized by the client or defined by a plan, a program, or a statement of policies. This chapter aims to present who defines, where to find, and how to refine the prerequisites for an urban design project. It also offers a guide for how to provide an organizational outline of a specific design process.

Step 3. Knowledge

Usually the client provides some of the background information about the study area. In competitions and workshops, such information is included in a briefing. In direct assignments, only partial information is normally supplied by the client.

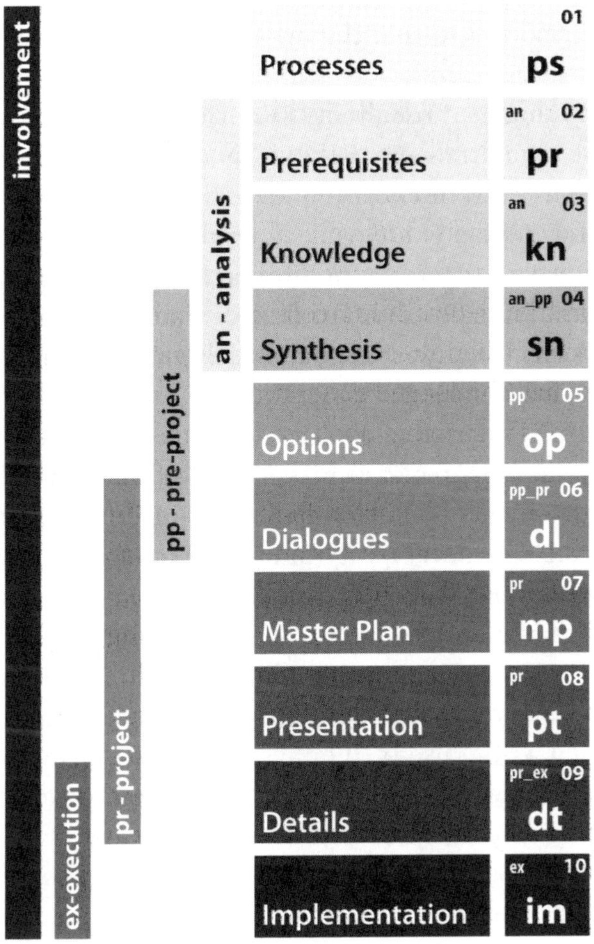

Figure 0.7 The not-only-one-solution process and its ten phases. (Drawing by Danilo Palazzo and Angela Colucci.)

This information often needs to be verified, improved, and completed in order to reach a more comprehensive understanding, or *knowledge*, of the study area to support the subsequent design steps. In every community, there are "competing ideas about *knowledge*" for any site. Recognizing that fact, and making the ideas visible at the onset, increases the likelihood of producing transformational synthesis in the next step. In other words, conflict is good, at least at the beginning stages of a design process. Often the quantity, quality, and variety of information need to be increased through original surveys and analyses. The designer may need to conduct independent surveys and analyses or to involve the people affected by the urban design project in order to collect data and opinions. Direct acquaintance with the site is a crucial experience for a designer. A fundamental part of this step is the site visit. The purpose of this chapter is to present some of the methods to complete, gather, and process information so that the urban designer achieves a comprehensive knowledge of the study area.

Although ecological thinking is valuable throughout the not-only-one-solution process, it is especially so in this step and the next. Ecology involves the relationship of all organisms, including humans, to one another and to their environments. As a result, an ecological approach can help guide what types of information are collected and how the information is understood. A preliminary ecological analysis of the site is integral to the urban design process. The field of study that considers the relationship between the design of built spaces and their environments is called ecological planning and design.

The term *environment* refers to our surroundings, while the term *ecology* encompasses the study of the reciprocal relationship of organisms to one another and to their biological and physical environments. When we add *planning* or *design* to these terms, the combined term refers to developing future options for our surroundings, for the interrelationship among biological and physical processes, and for the visual manifestation of those relationships. Lewis Mumford's friend Benton MacKaye (1940, 351) even declared that "regional planning is ecology. It is *human ecology*; its concern is the relation of the human organism to its environment." Ecological planning may be defined as the use of biophysical and sociocultural information to suggest opportunities and constraints for decision making about the use of the landscape (Steiner 2008). Or, as explained by Ian McHarg (1997, 321), it is the approach "whereby a region is understood as a biophysical and social process comprehensible through the operation of laws and time. . . . A survey will reveal the most fit locations and processes." Anne Whiston Spirn (1998) refers to such regional processes as the "deep structure" and the "deep context" of a place.

Ecological planning, according to Forster Ndubisi (2002),

> is a way of directing or managing changes in the landscape so that human actions are in tune with natural processes. . . . Ecological planning is more than a tool or technique. It is a way of mediating the dialogue between human actions and natural processes based on the knowledge of the reciprocal relationship between people and the land. (2, 5)

Step 4. Synthesis

Once the information is collected and the surveys are completed, the knowledge acquired needs to be summarized for two reasons. First, the designer needs to be precise. The information and analysis need to be as accurate as possible to direct and shape the final project. Second, a *synthesis* will be useful for informing and communicating with the involved public and the client. This chapter will describe five synthesis techniques: Strengths, Weaknesses, Opportunities, and Threats (SWOT) analysis; constraints and opportunities mapping; transects; exploded axonometric drawings; and suitability analysis. These five techniques have the advantage of being relatively easy to do and of being effective. Other parts of this chapter are devoted to techniques for understanding the spatial dimension of the site, for approaching the design task, and for diagnosing suitable uses.

Step 5. Options

This point of the process is characterized by the specification of the project goals and *options* by the designer. Once the purpose of the design has been defined, clarified, and summarized by the client, and once the information is collected, the surveys completed, and the data summarized, the designer needs to decide which direction to take, which goals and strategies to follow. At this point, the designer selects preferences and priorities. The designer develops different options to select a preferred course of action. The purpose of this chapter is to present different means of arranging a design goal setting: from setting a list of goals in order of priority to defining a concept plan or a vision, to processing and choosing among design possibilities.

Step 6. Dialogues

The discussion and confrontation of the designer's ideas, solutions, and ways to progress with the client and other interested parties is a central point of any urban design process. *Dialogue*, in an urban design process, designates the opportunities of the relationship both between the designer and the client and between the designer and the public involved directly, or even indirectly, in the transformation promoted by design. There are different types of participation depending on the phase in the process it takes place, on the people involved, and on the purposes of the participation. This chapter will present the role of participation in an urban design process and will explore its effectiveness. Selected techniques used in design and planning processes will be described.

Step 7. Master Plan

The definitive form and configuration of an urban design project is presented in a *master plan*. The master plan describes the proposed change of a given site. It is a physical plan that shows and maps, through writing and graphics, the overall development concept for the study area. The purpose of this chapter is to describe the contents of a typical master plan and to introduce the potential issues that a master plan can consider and satisfy.

Step 8. Presentation

After the urban design master plan is completed, the outcomes need to be *presented* to the client and possibly to a wider public. A good project can be damaged by a bad presentation. The means of presentation vary with the specific circumstances of the endeavor. The master plan report may be communicated differently, from a verbal presentation supported by a slide show to a project presentation in a poster. This chapter will discuss the use of images, renderings, physical models, and hand-drawn sketches to illustrate the outcomes of the urban design proposals.

Step 9. Details

After the master plan is completed and has received the approval of the client and/or the public involved, it is often necessary to *detail* some of the design components. These might concern mobility, green and open areas, public spaces, buildings, and street furniture, in addition to such topics as an economic assessment, fund-raising, and partnerships. Some of these details may be included in the design guidelines or in other detailed studies to pave the way for implementing the master plan. Using various examples, this chapter shows how design guidelines can be prepared as well as studies to assess the master plan before its implementation.

Step 10. Implementation

The master plan can be translated into precise rules that define distances, elevations, constraints, and spatial rules to be conveyed to architects, landscape architects, planners, and engineers, as in plans regulating the use of land and building shapes. When the master plan has been completed, presented, and detailed, most of the time it has to be adopted and approved by an administrative body or a planning authority. After that, the urban design project is ready for its *implementation*, the realization of the goals and policies that were considered in the process. This chapter presents some of the tools and techniques used to implement and execute the project.

Notes from the Authors

We apply some conventions throughout this book for the sake of convenience. For example, we call the design project author the *designer*. The term *design* could be defined as a team of designers (a multidisciplinary group in charge of or involved in a design process) or as several designers who act separately in space and time. The designer may be an architect, a landscape architect, a planner, or an individual with a cross-disciplinary background. We use the term *client* to mean the individual or individuals who commission an urban design project. The client can be a governmental body (a city, a public utility, a public agency) or a private entity (a developer, a real estate company, a group of investors, a landowner), a combination of public and private organizations (along the lines of the Community Development Block Grant Program promoted by the U.S. Department of Housing and Urban Development or the Italian Società di Trasformazione Urbana [Urban Transformation Company]) or a community, an ad hoc association, or an organized group of citizens. The client can also be a combination of all these groups. The *assignment* is the mandate or task given to the designer by the client. The *study area*, or *site*, is the place where the urban design occurs. A study area (or site) may be at a scale ranging from an entire city to the larger region or a smaller part of it.

We acknowledge the differences between North American and European urban design, especially in education (Palazzo 2011). In general, urban design education is more advanced in Anglo-American universities than elsewhere (Table 0.1). As it is, much urban design practice is undertaken by large multidisciplinary, multinational firms with roots in the United States, such as AECOM (formerly EDAW), WRT, SWA, Sasaki, and SOM; as well as in Canada, such as IBI; and, increasingly, in China, where there are many academic-based firms.

Contemporary urban problems require urban designers to be prepared differently from the past (United Nations 2004; Rodiek 2005). The education of urban design could be the means for preparing professionals who see urban design not as an "exercise in beautification of public spaces" but, rather, as an activity that will "reshape urban spaces . . . in the overall transformation of cities . . . to accommodate the new urban conditions" (Madanipour 2006, 174, 191) and to participate in the production and reproduction of urban form as social space (Cuthbert 2007). Urban designers must also be prepared to produce more sustainable, even regenerative, cities (Gore 2009).

Urban designers who have the aptitude to express creative intentionality matched with scientific knowledge and the capacity to manage processes need to improve the recognition and the concern of sites' ecological and cultural characteristics, to unlearn generic solutions and concepts valid elsewhere, and to find a balance among technical knowledge and creative expression. The classic argument, since the time of Plato and Aristotle through to Heidegger, is that there is a need to distinguish between *téchne* and *poiesis*, where "*téchne* was the dimension of

Table 0.1 Graduate Programs in Urban Design Taught in English as of 2009

Country	Institution	Course Title
Australia	Curtin University of Technology	Master of Urban Design[£]
	The University of Western Australia	Master of Urban Design[£]
	University of Adelaide	Master of Urban Design[£]
	University of Melbourne	Master/PGDip in Urban Design[*£]
	University of New South Wales, Sydney	Master of Urban Development and Design (MUDD)[*£]
	University of Sydney	Master of Urban Design[*£]
		Graduate Certificate in Urban Design[£]
Canada	University of Toronto	Master of Urban Design Studies[*$]
Germany and China	Technische Universität Berlin and Tongji University, Shanghai	Dual Master Program Urban Design (Berlin and Shanghai)[*]
India	Centre for Environmental Planning and Technology, Ahmedabad	Master of Urban Design[*]
	School of Planning and Architecture, Delhi	Master of Urban Design[*]
Ireland	Queen's University Belfast	MSc in Urban and Rural Design[@]
	University College Dublin	MSc in Urban Design[*]
New Zealand	University of Auckland	Masters of Urban Design (MUrbDes)[*]
Singapore	National University of Singapore	Master of Arts (Urban Design)[*]
		Master of Architecture (Urban Design)[*]
South Africa	University of Cape Town	Masters of Urban Design & City Planning[*]
		Masters of Architecture (Urban Design)[*]
Sweden	Lund University	Master of Sustainable Urban Design[+]
	Royal Institute of Technology, Stockholm	Masters of Urban Planning and Design[*+]
USA	Arizona State University	Master of Urban and Environmental Design[$]
	City College of New York	Master of Urban Design[§]
	Cleveland State University	Master of Urban Planning, Design and Development[§$]
	Harvard University	Master of Architecture in Urban Design: MAUD[*§]
		Master of Landscape Architecture in Urban Design: MLAUD[*§]
	Kent State University	Graduate Certificate/Master in Urban Design[*]
	New York Institute of Technology	Master of Architecture in Urban and Regional Design[§]
	Pratt Institute	MSc in Architecture and Urban Design (Post-professional)[§]
	Savannah College of Art and Design	Master of Urban Design[*]
	University of California, Berkeley	Master of Urban Design Degree[§]
	University of Michigan	Masters of Urban Design[*]
	University of Pennsylvania	Certificate in Urban Design[§]

Table 0.1 *continued*

USA (cont.)	University of Texas at Austin	Master of Science in Urban Design[*] and Certificate in Urban Design
	University of Washington	Certificate in Urban Design*[§]
	Washington University, Saint Louis	Master of Urban Design[§]
UK	Anglia Ruskin University	MPhil/PhD in Urban Design
	Bartlett School of Planning, University College London	MSc in Urban Design[#] MSc in Building & Urban Design in Development[#]
	Birmingham City University	MA/PGDip/PGCert in Urban Design[#]
	Cardiff University	MA in Urban Design[@#]
	Edinburgh College of Art	PGDip/MSc in Architecture and Urban Design[#] PGDip/MSc in Landscape Architecture and Urban Design[#]
	Heriot Watt University	MSc/PGDip in Urban Design[#]
	Lincoln University	MSc/PGDip/PGCert in Urban Design[#]
	Liverpool John Moores University	MA in Architecture and Urban Design[#]
	London South Bank University	MA in Urban Design[@]
	Newcastle University	MA/PGDip in Urban Design[#]
	Oxford Brookes University	MA/PGDip/PGCert in Urban Design[@#]
	University of Birmingham	MA in Urban Design[@]
	University of Dundee	MSc Spatial Planning with Sustainable Urban Design[@]
	University of Greenwich	MA in Urban Design[#]
	University of Liverpool	MA in Civic Design[@#]
	University of Nottingham	MA/PGDip in Architecture and Urban Design[#]
	University of Sheffield	MA in Urban Design[#]
	University of Strathclyde, Glasgow	MSc in Urban Design[@]
	University of the West of England	MA/PGDip in Urban Design[#]
	University of Westminster	MA/PGCert/PGDip in Urban Design[@#]

Sources: Resource for Urban Design Information (RUDI) 2009a[*]; RUDI 2009b[#]; http://www.studyinsweden.se[+]; http://www.gradschools.com[§]; Association of Collegiate Schools of Planning 2007[$]; http://www.studyinaustralia.gov.au[£]; http://www.urbandesigninstitute.co.za[*]; Royal Town Planning Institute 2008[@]. Urban design programs can also be offered as certificate—which is achieved combining subjects in different but related programs—such as those offered at the University of Pennsylvania, Harvard University, and Washington University or found at the doctoral level.

Note: PGDip: postgraduate diploma; PGCert: postgraduate certificate; MA: master of arts; MSc: master of science.

revelatory knowledge about the world, and *poiesis* was the dimension of creative, symbolic representation" (Corner 2002, 20). *Téchne* and *poieses* need to be reconsidered in urban design practice and teaching in order to face urban problems; to understand places, social needs, and community roles; and to deal with decision makers. This can be done by strengthening the teaching of processes and methods for approaching issues and sites (Roberts and Greed 2001; Moughtin et al. 2003; Lang 2005; Steiner and Butler 2007; Palazzo 2011). Another way is to confirm the role of the studio (or design workshop) as the place where the final product, with its aesthetic dimension, is assembled by means of a dialectic exchange. The ideal balance between techniques and creativity is also relevant in the *praxis* where urban designers apply their skills and knowledge in different places, within different cultures. The aim is to reinforce the role of the urban designer as an honest broker and a promoter of design processes, an active agent of social creativity for the realization of the public realm. To accomplish this aim, we suggest through this book a specific design process.

The urban design process that will be described in the following chapters is linear and consequential—that is, every phase builds on the previous one or affects the next. This method of presenting phases corresponds with descriptive and organizational requirements but does not necessarily coincide with what really happens in a design process. Many of the phases described in the following pages can, in practice, be merged; "generally, [the phases of a design process] do not arise in a fixed, logical order; designing is not a linear process, with a specific task leading to one and only one possible solution" (Leupen et al. 1997, 13). An analogy can be drawn to music, especially jazz, in which the musician begins with a score but adapts it for the performance, possibly requiring considerable improvisation.

1. Processes

Urban design connects knowledge to action through a systematic process that adapts to the specific circumstances of the project. The urban designer brings knowledge from previous experience, generates new intelligence about the project, and guides the process through to its realization.

We apply a model to urban design to help designers be more effective project managers. In this capacity, the designer plans, controls, and coordinates "a project from conception to completion . . . on behalf of a client [and] is concerned with the identification of the client's objectives in terms of utility, function, quality, time, and cost and in the establishment of relationships between [available] resources" (Blyth and Worthington 2001, xii).

Sticking to a process does not necessarily guarantee a successful project. However, an organized process can aid in collaboration and can clarify expectations of all involved parties. It can also help to make the best use of available resources, including time and money.

In the design and planning literature, several examples of processes and models are useful in considering a specific process for urban design. Michael Brawne (2003, 8) investigates the architectural design process or, to say it in a different way, how architects and designers "proceed from the past and present to a forecast of the future." Brawne assumes that the way architects proceed can be assimilated to sequence in the same way Karl Popper explained how scientific theories come into being. Popper's explanation appeared mainly in *The Logic of Scientific Discovery*, first published in German in 1935 and then in English in 1959. Brawne described the Popper sequence as a process that starts with "the recognition of a problem, then put[s] forward a hypothesis, a kind of tentative theory which need[s] to be tested in order to eliminate errors and end[s] with a corroborated theory which is, however, the start of a new sequence in which it becomes the initial problem" (Brawne 2003, 38). Brawne then concludes that "although clearly architecture is not a scientific pursuit . . . I nevertheless believe that the problem, tentative solution, error elimination, problem sequence is the most accurate description of the design process" (38).

In the field of planning, a well-known and heavily discussed dictum is *survey before plan*, coined by Scottish biologist and planner Patrick Geddes and then further elaborated on by English planner Patrick Abercrombie (Hall 1995). This succinct dictum establishes the framework for linking knowledge to action in the process. Theoretical reflections on planning and design, particularly after the Second World War, have resulted in many examples of processes applied to planning and design. Some examples, in order of appearance in the literature, follow.

In 1980, the Royal Institute of British Architects, in the *Handbook of Architectural Practice and Management*, proposed in the field of urban design a process model divided into four phases (RIBA 1980, quoted in Moughtin et al. 2004, 6):

1. *Assimilation*—the accumulation of general information and information specifically related to the problem
2. *General Study*—the investigation of the nature of the problem; the investigation of a possible solution
3. *Development*—the development of one or more solutions
4. *Communication*—the communication of the chosen solution/s to the client

Hamid Shirvani (1985) distinguishes six groups of design methods: internalized, synoptic, incremental, fragmental, pluralistic, and radical. The *internalized* method is the intuitive one: "The designer who uses the intuitive method first develops a design for the project in his or her mind, with the benefit and assistance of memory, training, and experience" (106).

The *synoptic* method, which is also commonly described as "rational" or "comprehensive," is usually composed of seven steps (Shirvani 1985, 111):

1. Data collection, survey of existing conditions (natural, built, and socioeconomic);
2. Data analysis, identification of all opportunities and limitations;
3. Formulation of goals and objectives;
4. Generation of alternative concepts;

5. Elaboration of each concept into workable solutions;
6. Evaluation of alternative solutions; and
7. Translation of solutions into policies, plans, guidelines, and programs.

The *incremental* method is described by Shirvani as another version of the synoptic method in which "the designer establishes a goal and then develops incremental steps to achieve it" (116). The *fragmental* process is similar to the synoptic, except that it is incomplete. The designer can "go through four out of the total *seven* steps suggested for the synoptic process" (116). The *pluralistic* process is an approach that incorporates into the design process the inhabitants' value system and the functional/social structure of the urban area involved in the design. Shirvani's final approach, the *radical* process, has as an underlying concept that "in order to understand and design for a complex urban setting, social processes must be understood first" (118).

A process of ecological planning, consisting of eleven steps, was proposed by Frederick Steiner in *The Living Landscape* (2008) (see Figure 1.1). These eleven interacting steps are as follows:

Step 1. Problem and/or opportunity identification
Step 2. Goal establishment
Step 3. Regional-level inventory and analysis
Step 4. Local-level inventory and analysis
Step 5. Detailed studies
Step 6. Planning concept
Step 7. Landscape plan
Step 8. Education and citizen involvement
Step 9. Detailed designs
Step 10. Plan and design implementation
Step 11. Administration

This ecological planning model synthesizes other processes of regional and landscape planning. Its main references are the ecological methods for design and planning formulated since the 1960s by Ian McHarg (1966, 1969, 1981) (see Figure 1.2). The principal idea links environmental information through ecological knowledge to design and planning decisions by what McHarg called the "layer-cake model."

In the field of urban planning, Larz Anderson, on behalf of the American Planning Association (1995), defines an urban planning process as composed of nine strongly interconnected phases. The process of plan making was viewed as a

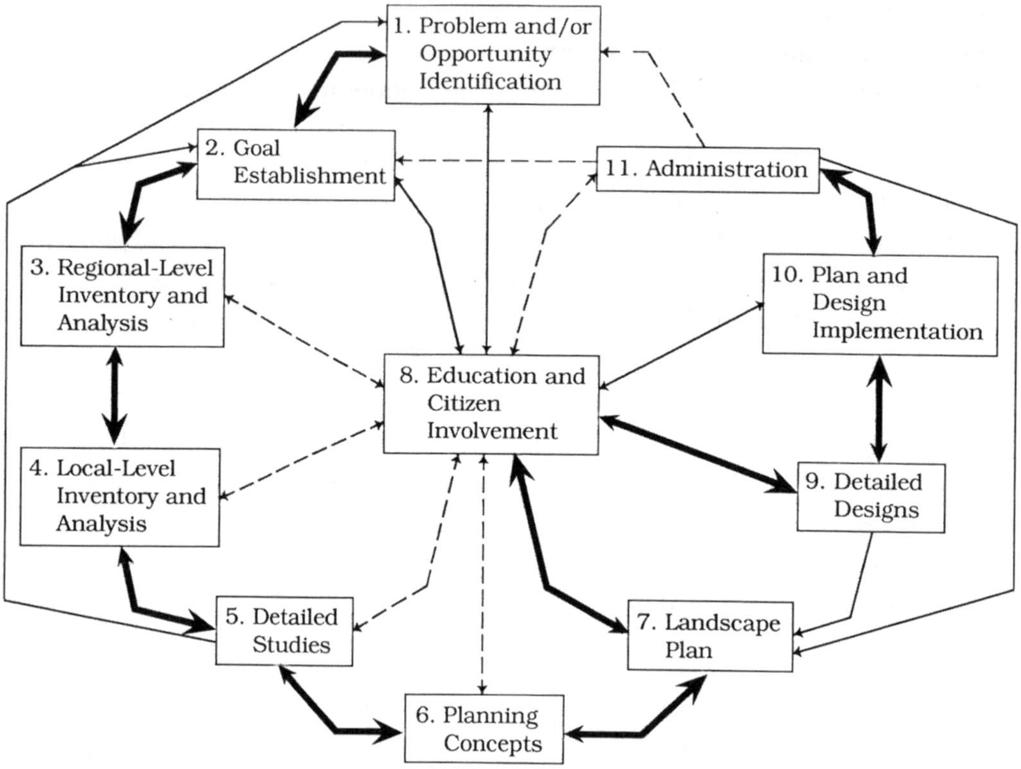

Figure 1.1 Ecological planning model. (From Steiner 2008, 11.)

continuous cycle that recognizes the iterative and interactive nature of planning (see Figure 1.3; Steiner and Butler 2007, 3):

1. Identify issues.
2. State goals, objectives, and priorities.
3. Collect and interpret data.
4. Prepare plans.
5. Draft programs for plan implementation.
6. Evaluate impacts of plans and implementation programs.
7. Review and adopt plans.
8. Review and adopt implementation programs.
9. Administer implementation programs.

Planning involves managing land uses in cities, agricultural areas, and forests. Planning is studied and practiced in terms of process. The planning and management of natural resources can be accomplished using the principles of *stewardship*, which can be defined as "the call to care for the Earth," counting on human and

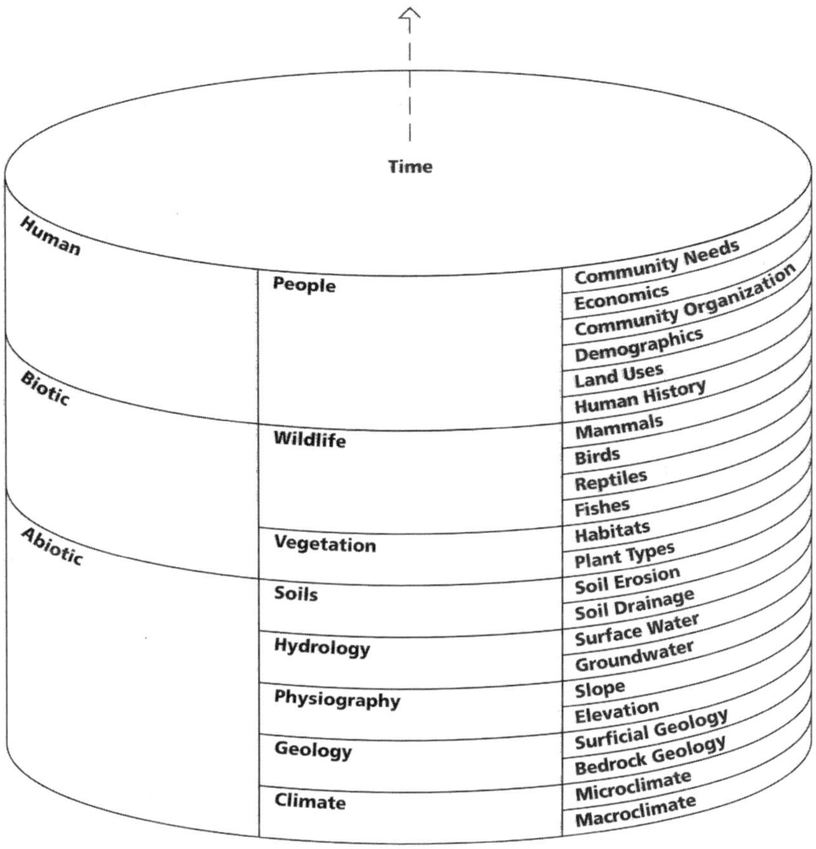

Figure 1.2 Layer-cake model. (From Steiner 2008, 15.)

individual responsibility to "guide individuals toward the common goal [. . . of the preservation of] Earth's beauty and productivity for future generations" (President's Council on Sustainable Development 1996, 8) and can be undertaken, according to Sexton et al. (1999), using the seven-step process summarized below:

1. Identify the problem, decision makers, their authorities, the stakeholders, and the decision-making process.
2. Define the problem and refine the objectives.
3. Develop alternative actions to achieve the objectives.
4. Compare each alternative with the objective.
5. Choose a preferred alternative.
6. Implement the chosen alternative.
7. Monitor and evaluate. (Reynolds et al. 1999, 690–92)

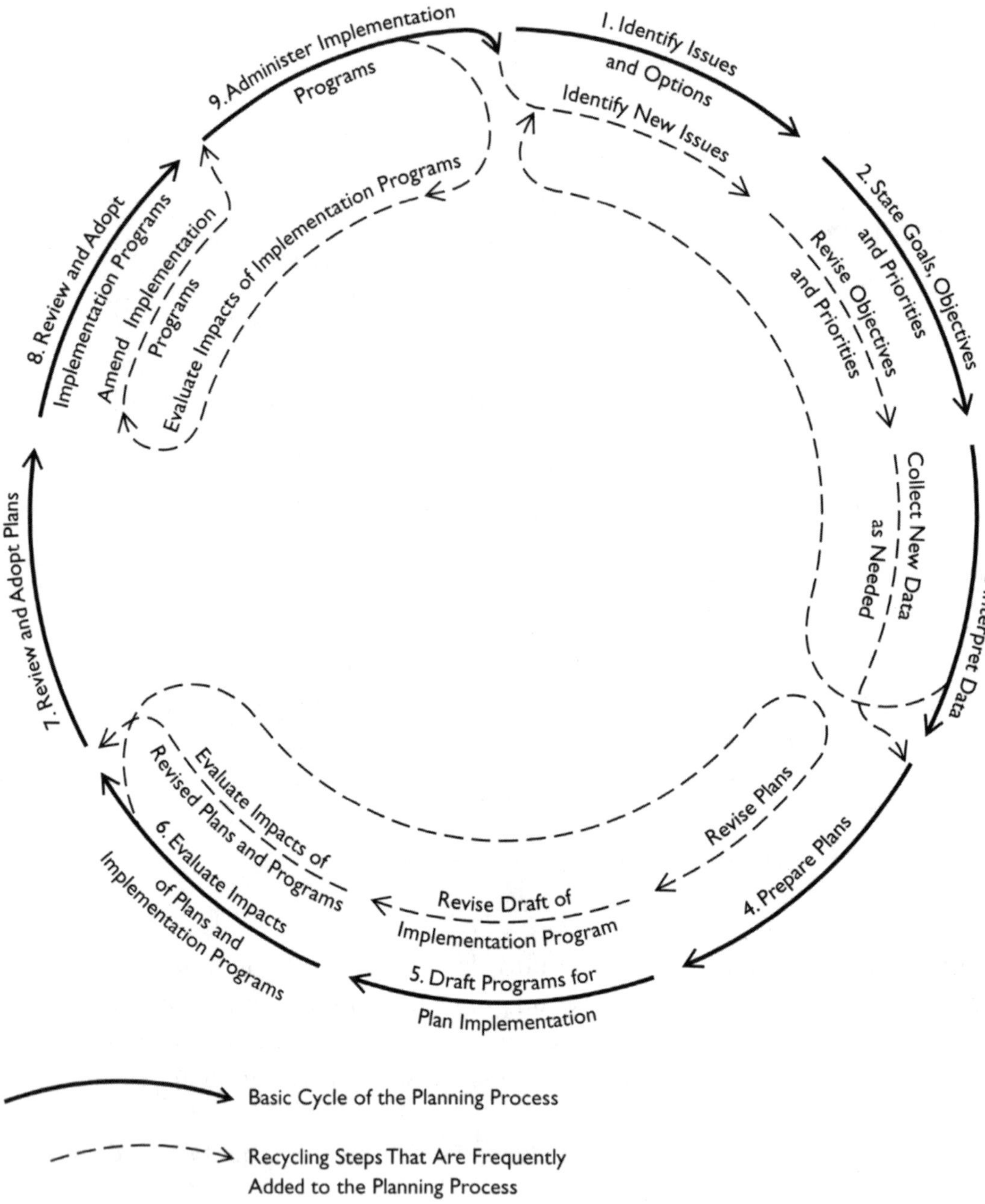

Figure 1.3 The process of plan making as a continuous cycle. (From Anderson 1995, in Steiner and Butler 2007, 3.)

Tony Lloyd Jones (2001), discussing the urban design process, distinguishes between artistic inspiration and Geddesian analysis. The first approach (which barely can be considered a process) is driven by the view of "many designers who see themselves as . . . gifted artists" (51). Therefore, according to Lloyd Jones, "the stress is on beautifying the city through grand and often formal street layouts and landscaping interventions" (51). This very clearly relegates the landscape to decoration ("landscaping") in the grand plan, rather than the deeper meaning of landscape as a synthesis of nature and cultural processes with clear ecological implications. On the opposite side of the "artistic inspiration," there is the Geddesian approach that views the design action as a problem-solving activity

> concerned with the issue of spatial organisation to meet functional need. . . . [This] approach [also labeled "functionalist" because of its engineering origin] suggests that if we analyse the problems that the design sets out to address in sufficient detail and in a scientific manner, a spatial solution will emerge from this analysis or "programme". It suggests that design is a linear process, which, if carried out with sufficient rigor, will lead to a single, optimum solution. (51)

Lloyd Jones suggests that there is a third option that overcomes the inspirational and the deterministic approaches. This approach takes the form of a cyclic process of analysis-composition-evaluation: "an attempt to reconcile factors that relate to client or user needs, factors that relate to the site or area under study and its context, and factors that relate to the constraints of planning policy and local planning regulation. It involves understanding the problems that are to be addressed and refining, abstracting and prioritizing the essential issues" (52). Lloyd Jones's third option lends itself to an ecological interpretation that emphasizes cyclic process and interaction.

Following are the four steps of the urban design process:

1. *Defining the problem*—starting from a study area appraisal and the project brief
2. *Developing a rationale*—taking into account summary analysis on planning/socioeconomic context; built form/townscape; land use/activity; movement and access; physical and natural environment; public realm and social space; and perceptual and cultural factors
3. *Summarizing development opportunities and constraints*—balancing the potentials of the site for its projected uses
4. *Conceptualizing and evaluating design options*—envisioning the possibilities for the study area with relative merits and shortcomings

Urban design can be considered "a continuous process of trial-test-change, involving imaging (thinking in terms of solutions), presenting, evaluating, and re-imagining (reconsidering or developing alternative solutions)" (Carmona et al. 2003, 55), a process characterized by cycles and iterations "by which solutions are gradually refined through a series of creative leaps or conceptual shifts" (54).

Process Strategies

As the process begins, it helps to provide an outline of future steps that should be considered during the project development. Available time, project character, and necessary materials to achieve the brief's requirements are important criteria for defining the process scope. In environmental impact assessments, scoping is used to define the proposed action, identify significant issues, eliminate peripheral issues, identify project requirements, indicate the decision-making schedule, and identify cooperating agencies. These activities are generally relevant to many urban design projects as well (especially if an environmental assessment is required by law).

The urban design process described in this book can be used as a reference basis, but every design project will possess its own particular characteristics (see Figure 0.7 in the introduction). Defining the times, responsibilities, meeting schedules, and interim deadlines is useful. However, as the project progresses, the outline will need to be amended as a result of factors that are often unpredictable in the idealized planned process.

Any urban design process should have a strategy, as Kevin Lynch and Gary Hack explain (1984, 369):

> Plans imply agreements. Without the agreement of those with the power to make changes, and at least the passive assent of those who could stop them, plans remain on paper. To have an effect beyond that of an influential intellectual model, the process of site planning must follow a strategy: it must organize the analysis, programming, design, and implementation so that ideas and decisions are meshed. A strategy includes many choices: how to define the problem, the particular design approach, the use of intuition or rationality, the response to uncertainty, the technique of learning, the degree of participation, the linking of form and management, the use of professionals, and the relation to the client and other decision makers. A good many of these decisions are in the usual case simply customary. But . . . such choices should be made explicitly.

The Process Strategy in the Workshop on Chisinau, Moldova

Organizing the design process takes into consideration the time available, the competencies, the prerequisites, and the nature of the assignment. When time is particularly short, as is usually the case in a workshop, the process organization has a significant value. In 2007, an urban design workshop was conducted in Lecco, Italy, for a strategic area of Chisinau, the capital of Moldova, the Eastern European state that borders Romania to the west and the Ukraine to the east (see Figure 1.4).

Chisinau is the political, industrial, and commercial center of Moldova. Located on the Bîc River in the center of the country, it is the largest city of Moldova, with 650,000 inhabitants. During the Soviet domination (1944–1991), the heavy industry of the country was located along the Bîc River. Today, the industrial areas have been largely abandoned. Some buildings were demolished and replaced by retail centers; others are only partially used. The Bîc River and its adjacent soils are heavily polluted.

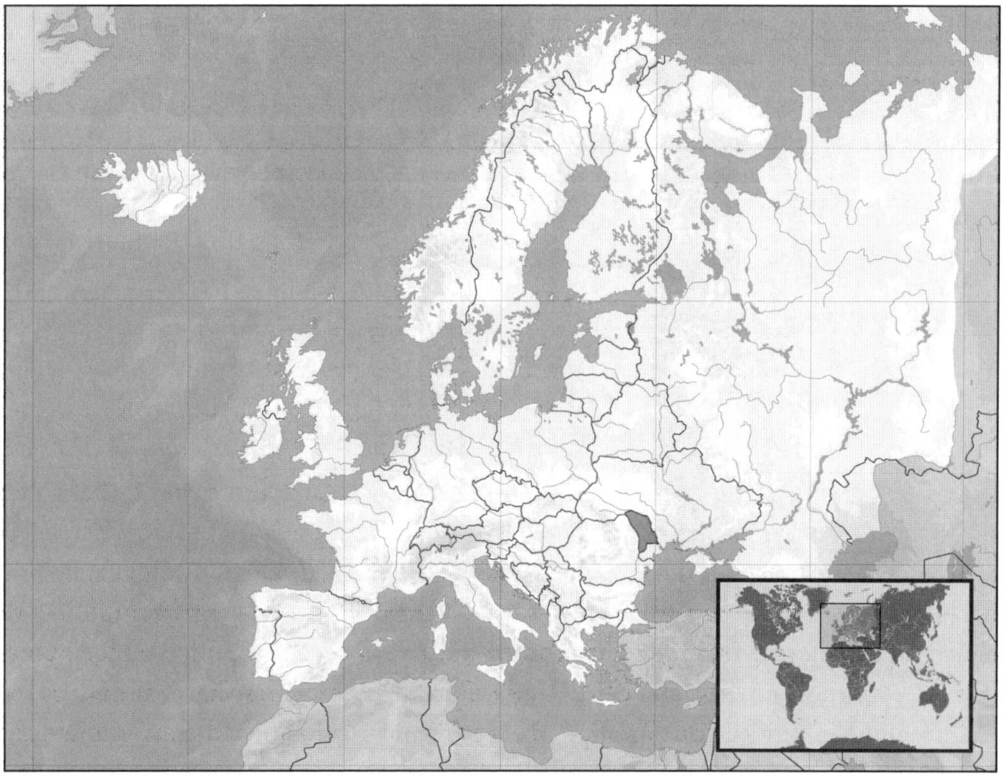

Figure 1.4 Moldova in the European continent. (Map by Danilo Palazzo.)

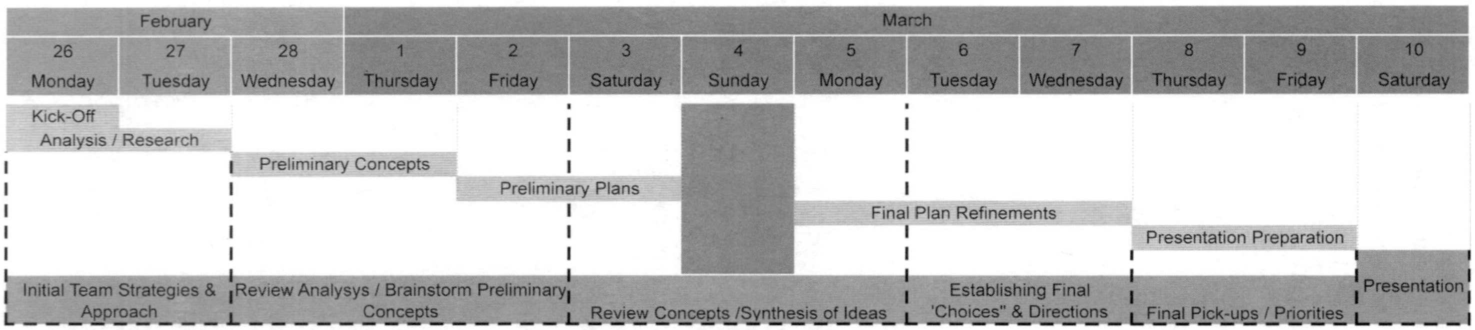

Figure 1.5 The phasing table for the Chisinau workshop. (By Danilo Palazzo.)

The municipality of Chisinau and Milan Polytechnic promoted a design initiative to define some ideas for the area along the river. A two-week workshop was organized to produce a proposal for the City of Chisinau. The workshop was held with practitioners from the London office of Skidmore, Owings & Merrill (SOM), with academics from the Universitat Autònoma de Barcelona (Autonomous University of Barcelona) and Milan Polytechnic, and with students from various European and Asian countries. In addition, four design and planning professionals from Chisinau communicated daily via computer with this group of twenty-one people. To redefine the function of the whole area (7,400 acres, or 3,000 hectares), the team decided to work on different issues:

- *Transportation* at national, regional, and urban levels
- *Mobility* of people and goods
- *Environment and landscape*, including the pollution of the river and soils and the need to redesign the areas along the river in terms of hydraulics and for recreational uses
- *Agriculture*, one of the most important resources of the nation and the major land use outside Chisinau
- *Energy*, the need to understand how to reduce natural gas use by introducing biomass plants
- *Finance*, finding the financial sources to implement the workshop proposals
- *Administration and management* of the whole project

To perform these tasks, the twenty-five-member team was split into different groups focusing on specific issues. A phasing table was proposed to organize the process and to give the team pace and rhythm (see Figure 1.5). The process was determined at the very beginning of the two-week workshop on the basis of the time available, the strengths of the team, the request of the "client," and a rational organization of the steps from initial research and analysis (which correspond to the "knowledge" and "synthesis" steps described in this book) to preliminary concepts ("options") to final plan ("master plan") and then the final presentation. The "prerequisites" were contained in a briefing book prepared in advance and distributed to workshop participants and in "dialogue" between the Milan team and the local participants in Chisinau.

Summary

Usually, the designer provides an early version of the project plan, perhaps only roughly sketched. The idea is to begin imagining the final outcome but to avoid getting locked into a fixed solution. This "open-endedness" permeates the entire process and is indeed important, even if it is difficult to manage. The project is the process target, its goal. It is therefore natural and expected that designers direct individual thought, their own actions, toward that final outcome during all the steps of the process.

In the design process, as in planning, improvisation can occur so that information is synthesized before the data survey is completed as part of the knowledge phase.

2. Prerequisites

In this chapter, we introduce the various types of prerequisites that help frame the urban design process. As explained in the introduction, we describe in situ requirements and assumptions of the word *prerequisites*. Prerequisites provide the starting point of an urban design project. They may be established by the client, and they can be defined by the natural and cultural conditions of the site and therefore included in the initial information provided by the client or by the law, the local plan, or the zoning ordinance. Specific environmental characteristics of a site establish a framework for the design. For instance, it would make no sense to propose an urban design of igloos in the tropics or of grass huts for the Arctic. The environmental characteristics may be less obvious in the cities of Europe, the Americas, Asia, and Australia as they can be masked by technologies, such as air-conditioning and heating systems. Nevertheless, the specific environmental conditions of each site need to be recognized so the urban designer can incorporate elements into a project that will reduce energy costs and the production of greenhouse gases while creating a healthy and productive place for people to live.

The public may also help to define the scope of an urban design. Charrettes and workshops assist the urban designer in understanding public values and aspirations. Prerequisites help the urban designer understand the scope and programmatic boundaries of the project.

Urban environments change constantly, often by design and sometimes by accident. An urban design project can be initiated for many reasons and in many ways. For simplicity's sake, four general types of project origination will be considered here.

- *Commissioned design.* The landowner (public or private) commissions the design.
- *Design competition: public or private entity.* Sometimes in partnership with nonprofit organizations or businesses, or through a public-private partnership, a public or private entity decides to initiate a competition, either open or subject to invitation, to solicit plans to transform an area under its jurisdiction.
- *Informal proposal.* A community of citizens or a neighborhood committee, with or without the support of elected officials or a public agency, addresses issues facing the place where they live through an informal proposal to a governing body, forestalling a decision to develop or promoting the improvement of general conditions in the area.
- *Plan assessment for project implementation.* A city planner carries out an assessment of some regulatory, political, and planning proposals, included in an official city plan, to anticipate and evaluate the plan's morphological and spatial consequences.

The four possible starting points suggested here can be expanded to include most circumstances in which an urban design project begins or is requested. At the outset of the process, the designer will consider the client's demands—be it a private owner, a public entity, a competition-organizing authority, a nonprofit (or nongovernmental) organization, or a community of citizens—as well as the characteristics and environmental conditions of the place. In addition, there may be legal prerequisites the urban designer must follow. For example, a zoning ordinance may regulate the density or the use of a site.

Environmental Characteristics

The environmental and site characteristics can guide or limit the development of a project. In some cases, environmental characteristics can be included in the documentation the client provides for the designer. For example, competitions frequently include detailed descriptions of the site's environmental characteristics. Because competitions seek broad, international teams who usually cannot visit the site, environmental information is provided for them. The environmental characteristics can be ecological, historical, morphologic, climatic, visual, and political. They can also include road conditions, public spaces, and the presence, efficiency, lack, or scarcity of facilities (e.g., mass transportation). Ecological and landscape qualities can, for example, direct some settlement choices by suggesting orientation, localization, and building shapes. An understanding of ecology can also limit bad choices, such as locating uses or activities in places that are inherently dangerous for people or property. An ecological understanding enables the designer to see relationships and make connections between the present conditions of a site and its past.

Environmental characteristics may be documented in official reports of a jurisdiction. In other cases, one of the first tasks for the designer is to collect and process data and information to define a framework of the conditions as completely as possible. We will discuss this *knowledge,* how it is acquired through surveys and analyses, and how it may then be *synthesized* later in the book. Such characteristics can be taken as prerequisites for an urban design project and can be further explored at the site scale.

The client demands component of the prerequisites can be expressed explicitly or only partially. Explicit demands are those contained and organized in a document (the brief for a competition or workshop or the legal regulations for an urban plan). The client may express with precision and transparency the expectations as part of the assignment. In some cases, a client's demands may not be completely disclosed when the client does not want to expose market information to competitors. In these situations, the designer works with the client to elicit a set of values to be converted into goals and issues to be resolved during the design process.

Techniques for Listening to Client Demands

The urban designer can seek suggestions, instructions, information, and orientations for a project from groups composed of the public, professionals, elected officials, academics, and researchers. Some common techniques used by designers and planners to elicit participation or to clarify demands follow.

- *Task forces* are ad hoc agency-sponsored citizen committees, or small groups of people, "representing various interests, points of view, or fields of expertise" (Creighton 2005, 103) with a well-defined task, often relating to a single problem or issue. Such a specific task may be to establish goals and propose actions for an urban design project.
- *Citizens' advisory committees* are appointed to represent the ideas and attitudes of local groups. Their purpose is to advise a decision-making body, such as a planning commission, an agency staff, a developer, or an urban designer.
- *Technical advisory committees* are groups that represent bodies of technical or scientific information that is important to a planning commission, an agency, a developer, or a designer. Often these groups are multidisciplinary. A technical

advisory committee may be an interagency committee, or it may be a group composed of university or consulting company members.

- *Neighborhood planning councils* are organizations formed by citizens or an outside community organizer that engage in various neighborhood programs as well as in advocacy.
- *Group dynamics* is a generic term for a variety of problem-solving techniques used to define and to clarify goals, to encourage group interaction, and to resolve conflict within citizen groups.
- The *charrette,* an example of group dynamics, is "an intense effort that lasts for several days to solve a problem or come up with a design in a limited time: it is focused on a single issue" (Creighton 2005, 105). Charrettes may also be used to find general agreement on design issues.
- *Nominal group workshops,* another form of group dynamics, are built on the premise that any reasonably representative group of people who are concerned with a project or an issue can identify virtually all of the problems associated with the project or issue and can make the individual compromises necessary for reaching priorities or preferences (Institute for Participatory Management and Planning 1978, 5–6; Gil and Lucchesi 1979; Creighton 2005; Steiner 2008).

During the preliminary phase of a design process, the designer should ask and consider a variety of specific questions. Some of these can be shared with the client or the public in the first steps of the process, or they can become the starting points for involvement activities. Questions can be related to the following:

- *Past experience.* What kinds of issues have cropped up in similar projects in the past? What kinds of solutions were adopted? Were these solutions applied? Can they be visited or have they been described in journals or books? Have users or others described or evaluated similar projects? Is it possible to meet the designers, the clients, or the people involved in similar projects? What are the positive and negative aspects affecting similar projects? What went wrong? Why?
- *User groups.* Who will be the regular users? Who will be occasional users? What might their concerns be? Which groups of people might be consulted and how? How might user-group needs change in the future demographically— (e.g., obsolescence, immigration, or gentrification)?
- *Uses.* When will the site be used: daytime, nighttime, seven days a week, twenty-four hours a day? Are there differences between day and night use or between

workdays and weekends? Should the design address the issue of evening or night use? Are there potential conflicts among the foreseen uses? When? Why? How can these conflicts be solved?

Some of these questions can also be used in formal and informal meetings with the client or any interested or involved parties.

The Brief

At the very beginning of the design process, it helps for the designer to receive a brief to better understand where, how, and with whom to arrive at the design solution. A brief is a document—with written descriptions, images, and maps—that states project requirements. Briefs are typical for competitions and workshops. In competitions, the brief is the linkage and agreement among the subject initiating the process, the competing teams, and the jury that will evaluate the submitted proposals. In a workshop, the brief works in the same way but with only two participants: the entity commissioning the project and the participating team.

A brief can also be prepared for direct assignments to better define the client's aspirations, to stimulate the design team, and to help manage the design process. According to Alastair Blyth and John Worthington (2001, 3), "briefing is an evolutionary process of understanding an organization's needs and resources, and matching this to its objectives and its mission. It is about problem formulation and problem solving. It is also about managing change. . . . Effective briefing begins without pre-conceived solutions. Briefing is a process by which options are reviewed and requirements articulated." A typical urban design brief seeks to define the particular needs of the area, places the site into a regional context, and explains the interests of the client and other participants. The objective of an urban design brief, according to Blyth and Worthington (179), is to accomplish the following tasks:

- Identify the range of stakeholders and their expectations.
- Set out the conditions, constraints, and opportunities of the site.
- Test alternative uses and design strategies to meet the different expectations.
- Focus on an achievable vision by presenting precedents of best practice from local examples and abroad.
- Establish goals, objectives, and a plan of action.

Typical data needs for preparing a brief are listed in Box 2.1.

Box 2.1 Data Needs for Preparing a Brief

Maps and Images

Base maps
Aerial photographs
Existing land uses
Historical images
Historical maps
Photos and other representations of the area

Natural Environment

Climate
Topography
Soils
Water features
Vegetation habitat areas
Natural hazards
Natural resources

Housing

Conditions
Vacancy rates
Affordability
Market prices
Proportion of public versus private

Transportation

Street networks
Street capacities
Traffic-flow volumes
Parking supply and demand
Transit facilities by mode
Bicycle and pedestrian networks

Public Utilities

Water supply
Wastewater disposal
Stormwater management
Solid waste management
Telecommunication services
Heating networks

Community Services

Administrative centers
Education facilities
Parks and recreation facilities
Health services
Public safety facilities
Religious centers

Population and Local Economy

Population size
Population characteristics
Vital statistics
Labor force characteristics
Businesses and enterprises (sectors, workforce, and employees)
Cost of living

Planning and Special Topics

History of the area
Urban studies, ethnographies, and local history
Urban plans and zoning
Policies and regulations (national, regional, and local)
Projects under evaluation or under construction that can influence the study area
Historic sites and buildings (types of constraints and applicable rules)
Archaeological sites

Source: Adapted from Anderson, Klein, and Meck 2007, 5.

The Brief for the Vatnsmýri Airport Area Competition, Reykjavík
A competition brief was issued in 2006 by the City of Reykjavík, the capital of Iceland. The organizers called for ideas for the airport area of Vatnsmýri, a large site (370 acres, or 150 hectares) south of Reykjavík (see Figure 2.1). The competition goal was "to maximize the opportunity offered by Vatnsmýri to strengthen and consolidate the city for the twenty-first century, providing quality and a strong sense of community. By creating a contemporary and robust urban fabric with the flexibility required for research, technology, and knowledge based enterprises mixed with significant housing, services, and new residential forms, Reykjavík will strengthen its international role and competitive edge" (Reykjavíkurborg 2007, 2). The "Call for Ideas" document was considered to be the brief. It was included in the material distributed to the participants to inform them about the project requirements. The Call for Ideas contained the following:

- An explanation of the procedure and of the project proponent
- The project description with maps and written descriptions of Iceland, Reykjavík, the site, the adjoining areas, and the planning provisions
- Goals and assessment criteria
- Procedures, with participant registration rules, for accepting entries and for assessing the proposals
- Information on
    - history and archaeological remains
    - nature and ecology
    - weather and sunlight
    - transportation and traffic planning
    - Reykjavík's economy and plans
    - consultations with the public and other affected parties

The material organized for the Vatnsmýri competition also included large maps at regional and municipal scales, projects already proposed for the adjoining areas to consider in the design process, and annotated photos of the site and of the surrounding areas. Also included was a document called "Consultation Days," which contained a summary of the two-day participation process through which the City of Reykjavík promoted the project and prepared people for the transformation of the site. The document included suggestions from participants about forms, densities, and future development; the urban environment they envisaged; and the results of an experiment with wooden blocks (see Figure 2.2) that corresponded

Figure 2.1 Aerial map of the Vatnsmýri site. (From Reykjavíkurborg 2007, II.)

Figure 2.2 Participants at the "Consultation Days" event had the opportunity to use wooden building blocks to create the kind of development they liked. Twenty proposals were prepared by individuals or groups. Each proposal was then sketched and displayed on the wall. (From City of Reykjavík 2007, 23.)

to single buildings and urban blocks. The participants arranged these blocks to visualize land use, shapes of urban patterns, recreational spaces, and connections with existing natural features. Another document, called "Stakeholder Meetings," included the minutes from meetings with interested parties in preparation for the competition. Stakeholders' expectations for the site were collected during consultations organized by the municipality in the months before announcing the competition.

Summary

An urban design project usually results from a request by a client to a professional designer. The client's requirements are not the only aspects that will guide the design, however. Other factors will emerge from the environment in which the design will take place as well as from regulations and plans that shape the site and its environs. The affected community commonly influences the forthcoming project and can help define the aims and goals of an urban design. The combinations of all these aspects, expectations, assumptions, and restrictions are here considered as *prerequisites*.

3. Knowledge

Although prerequisites involve the complex requests and information that the client gives to the designer, the urban design team needs to take additional steps to delve more deeply into the site and its context, parts, and components. This is the part of the process we define as *knowledge*. This stage is pivotal in the process. It is the time when designers investigate a site and its surroundings to understand the place that they will attempt to transform. Kevin Lynch states: "Every site, natural or man-made, is to some degree unique, a connected web of things and activities. That web imposes limitations and offers possibilities" (Lynch and Hack 1984, 5).

In most cases, the information and data provided by clients need to be expanded. The designer should review the information provided in the brief and the data gathered during workshops or for the competition. In addition, data may be available from the public agencies with jurisdictional responsibility for the study area. Information and data can be enhanced through research in books, journals, reports, and websites. Whenever possible, the designer should visit the site. But there are some situations in which it is almost impossible, because of time, distance, and money, to visit the site, to undertake an original survey, or to elaborate on information that has been provided.

With competitions, site visits are typically difficult, and it can be a challenge to make direct and original surveys. Frequently, competitions are for areas distant from the home of the team. Workshops are situations in which it is not easy to collect new data and elaborate on them. Time constraints are also common. But even in such circumstances, it is possible to prepare an analysis with the documentation provided or to look for other information apart from that given in the brief. This chapter describes different techniques for improving information and combining data to compose the knowledge of the site and its surroundings. The site should be viewed in ecological terms, that is, as a system of organisms—humans and non-humans—interacting with one another and their environments, including those beyond the project boundary.

A total knowledge of the place is practically unachievable. Time, money, and abilities are not constantly available, and it is not realistic to know everything of a place and of its connected webs. Urban designers will look ultimately for a reasonable knowledge that will allow them to understand data and information well enough to begin the design. Lynch writes: "Understanding a locality demands time and effort" (Lynch and Hack 1984, 5). Such understanding also requires some detail to describe the potential analyses that can be undertaken during an urban design process. As a result, this chapter is lengthy.

Survey and Analysis

Survey and analysis techniques and procedures depend largely on the nature and scale of the urban design project. The techniques outlined here focus on urban sites at different scales. The aim is to define a potential framework of surveys and analyses. This section does not claim to be comprehensive or to be universally applicable. Designers adapt such tools based on the specific circumstances, just as a carpenter adjusts tools to fit a particular project.

Several analysis and survey techniques have been developed for urban design activities, and many good examples of typical working methods to understand a place are available. Urban Design Associates (UDA), a Pittsburgh, Pennsylvania, firm, published *The Urban Design Handbook* (2003), which includes several techniques, including UDA X-ray drawings. These drawings are a graphic analysis technique to represent existing conditions at different scales and, in a later phase, to show proposed future conditions (UDA 2003, 73). Similarly, Ian McHarg (1969) used the X-ray metaphor when describing his ecological map overlay system, which, Anne Spirn (1998) observes, reveals the deep structure and the deep context of a place.

Additional examples can be found in other handbooks. *Urban Analysis* (Schwalbach 2009) provides basic insights of historical urban analysis of social spaces, land use, open spaces, and transportation structures, while *Urban Building Blocks* (Bürklin and Peterek 2008) describes a survey technique as well as the roles and functions of different building blocks. The student edition of *Planning and Urban*

Design Standards (Steiner and Butler 2007) describes social and demographic analysis. *Urban Design: Methods and Techniques* (Moughtin et al. 2004) emphasizes the role of sieve mapping and Geographic Information System (GIS) technology to collect and connect data related to physical, functional, socioeconomic, and behavioral aspects. *Graphics for Urban Design* (Meeda, Parkyn, and Walton 2006) offers good examples on how to visualize contextual, spatial, statistical, and conceptual analysis. *Urban Design Toolkit* is a compendium of techniques prepared by New Zealand's Ministry for the Environment (2009). Now in its third edition, it offers synthetic descriptions of research and analysis tools, such as the space syntax analysis (Hillier and Hanson 1984) and the legibility analysis advanced by Kevin Lynch in *The Image of the City* (1960).

To adapt techniques to the task at hand and to the specific characteristics of the place, urban designers need first to consider such variables as the time available for accomplishing the task, the information available, and the type of the design commissioned. Several principles should be considered when beginning to collect data and undertake analyses:

- There is no set framework of analysis to follow that fits every situation.
- Site visits can lead to unexpected outcomes that might contrast with initial design sketches and concepts.
- The urban designer should be able to adjust to such discrepancies without falsifying the analytical outcomes just to have them fit a preconceived design.
- Analyses are executed not to correspond to some categorical imperative or some ethical or normative obligation or to a mandatory checklist but to guide the design process.

When a design has been fed exclusively by the designer's "creativity" without regard for the analyses, or when there is a recognizable gap between the outcomes of the analyses and the final results, the project will become distorted and, frequently, a failure.

Site Visits

Direct familiarity with the site is a crucial experience for any designer. Moreover, direct acquaintance with the place prior to other activities helps designers to define the types and kind of surveys and analysis necessary for the project. Even if complete information is available in the form of pictures from several diverse points of view, detailed reports, meticulous surveying, analyses, and sophisticated elaborations, the visit to the site presents a decisive event in the design process. The designer should have an opportunity to walk around the study area with a camera, a pencil, and a sketchbook. During a site visit, the designer should be receptive to signals coming from the place; its context can reveal its component parts, such as sounds, colors, smells, shapes, combinations, and expressions. This is called the *sense of place* (or *genius loci*). Such insight enables the designer to direct the plan toward unexpected and otherwise unforeseeable destinations.

The experiences of urban designers, landscape architects, and architects reveal the importance of the visit and its determining role in the design process. The site visit also provides the moment when preconceptions falter and new ideas take shape. Exploring the *genius loci* has challenged generations of urban analysts. Christian Norberg-Schulz (1980, 5, 6, 8) says in his book of the same title:

> A place is a space which has a distinctive character. Since ancient time the *genius loci*, or "spirit of place," has been recognized as the concrete reality man has to face and come to terms with in his daily life. Architecture means to visualize the *genius loci* and the task of the architect is to create meaningful places where he helps man to dwell. [. . . A place is] something more than abstract location. We mean a totality made up of concrete things having material substance, shape, texture and colour. Together these things determine an "environmental character," which is the essence of place. In general a place is given as such a character or "atmosphere." A place is therefore a qualitative, "total" phenomenon, which we cannot reduce to any of its properties, such as spatial relationships, without losing its concrete nature out of sight.

A specific type of site visit is the "walking tour" or "guided walk," in which the urban design team visits the site together with interested people from the community who could be affected by the project. Sometimes, before the start of a project or prior to writing the brief, it can help to bring interested parties to the site to listen to their opinions about the place. An organized record of comments, suggestions, and recommendations can become an important tool for the designers.

The Visit to the Sea: Renzo Piano

A meaningful episode about experiencing the site was told by Renzo Piano to Fulvio Irace in the interview that opens the catalogue of the exhibition Città Visibili to the Triennale of Milan in 2007. Piano speaks about the plan for the international airport Kansai in Japan, which rises on an artificial island:

> When with Peter Rice we began the Kansai project, between the not familiar waters of the Yellow sea, we asked to go to see the site and they answered that there was not a site, because the island had not been built yet. . . . For half a day we were berthed on a boat to imagine a building where there was only water and in that silence we practiced our usual initiation rituals to the project. It is never bad to exercise your imagination: to go in a place thinking that, where there is nothing, there will be something. . . . It is like a physical exercise: you go to the place and memorize the context, then you close your eyes and you can imagine the project, therefore when you reopen them you can position the building in its place. This nearly cinematographic technique is faster than the computer and it is fundamental because when you have captured the place you can also see it again at home; to go to the place is essential. (Irace 2007, 8, 11)

The site visit helps the designer understand what that place means for those who live there. When talking about this activity, Piano also says that

> to listen is useful because it is the art of stealing, of taking, of capturing: it is bare-faced robbery, with a noble goal. We often chat with the clients or the inhabitants of the place, and I return home with my sheets of notes and sketches: the list of the stolen property. Going around, hands in pockets and nose in the air in order to absorb, is the art of listening, because also places speak and too often the architect does not listen to them. The places speak, people speak. . . . It is necessary to listen to the thin voices, the silent and weak voices; to capture the essence of the things implies a training in listening that is not learned at school, but through life experiences. (Irace 2007, 14)

The experiences of great interpreters of architecture convey principles that, in most urban design situations, need to be combined with surveying the urban texture and listening to people (discussed further in Chapter 6, Dialogues).

Photos and Sketches

Photographs and hand-drawn sketches enable the designer to record key features of the site. The designer can try to capture the overall spirit of the place as well as specific details (see Figures 3.1 and 3.2). Positive and negative attributes can be recorded as well as historical buildings and places and natural characteristics. Designers frequently use site photographs in subsequent phases of the process, especially in the master plan and when communicating with the client and the public.

Figure 3.1 Parliament from the River Thames, London. (Drawing by Carl Steinitz.)

Figure 3.2 Piazza San Marco, Venice. (Drawing by Carl Steinitz.)

During a site visit, notes are taken in various ways. First, the designer builds a mental inventory, a personal geography of the place. Urban areas are composed not only of solids or voids but also of sounds, smells, lights, and feelings tied to the presence or absence of people—activities that are carried out or, alternatively, their absence. When visiting a site, the designer envisions a series of images, more or less clear and precise, that foresee the future order. The designer imagines persons, masses, and volumes where there are empty spaces, and conceives functions in place of abandoned buildings or skeletons and abandoned structures. The designer sees trees and open spaces where there are worn-out asphalt and ruins. Designers cover the real image with their own knowledge, with personal professional experiences, with projects already in existence.

This mental geography occurs many times throughout the design process. Sometimes designers will notice that their projections overlap with the actual map of the place, or that some impressions and feelings that they had during the visit could not be recorded with a camera or a sketch. The image survives in the designer's memory and imagination.

During the visit, it is useful to also employ less evanescent tools, such as photography. Digital cameras have advanced our ability to capture images of the study area. With film cameras, fewer shots were taken than are now with digital cameras that have virtually limitless memory. Having to change the film every twenty-four or thirty-six shots or to decide in advance whether to use color or black-and-white film, negative film, or slides and having to wait for the pictures to be printed after having chosen the format and the number of copies are aspects far surpassed with digital photos. In addition, digital cameras, like their film predecessors, record the date and the time the image was captured, which can be helpful in design.

A site visit should be well organized starting with reading the map of the site. The designer should know ahead of time which questions to ask residents. It is necessary to organize the tasks among the participating design team members (to avoid double coverage of the same areas by different team members), to share responsibilities for large or complex areas, and to organize site exploration from a variety of vantage points: on top of a nearby building, on the ground, far away, who will photograph the existing buildings, the empty spaces, and so forth.

Taking a picture is never an objective act. The choices of lens, shot, light, and the moment when the picture is captured are all decisions that influence the result. It is often useful to record these decisions.

Sketches, drawings, and notes on a map are additional ways to know a place. In a sketch, it is important to understand the relationships between places, between solids and voids. As Carl Steinitz (2009, 79) observes: "My main purpose in drawing is to record the event of being there." He uses field drawings as "a kind of visual diary." To understand a place, it can help to hand-draw a section or a plan (see Figures 3.3/Plate #3 and 3.4/Plate #4).

In *Townscape* (1961), Gordon Cullen demonstrates that a skillful hand is not the only means for reading a city atmosphere to transform it. A map is the most meaningful companion in a site visit. On the map, it is possible to mark buildings that no longer exist, new buildings, and other changes. The designer can also record what is seen and observed as well as viewpoints and questions to explore further.

Graphic comments can be added to the map, using color pens or pencils, or graphic software once images are loaded onto computer. The designer should also

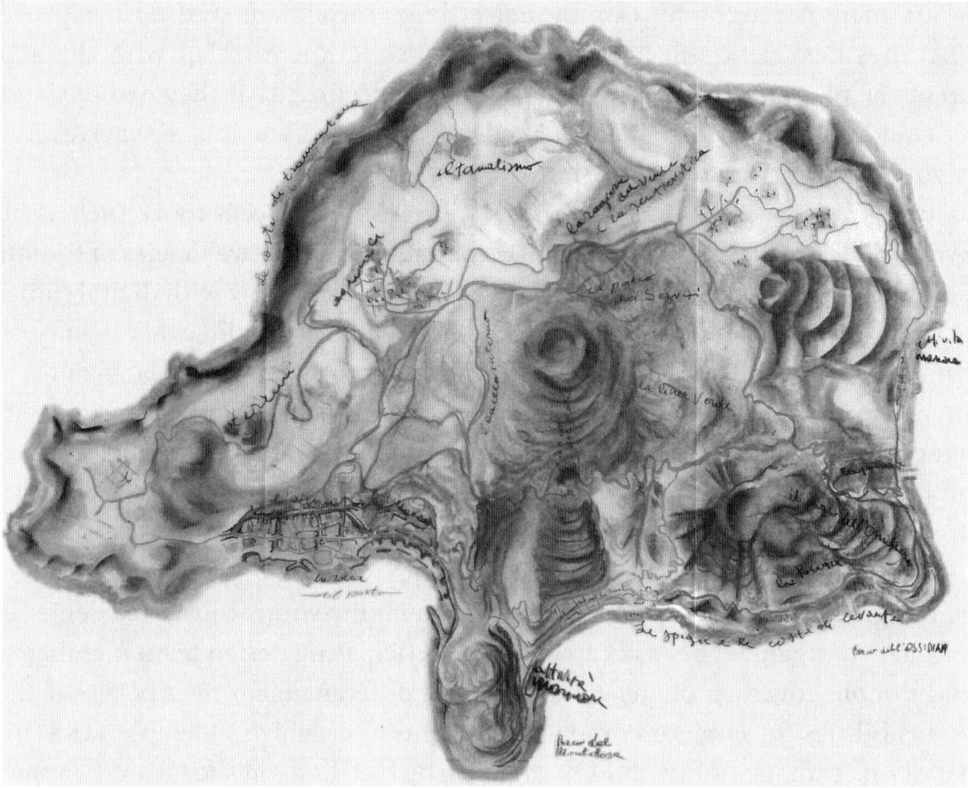

Figure 3.3 (also Plate #3) Isola di Lipari, Messina, Italy: the natural and human-made environments. (From Leone 2004, p. C XII.)

record the time and date of the visit on the map. Before the site visit, a list of features to visit can be made with spaces for comments. The designer can also plot routes to follow before the visit. Archaeologists and ecologists use a grid system for sampling during their site inventories. Designers can adapt this technique to ensure that they cover the whole site during their visit.

A widespread tool for organizing a site visit is an aerial or satellite photo. Such photos can be used during several phases of the process in addition to the site visit. Aerial and satellite photos, tridimensional images of buildings, or photos of street facades or entire urban quarters are widely available on the Internet. Aerial pictures can be used to prepare a visit but should not replace it. Google Earth and ArcGIS Online are useful tools to visit a place virtually, before an actual visit. The designer can also return to Google Earth or ArcGIS Online to check site elements and characteristics.

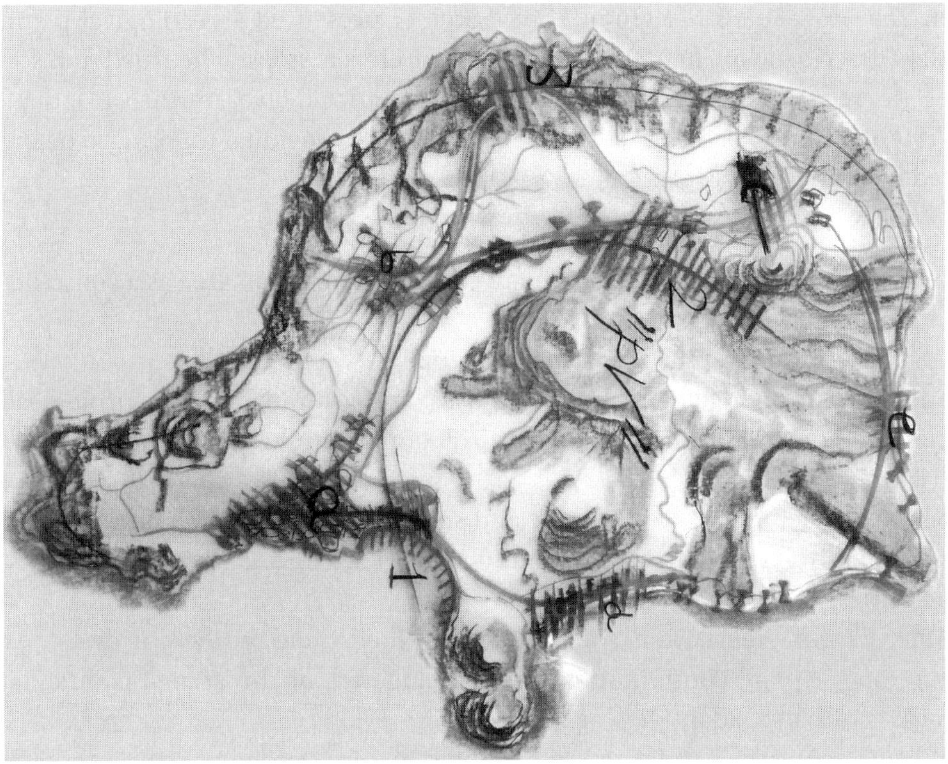

Figure 3.4 (also Plate #4) Isola di Lipari, Messina, Italy: ideograms to interpret the natural and human-made environments. (From Leone 2004, p. C XII.)

During the visit, the designer will usually engage site users in conversation, which can be as useful as taking photos or making sketches. A group of visitors with cameras, notebooks, and maps always stimulates the attention and curiosity of the inhabitants and users of the place. This should be the beginning of a dialogue that can help the designer to understand the place from the perspective of those who live or work there.

Ecological Planning Methods

Ecological planning emerged in North America during the 1960s. The pioneering studies of McHarg and others, including George Angus Hills in Canada and Philip H. Lewis in Wisconsin, became well known among professionals, scholars, and students. These studies and applications, which originated from many precedents in regional planning and landscape architecture (Palazzo 1997; McHarg and Steiner 1998; Ndubisi 2002), have evolved rapidly since the 1980s.

In *The Living Landscape* (1991, 2008), Steiner presented an ecological planning model (described in Chapter 1) composed of eleven steps. The third and fourth steps are, respectively, dedicated to "regional and local level inventory and analysis." Steiner's book provides a list of elements, from regional to local, to be inventoried in the design process:

- *Regional climate*—temperature and precipitation
- *Geology*—geological maps to evaluate the suitability of an area as a construction site
- *Terrain*—physiography (elevation and slope)
- *Water*—water budget (precipitation, uses, and groundwater), hydrological cycle, flooding areas, water quality, hydrologic system, water supply, and sewage treatment systems
- *Soils*—characteristics, soil survey, and soil capability classification (the survey particularly helps with understanding land uses and land values for specific activities)
- *Microclimate*—ventilation, solar radiation, albedo, and temperatures
- *Vegetation*—plant communities; rare, endangered, or threatened plants; native and disturbance adaptive plants
- *Wildlife*—species; habitat values; habitat of rare, endangered, or threatened species
- *Existing land use* and *land users*—the physical arrangement of space utilized by humans, ownership (public and private), settlement patterns, buildings, and open space types

In *The Granite Garden*, Anne Spirn (1984) advances McHarg's method for urban areas. She uses the clever subtitle "Urban Nature and Human Design" to explain her approach. Spirn illustrates the importance of understanding the natural settings of cities, including their air, geology, water, plants, and animals, to create better urban spaces.

Ecological Footprints

The ecological footprint concept was developed by Mathis Wackernagel and William Rees (1996) at the University of British Columbia. They were interested in measuring the consequences of human actions, especially urban uses, on ecosystems. In urban design, the concept can be applied to determine how much of the earth will need to be used for the proposed project. The analysis compares the resources needed to support the project with nature's ability to regenerate those resources and to produce ecosystem services. As a result, the designer could estimate demand for water, food, and energy as well as waste and carbon produced by the project.

> The Ecological Footprint measures the impact of consumption and subsequent waste discharge (including consumption of food, housing, transportation, consumer goods and services) by converting impact variables into the single unit of land. This includes land appropriated by fossil energy use, the built environment, gardens, crop land, pasture, managed forest and land of limited availability, including untouched forests and non-productive areas such as deserts and icecaps. It has been applied at various scales, but it appears to be especially popular at the national, urban and personal scales, although recently, it has been acknowledged that the approach perhaps works best at the national level, and that particularly for comparative purposes more work needs to be done to improve its application at the urban level.
>
> In the case of a city, the approach can be used to calculate the equivalent amount of land consumed in order for a city to function. This equivalent amount of land is influenced by changes in both population and per capita material consumption (McManus and Haughton 2006, 115).

Phil McManus and Graham Haughton note that the ecological footprint concept has been applied at several scales in Europe, Australia, and North and South America (2006). The two authors maintain that "the Ecological Footprint is a very effective way for officials and politicians to convince the public of their environmental policies, by appealing to the apparent common sense and fair play aspects of reducing the negative impacts of a city on areas beyond its boundaries" (123), but at the same time they retain that "although the tool is intended to be used sensitively by those developing it for different places, this caveat is not enough to overcome our concerns about the tendency inherent in a universalizing tool to reduce issues to over-simplistic readings of problems, and from this, their solutions" (126). The Center for Sustainable Economy and the Global Footprint Network maintain websites where one's ecological footprint can be computed (http://www.myfootprint.org and http://www.footprintnetwork.org).

The Collection and Analyses of Historical Data

Historical analyses highlight the role of the past for transformations being considered for the future. Many urban projects take place in already developed areas of towns and cities. The phenomenon of industrial areas being abandoned or waning

Figure 3.5 Piazza Santissima Annunziata, Florence, Italy. (Photograph by Danilo Palazzo.)

has characterized the evolution of European and North American towns starting from the last quarter of the twentieth century and will no doubt affect urban areas in Asia, Latin America, and Australia in the twenty-first century. The urban environment has always been shaped by additions, integrations, redevelopments, restorations, replacements, eliminations, or removals, as a causal walk around a city like Rome amply illustrates. To work through an urban design, it is necessary to know the phenomena and the complex circumstances that led to forming the present-day town. Kevin Lynch, opening his masterpiece *The Image of the City* (1960, 1), wrote:

> Like a piece of architecture, the city is a construction in space, but one of vast scale, a thing perceived only in the course of long spans of time. . . . At every instant, there is more than the eye can see, more than the ear can hear, a setting or a view waiting to be explored. Nothing is experienced by itself, but always in relation to its surroundings, the sequences of events leading up to it, the memory of past experiences.

Lynch combined the role of time for the city itself and for our personal experience. As urban designers, we should consider how time affects the city and influences our observations.

Edmund Bacon, in *Design of Cities* (1974, 109), formulated the "principle of the second man" according to which "it is the second man who determines whether the creation of the first man will be carried forward or destroyed." Bacon proposes—through positive historical examples such as Piazza SS. Annunziata in Florence, Italy (see Figure 3.5), and the more recent but negative example of the Norrmalm plan in Stockholm, Sweden—that in every moment of history when designers operate in the urban texture of their contemporary city, they act like the "second person," because before them, anonymous or famous designers have shaped the city. One cannot ignore Gaudí in Barcelona, or Burnham and Wright in Chicago, or Olmsted in New York City, or Marx in Rio. "It is the second person involved in a project who determines if the design forces set in motion by the initiator are achieved, developed and enhanced, or destroyed. It is the second designer who has to forgo his or her own egotistical instincts in order to develop the vision of another" (Moughtin et al. 2004, 35)

Bacon (1974, 108–9) described the principle of the second man with an example that links the very end of medieval time and the beginning of Renaissance:

> The great beauty and elegance of Brunelleschi arcade of the Founding Hospital, shown on the right [of the picture], found expression elsewhere in the Piazza della Santissima Annunziata, whether or not Brunelleschi intended to be so. The first significant change in the square, following the completion of the arcade in 1472, was the construction of a central bay of the Santissima Annunziata church. This was designed by Michelozzo in 1454 and is harmonious with Brunelleschi's work. However, the form of the square remained in doubt until 1516, when architects Antonio da Sangallo the Elder and Baccio d'Agnolo were commissioned to design the building opposite to Brunelleschi's arcade. It was the great decision of Sangallo to overcome his urge toward self-expression and follow, almost to the letter, the design of the then eighty-nine-year-old building of Brunelleschi. This design set the form of Piazza della Santissima Annunziata and established, in the Renaissance train of thought, the concept of a space created by several buildings designed in relation to one another. . . . The quality of Piazza della Santissima Annunziata is largely derived from the consummate architectural expression that Brunelleschi gave the first work, the Innocenti arcade, but it is really to Sangallo that we owe the piazza in its present form.

In Stockholm, the principle of the second person resulted in a great fallacy, as Bacon underlines. The lower Norrmalm project, designed by David Helldèn in the 1950s to give form to a new and modern city on top of the subway, substituting the existing Klara quarters, was one of the larger city renovation projects in Europe in the postwar period (see Figure 3.6). The Helldèn project

> with its five tall towers, is concentrated, carefully designed, internally logical, and functionally related to the development of the region, the beauty of the historic Stockholm is not destroyed. . . . The precise position, form, and size of the five towers were fixed by the government. David Helldèn designed the first one himself. . . . Then came the second man. The architect of the second building determined what the relationship would be between the two, just as Sangallo decided in Piazza della Santissima Annunziata. He designed a building very similar to Helldèn's in materials, color, and design expression, but just slightly different. And with this example before them, the same thing was done by the next and the next, the fifth being strikingly different, as was the original intention. The result is a dissonance, as in a quartet in which each person is performing slightly off key. (Bacon 1976, 312–14)

Figure 3.6 The Five Towers in Norrmalm, Stockholm, Sweden. (Photograph by Alessandro Palazzo.)

In general, the second person is asked to intervene in a context in which the existing component can be considered a relevant driving force for the expected urban transformation. The appraisal of the urban components can consider the following topics:

- *Nature of the place*—what were the ecological conditions prior to human settlement and how have people interacted with the environment through time
- *Urban texture*—how the city has been formed, which actions and forces molded it, when the main transformations occurred
- *Patterns of blocks and their characteristics*—their evolution, their density, and the formal composition (heights and masses) of the buildings within city blocks
- *Density*—the number of people per square feet (or square meter) on a given area of land
- *Single functions or mixed use*—what marks or has marked neighborhoods and districts

- *Armatures*—those urban elements that act as "a polar arrangement in which urban space is arranged on an axis between two key attractors, as the poles of a magnet" (Wall and Waterman 2009, 168) (Examples of armature are the Rambla in Barcelona [Figure 3.7], the Galleria Vittorio Emanuele II in Milano [Figure 3.8], and the linear spaces connecting in Washington, DC: Capitol Hill, the National Mall, the Washington Monument, the World War II Memorial, and the Lincoln Memorial.)
- *Building typologies*—what they are, how they have evolved, which of them have lasted through time
- *Single buildings*—buildings protected by law, such as landmark buildings, buildings of value for their historical or architectural features, buildings distinguished for their function, buildings by famous architects, and buildings by unknown designers that are distinguished from their neighbors because of their ability to interpret the typology or the relationship with the streets and the public space or, on the contrary, provide a negative example
- *Building components* and *relationships with the exterior*—that is, the facade pattern of windows, entrances, balconies, loggias, porches, and arcades, and what has been the evolution of the facades and the skins of the buildings
- *Private space*—how the external space of private buildings is organized and how it is utilized (courtyards, gardens, parking lots, and commercial uses)
- *Street network*—their sections, what functions they had and now have, their role when they were designed, and which parts are still in use
- *Public space*—how the meeting, ceremonial, representative, and recreational spaces have changed, which functions are carried out now in public spaces compared to those originally planned (Particular attention can be paid to understand how spaces are shared among different age groups; by different means of transportation and mobility, including bikes, walking, cars, and public transportation; and how uses change during weekdays as well as between daytime and nighttime.)
- *Paving* and *street furnishing*—which are the elements that characterized the original design site, which ones have remained, and which have been replaced
- *Markers of places*—which are the markers and landmarks people use to move through the city (Tall buildings, bridges, statues, sculptures, and signs can act as elements of the mental map of everyone traveling, walking, or biking through the city structure; see Figure 3.9.)
- *Planning tools*—urban plans and policy documents for the city or the precincts for managing transformation and changes

- *Previous projects*—the site may have been affected in the past by projects that partially or totally involved it, as the Norrmalm example illustrates. Competitions may have been launched whose results were never implemented. By understanding such failures, the urban designer may avoid past mistakes.

Such topics can be studied by consulting several sources. Current maps, site visits, previous urban studies, and historical papers, held in public or private archives or collected in monographs, can be useful for reconstructing the urban evolution of the city or its parts.

Historic Growth Pattern Map

To visualize the growth and the transformation of an urban area, a useful tool is the *historic growth pattern map*. Different historical ages, displayed on maps, can be laid over a recent base for comparison. Various colors can be used to illustrate historical cartographic borders (for instance, employing a color scale ranging from

Figure 3.7 La Rambla, Barcelona, Spain. (Photograph by Danilo Palazzo.)

Figure 3.8 The Galleria Vittorio Emanuele, Milan, Italy. (Photograph by Danilo Palazzo.)

darker to lighter to indicate the more distant past to the more recent, preferably using warm tones). The production of an urban pattern historical evolution map begins by collecting maps of different historical borders, preferably in the same scale. In Italy, for example, in public or university archives, it is possible to retrieve the Istituto Geografico Militare (IGM) maps that cover the entire Italian peninsula. The production of IGM maps began at the end of the nineteenth century (a few years after the unification of Italy in 1861) and were subsequently updated until more recent years. Generally, these maps show features for the 1880s, 1930s, 1950s, and 1970s. Maps produced by Italian regions are frequently current.

In the United States, Sanborn maps have a similar function. These maps were created between 1867 and 1970 to assess fire insurance liability for around twelve thousand U.S. towns and cities. They provide detailed information about buildings, city blocks, and streets and were drawn at a scale of fifty feet to one inch (http://sanborn.umi.com/).

After historical maps are collected, the process of drawing a new map of the

Figure 3.9 Chicago, Wabash Avenue: the elevated train and, in the distance, the Trump International Hotel and Tower designed by Skidmore, Owings & Merrill, 2008. The tower was completed in 2009. (Photograph by Danilo Palazzo.)

urban pattern historical evolution begins. Today, such maps can be created using digital programs such as CAD (computer-aided design) or graphical programs such as Adobe Illustrator or CorelDRAW. The most recent map is compared with previous maps chronologically. Depending on the level of detail, the buildings or blocks appear only on the most recent map to represent the transformation that took place over the years between the penultimate and the last map. This same process is applied to the past, using darker tones to color the urban parts that differ in the various historical periods (see Figure 3.10 as an example of historical evolution maps applied to Timişoara, Romania).

A similar technique was applied by Brian McGrath to the lower half of Manhattan Island. McGrath started Manhattan Timeformations in the 1990s with an exhibition and a book called *Transparent Cities* (McGrath, 1994). Subsequently, a permanent exhibition was installed at the Skyscraper Museum in New York City

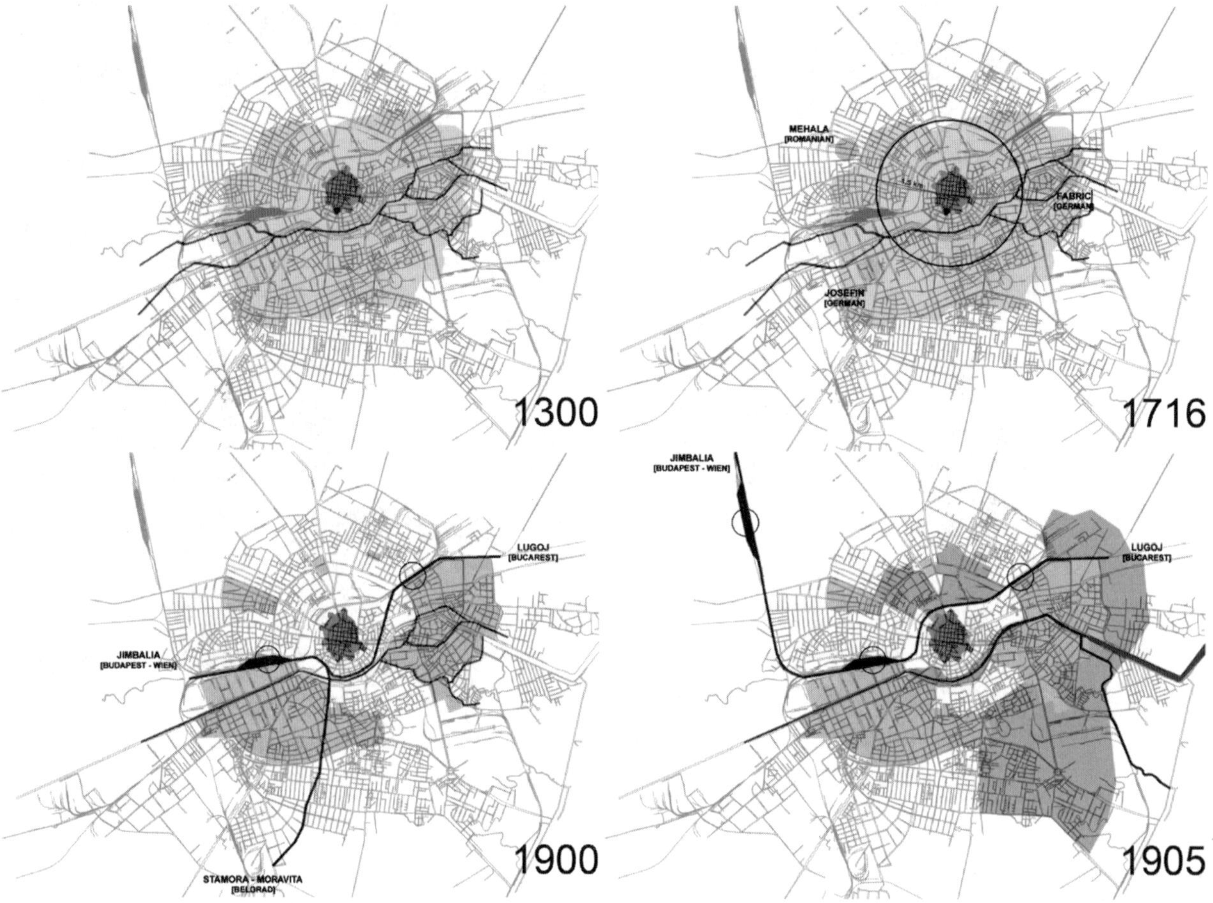

Figure 3.10 Timişoara, Romania: historic growth pattern from the fourteenth century to the twenty-first century. (By Massimo Tadi.)

and on an interactive and animated computer model on the web (http://www.skyscraper.org/timeformations). According to the Skyscraper Museum per its website, the exhibit simultaneously presents "a layered, cartographic history of the lower half of Manhattan Island, and an exploded time line chronicling the real estate development of high-rise office buildings which constitute the skylines of Midtown and Downtown Manhattan." For an even deeper natural history, see Eric Sanderson's marvelous *Mannahatta* (2009), a study of the island's landscape ecology prior to European settlement. In 2010, the Wildlife Conservation Society took this research beyond Manhattan to the other four New York boroughs in its

Welikia Project to reveal the original ecology of the whole city (http://welikia.org).

Collecting old photographs, drawings, newspapers, and books about the history of the place enables investigation into other elements, such as the role and the hierarchy of streets and public spaces, the functional evolution of historical buildings, and the architectural character of important buildings. Documents in local archives and other public or private records can sometimes make it possible to understand some of the design choices made in the past and the reasons why solutions were discarded while others were preferred. Local documents, written by amateur historians, can aid in understanding the role of the past in the contemporary urban design.

Collecting historical data can contribute to the design through the recognition of past values of site features. This process can help suggest a direction for developing and protecting valuable elements and can also distinguish those parts, either buildings or open spaces, that can be replaced or transformed.

Urban Morphology

Another aspect to consider in the urban design analysis is the site's morphology. University of Washington professor Anne Vernez Moudon (1997, 3) defines urban morphology as "the study of the city as human habitat. . . . Buildings, gardens, streets, parks, and monuments are among the main elements of morphological analysis."

Morphological analysis is particularly useful when the urban design takes place in a historical area or in a well-established urban texture. Such analysis can also help when the purpose of the plan is to substitute and to complete urban areas. This is typically the case in the redevelopment of former industrial areas in mature city contexts. In such cases, "the shaping of the city needs to go through a phase of research and design that, stemming from the very fact that construction is always linked to particular circumstances, finds a complement of knowledge grounded in historical research" (Malfroy 2001, 66).

Urban blocks are relevant elements of classical European cities that characterized some of the more important transformations, such as what happened in Paris with Georges-Eugène Haussmann (from 1853 to 1882); in Amsterdam, according to the plan by Hendrik Petrus Berlage (from 1913 to 1934); and in the British Garden Cities (at the beginning of the twentieth century). Urban blocks, beginning from the second half of the twentieth century, were discredited, according to Panerai and colleagues (2004), although they still remain "the interest in the 'physical dimension of the city' and the attempt to penetrate the mysteries of the 'urban tissue'" (ix). Nevertheless, the interest in urban blocks had a recent resurgence in the United States and the United Kingdom. In the United States, "the work of the New Urbanism and the Charter for the New Urbanism had returned to the street and blocks as basic elements of the urban tissue, whether in urban renewal projects or urban extensions. In the UK, the Urban Villages Movement [and other projects] demonstrate a similar return to traditional forms" (Samuels 2004, viii).

The Urban Morphology Analysis in the Fiera Catena Plan of Mantua, Italy

The planning of an area of the city of Mantua, Italy, called Fiera Catena provides an example of applying a historical and morphological analysis to an urban design. Toward the end of the 1990s, the municipality of Mantua commissioned the Milan Polytechnic to develop the analysis and preliminary hypothesis for the detailed plan of Fiera Catena, an area of approximately 76.6 acres (31 hectares) in the historical center of Mantua. The historical analysis was of fundamental importance to establish guidelines for orienting the buildings, identifying the strong concept to follow, and determining which elements to retain or to eliminate. The team asked a city historian to prepare a historical map of the area to help guide the transformation plan.

The Fiera Catena area, to the southwest of Mantua, was incorporated into the city following the works on the Pitentino water system and the construction of the third perimeter wall completed in the fifteenth century. This portion of the city evolved through the influence of nearby Porto Catena. From the end of the fourteenth and throughout the fifteenth centuries, the harbor was the main landing point for the city, and important trading activities moved into the surrounding zone, influencing the building development of the area. During the seventeenth century, the Duchy of Gonzaga's decline also affected the city's economy. Porto Catena lost its relevance, and the lack of periodic dredging works to maintain the harbor rendered it unfit for use. In 1707, Mantua was annexed to form part of the Habsburg Empire, becoming an important military fort because of its location. In 1709 and 1710, the government, in an attempt to restore the business activities of the harbor, arranged for a series of works that gave Porto Catena the layout still largely visible today. Increasing strategic-military requirements led, especially in this part of the city, to growth of the military infrastructure. For instance, two new munitions stores were constructed. After the closure of the convent complexes of S. Maria del Gradaro and S. Paola, located in the more southern zone, they became warehouses and artillery barracks.

During the nineteenth century, new operations were undertaken at the harbor site. Between the end of the nineteenth and the early twentieth centuries, the Società Ceramica Mantovana, which produced ceramic articles, opened its factory in the precinct. The military presence continued over a long time span, and the harbor remained a trading point until 1964, in spite of the railway construction and the enhancement of the highway network. During the 1960s, the Società Ceramica Mantovana closed and its vast area was abandoned, beginning a general continuous decline in the area. By the end of the 1990s, Porto Catena was used by just a few pleasure boats. The surrounding building situation was in a bad state, aside from sporadic redevelopments. The Urban General Plan—in the same area for which a competition had previously been held—required that approximately

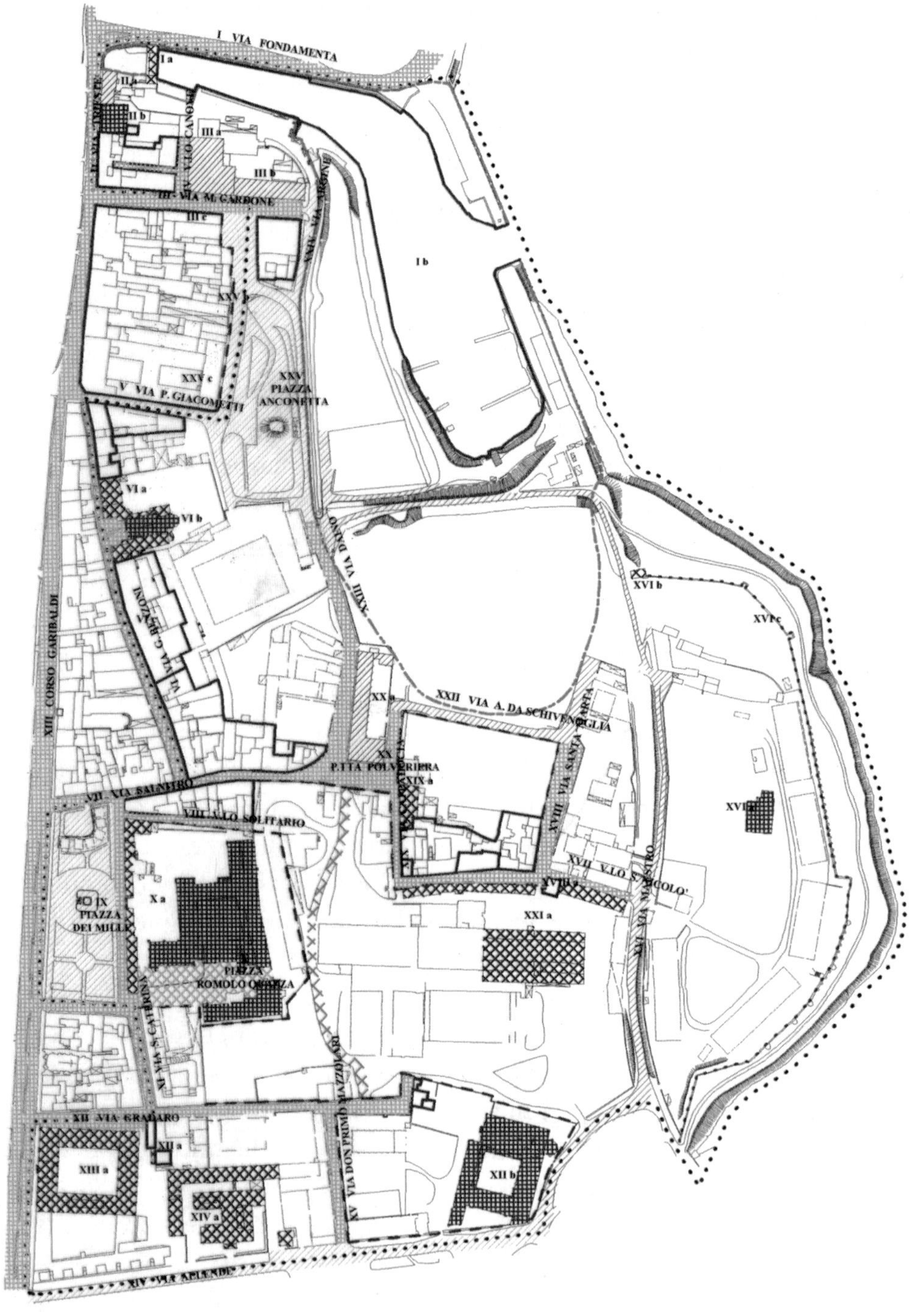

Figure 3.11 Historical map of the Fiera Catena area, Mantua, Italy, 1999. (From Treu 1999. Principal investigator: Claudia Bonora.)

1,291,669 square feet (120,000 square meters) of mixed residential and business functions together with city and regional services (the courthouse) be added to the existing 538,195 square feet (50,000 square meters).

The request to the city history expert was to supply a report and a summary map, which would effectively guide the development of the area. The purpose of the historical analysis was to inform the design of the area and to support the options for redeveloping the historic street network. The design would include how to orient new buildings, how to complete the existing urban design framework, how to recognize which buildings could be demolished, and how to protect, through regulations, valuable buildings and to replace or renovate those lacking in historic-architectural value.

Through analysis and study of publications, and comparison of the various historical maps, the characteristic elements of the evolution and the transformation of the urban fabric of this portion of Mantua were ascertained. The historical map (see Figure 3.11) illustrates that a great part of the street and road network is of undisputed value because it remained mostly unchanged for centuries. For some specific areas, the map displayed the following levels of preservation opportunities:

- Buildings of artistic and historic value as "monuments"
- Historical buildings with architectural value, but not enough to consider them monuments
- Buildings that for their specific features can be considered typical for their period
- Historical buildings with architectural value but having no special characteristics that would prevent their transformation
- Buildings with no obvious historical and architectural value
- Historical footprints of entire blocks or parts of blocks that have remained unchanged despite variations in the typological characteristics of the buildings
- The borders of historical interest kept unchanged
- The historical borders of the harbor, aligned with the old layout of Porto Catena

Socioeconomic Analyses

Demographic analyses are conducted using census or municipal data and by comparing the same data from different time periods. Such analyses show the changes in composition and character of the people who live in or near the site. More detailed investigations help reveal phenomena such as aging; the dependency of those who are not economically active (the elderly and schoolchildren) on the active population (people of working age, usually from fifteen to sixty-five years old); migratory balances (the number of persons who come from other regions or other countries offset by those leaving); and natural balances (the ratio between births and deaths).

Three types of population studies are relevant for urban design: trends, characteristics, and projections. Population *trends* include changes and rates of change in number and location of people as well as the consequences of change. Population *characteristics* include age and gender, composition, birth statistics, death statistics, ethnic composition, distribution, migration, and population pyramids. *Projection* techniques include the cohort-survival model, geometric interpolation, and simulation models.

Economic analyses help ascertain the phenomena connected with work activities, the composition of the workforce, and real estate market trends. The role of economic analyses in an urban design plan depends on the objectives and the mission of the project. At the start of the design process, if there is no clarity on the proposed functions for the site or about the number of functions, an economic analysis can help to envisage and to preview the possible scenarios.

Transforming an urban area always affects its surrounding context. Depending on the scale and the importance of the plan, the surrounding context can relate to the same neighborhood or to adjacent urban districts. In some cases, the effects of a transformation can be perceived at a larger scale. The impacts can be positive (e.g., when a transformation realizes its benefits and works as an example for nearby areas) or negative (typically as a result of an increase in traffic and congestion). More often, projects produce a mix of favorable and unfavorable externalities. The design process needs to consider this and attempt to forecast the unwanted economic outcomes in order to mitigate them.

Study of Transportation and Urban Mobility

A potential increase in traffic from the project should be considered from the outset of an urban design process. Software and predictive tools can model the potential effects at different scales. Traffic models analyze the primary ways people travel. Many software packages are available and are generally based on the same three parts:

- Representation of the road network
- Socioeconomic data
- A mathematical formula or an algorithm for distributing the routes

The network represents the major routes and how to get around within the study area. In simple models, this constitutes the road system for automobile traffic only. The network can show the new roads provided by the design. The road network is represented by nodes (intersections) and the links that connect them (roads). Each node or link also has information about its real physical data, such as capacity and speed. The network ends at external stations that represent connections to the outer road network.

Land use around the site is a major factor in how many trips people are likely to make. Estimates are determined for roughly how many trips are made to and from general types of land uses, such as shopping areas or residential neighborhoods. The model area is split up into areas of similar land uses. The demand for transportation is also based on socioeconomic information in each area, such as number and type of jobs and number of households, but also goods, services, and cultural and recreational activities. In short, what attracts and keeps people in metropolitan or urban areas is *accessibility* that has "the potential for interaction, both social and economic, the possibility of getting from home to a multitude of destinations, offering a spectrum on opportunities for work and play" (Handy and Niemeier 1997, 1175).

Thus, accessibility is an important characteristic of urban areas, and it affects urban design projects. As Handy and Niemeier (1997, 1175) explain:

> Accessibility is determined by the spatial distribution of potential destinations, the ease of reaching each destination, and the magnitude, quality, and character of the activities found there. Travel cost is central: the less time and money spent in travel, the more places that can be reached within a certain budget and the greater the accessibility. Destination choice is also crucial: the more destinations, and the greater the variety, the higher the level of accessibility. Travel choice is equally important: the wider the variety of modes for getting to a particular destination, the greater the choice and the greater the accessibility. Accessibility is thus determined both by patterns of land-use and by the nature of the transportation system, although two people in the same place may evaluate their accessibility differently, as wants and tastes vary.

One of the most diffused models to measure accessibility is the "gravity model," based on Newton's gravitational law, which states that the attractive force between two bodies is directly related to their size and inversely related to the distance between them. The gravity model for transportation uses network and land-use information to simulate traffic in the region. It weights opportunities in an area by an attraction measure (e.g., jobs, total retail floor space, opportunities of different kinds) and discounts attractions by a measure of impedance (travel time or travel cost) (see Handy 1992; Niemeier 1996; Handy and Niemeier 1997 Baradaran 2001; and Baradaran and Ramjerdi 2001). The resulting equation estimates the number of trips that will be made and the route each trip will take. The amount and type of land uses in a zone determines how many cars will be "attracted." Drivers will usually take the shortest, fastest routes. As traffic congestion makes one route less desirable, other routes will be used. The increase of functions determined by a new settlement can also be simulated.

According to the U.S. Department of Transportation, the gravity model has been the most widely used formula, mainly because it is simple in concept and because it has been well documented. "In essence the gravity model says that trip interchange between zones is directly proportional to the relative attraction of each of the zones and inversely proportional to some function of the spatial separation between zones. This function of spatial separation adjusts the relative attraction of each zone for the ability, desire, or necessity of the trip maker to overcome the spatial separation involved" (U.S. Department of Transportation 1983, I-2).

Accessibility, A_i for resident of zone *i*, based on the gravity model, is expressed mathematically as follows (Handy and Niemeier 1997, 1177):

$$A_i = \sum_j a_j f(t_{ij})$$

where a_j is the activity in zone *j*;

t_{ij} is travel time, distance, or cost from zone *i* to zone *j*, and

$f(t_{ij})$ is an impedance function.

The model requires calibration before it can be used for prediction of future travel demand. Calibration is accomplished

> to reflect how individuals and households perceive the travel and destination choices available to them. Travel surveys provide a basis for calibration. . . . Calibration is made difficult by the fact that revealed behavior—what residents

actually do—is not necessarily the same as preferred behavior—what residents would choose to do given a desired set of alternatives. Revealed behavior is shaped by the specific alternatives available. For example, if a community does not have good pedestrian access, then residents will make few pedestrian trips, but this does not imply they would not make such trips if pedestrian access were better. Traditional surveys of travel behavior deal exclusively with revealed behavior, and pay little attention to the reasons behind the behavior and the underlying preferences of residents. A careful analysis of revealed behavior may hint at underlying preferences and attitudes, but new types of surveys are needed to explore travel choices fully. (Handy and Niemeier 1997, 1180–81)

The final step is to interpret and translate the accessibility measures in a form useful for the urban designer and the project under design. Another important issue to be measured is the role of public transportation and existing bike and walking paths. The designer needs to consider the actual network of the different types of mass-transit facilities approaching the site as well as the network of bike and walking paths. A map of public transportation lines and paths in use, under construction, and planned is a useful tool for understanding the linkages between the site under design and its surroundings. The mapping should also help the designer to propose possible changes to the transportation network—for example, to change an existing bus route to the site or to add new bus stops closer to the area under consideration or to connect existing trails to the area under study.

The Guidance on Transport Assessment, prepared by the UK Government, Department for Transport (2007, 8, 9), suggests that during the preparation of a transportation assessment, the following concerns must be considered:

Encouraging Environmental Sustainability

- *Reducing the need to travel, especially by car*—reducing the need to travel, reducing the length of trips, and promoting multipurpose or linked trips by promoting more sustainable patterns of development and more sustainable communities that reduce the physical separation of key land uses
- *Tackling the environmental impact of travel*—by improving sustainable transport choices and by making it safer and easier for people to access jobs, shopping, leisure facilities, and services by public transport, walking, and cycling
- *The accessibility of the location*—the extent to which a site is, or is capable of becoming, accessible by noncar modes, particularly for large developments that involve major generators of travel demand

- *Other measures that may assist in influencing travel behaviour (ITB)*—achieving reductions in car usage (particularly single-occupancy vehicles) by such measures as car sharing/pooling, high-occupancy vehicle (HOV) lanes, and parking control

Managing the Existing Network

- *Making the best possible use of existing transport infrastructure*—for instance, by making low-cost improvements to the local public transport network and the use of advanced signal control systems, public transport priority measures (bus lanes), or other forms of Intelligent Transport Systems (ITS) to improve operations on the highway network (It should be noted that the capacity of the existing public transport infrastructure and footpaths is finite and that in some areas overcrowding already exists.)
- *Managing access to the highway network*—taking steps to maximize the extent to which the development can be made to "fit" within the available capacity by managing access from developments onto the highway network

Mitigating Residual Impacts

- *Through demand management*—using traffic control measures across a wide network to regulate flows
- *Through improvements to the local public transport network and to walking and cycling facilities*—for example, by extending bus routes and increasing bus frequencies, and by designing sites to facilitate walking and cycling
- *Through minor physical improvements to existing roads*—it may be possible in some circumstances to improve the capacity of existing roads by relatively minor physical adjustments, such as improving the geometry of junctions and so forth within the existing highway boundary
- *Through provision of new or expanded roads*—it is considered good transport planning practice to demonstrate that the other opportunities above have been fully explored before considering the provision of additional road space, such as new roads or major junction upgrades

Study of Social Facilities

Another factor in the transformation of urban areas as populations increase is meeting the growing demand for facilities. Schools, green spaces, hospitals, social services, religious sites, sports facilities, shops, community centers, and libraries are typically expected by new residents. Restaurants, bars, urban parks, and other facilities might be desired by office employees and occasional users. Cultural facilities, such as entertainment venues, cinemas, theaters, and museums, can be provided in some development areas.

An urban design plan with new housing should consider the influence that the fresh population will have on the existing community services. The plan should also account for additional services where the existing ones would not be able to satisfy the needs of the new population. The first step is to locate the existing services: schools, green areas, spaces and services for elderly and young people, sanitary services, and parking.

The survey of existing services needs to be compared with the current and projected populations to estimate whether present services can satisfy future needs. The dimensions of community services can be determined in various ways. For instance, a 1968 Italian law (Dm 1444, April 2, 1968) defines the spacing between housing and public spaces as well as for parking. The minimum is set at 194 square feet (18 square meters) for public spaces (excluding roads) per current or future inhabitant. This minimum quota is mandatory for urban plans and urban transformation. The designer should consider that each inhabitant, according to common interpretation, corresponds to 862–1,076 square feet (80–100 square meters) of housing. The 194 square feet (18 square meters) per inhabitant, according to the norm, should be divided as follows:

- 48 square feet (4.5 square meters) for educational facilities: daycare, nursery schools, primary and secondary schools
- 22 square feet (2 square meters) for common interest facilities: religious, cultural, social, charitable, sanitary, and administrative, or for public services
- 97 square feet (9 square meters) for public spaces, such as parks and sports facilities
- 27 square feet (2.5 square meters) for car parking

John Wiley & Sons has published standards books for architecture, landscape architecture, and urban design and planning that can help designers to understand, in the preliminary design analysis phase, whether the new population will find the minimal satisfaction of core community services (American Planning Association 2006; Hopper 2006; American Institute of Architects 2007; Steiner and Butler 2007). The urban designer, through consultations with public officials and the affected communities, will complete a community services framework with reference to the context and the actual conditions.

The Provision of Urban Facilities in the United Kingdom

The Final Report of the Urban Task Force, better known as *Toward an Urban Renaissance*, first published in the United Kingdom in 1999 and updated in 2005, addresses the topic of public facilities, starting from the number of inhabitants that can warrant neighborhood facilities. Each service corresponds with a population size that is able to support it (Urban Task Force 1999, 61):

- Primary school: 2,500–4,000 inhabitants
- Doctor: 2,500–3,000 inhabitants
- Corner shop: 2,000–5,000 inhabitants
- Public housing: 5,000–7,000 inhabitants
- Group of shops: 5,000–10,000 inhabitants
- Post office: 5,000–10,000 inhabitants

The Final Report also proposes another method for identifying core facilities combining distances and population. A diagram distinguishes facilities on the local, neighborhood, district, town, and city scales, and a chart differentiates facilities according to distance and catchments (see Figure 3.12/Plate #5).

The governments of England, Northern Ireland, and Scotland have defined planning policies and guidelines to deal with several aspects of planning—from nature conservation to transportation to waste management and so on. Some of these planning policies and guidelines deal with the provision of new facilities and give an appropriate balance between new provision and the enhancement of existing facilities.

In England, these policies are called Planning Policy Statements (PPS; formerly known as Planning Policy Guidance Notes, or PPGS), which provide "Central government guidance on planning matters." In the same way, Scotland has defined Scottish Planning Policies (SPP) and National Planning Policy Guidance (NPPG), while Northern Ireland also provided some PPS (Rydin 2003; Cullingworth and Nadin 2006).

The English "Planning Policy Guidance 17: Planning for Open Space, Sport and Recreation" (UK Government 2002b) states that

> the Government believes that open space standards are best set locally. National standards cannot cater to local circumstances, such as differing demographic profiles and the extent of existing built development in an area. . . . Local standards should include:

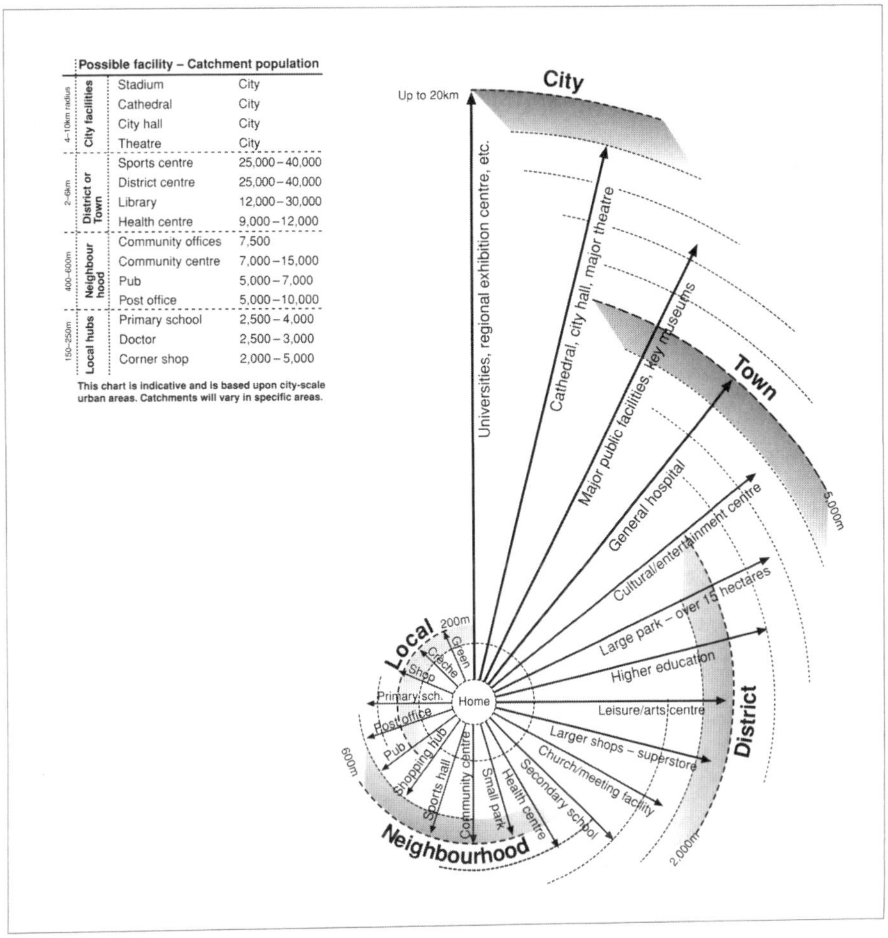

Figure 3.12 (also Plate #5) The city provides the framework for core institutions. (From Urban Task Force 1995, 31. Courtesy of Andrew Wright Associates.)

- quantitative elements (how much new provision may be needed);
- a qualitative component (against which to measure the need for enhancement of existing facilities); and
- accessibility (including distance thresholds and consideration of the cost of using a facility).

The *Planning Policy Guidance 17 Companion Guide* (UK Government 2002a, 2) aims to give "clarity and reasonable certainty for developers and land owners in relation to the requirements and expectations of local planning authorities in respect of open space and sport and recreation provision." The guide is intended to provide useful examples and indications for local authorities to fulfill the PPS. The PPG17 Companion Guide emphasizes the importance of the local context to define dimensions and character for open spaces and sports facilities.

> The need for most forms of open space and sport and recreation facilities is largely related to population and this should make it possible to derive broad benchmarks, which authorities may find useful. However, the number of people is only one of many factors affecting the amount of provision needed in an area. Other relevant factors include:
>
> - the age and social structure of the local population, together with its distribution and the density of development;
> - the proportion of natural to artificial turf pitches;
> - the extent to which authorities and their partners are promoting sports development and community events and activities in parks and other green spaces;
> - the extent to which sports facilities on school sites are open for community use;
> - the amount of private greenspace; and local traditions—for example, cricket is particularly popular in Yorkshire. (UK Government 2002a, 14)

The Northern Irish Government published the Planning Policy Statement 8 (PPS 8) in 2004, titled *Open Space, Sport, and Outdoor Recreation*. This statement recommends "a minimum standard for 'outdoor playing space' of 2.4 hectares [5.9 acres] per 1,000 population" (North Ireland Planning Service 2004, 12). The Northern Irish Government has also published a document defining parking standards for cars and bicycles—categorized for specific activities, including residential areas, hotels, schools, cinemas, theaters, and so on—that could be a useful reference to define spaces for parking (North Ireland Planning Service, 2005). Similar documents were issued by the Scottish Executive, such as the Scottish Planning Policy 17 (SPP 17), *Transport and Planning Maximum Parking Standards* (2003), and the *Minimum Standards for Open Space* (2005).

The objectives of the Scottish NPPG17 (National Planning Policy Guideline 17) include "promoting healthy living, fostering neighbourhood pride and community cohesion" (Scottish Executive 2003, 28). As a result, while encouraging recreation activities, NPPG17 also includes guidance for protecting natural features and water, areas of outstanding natural beauty, and greenbelts.

Standards in the United States

Tony Veal (2008, 3, quoting Wilkinson 1985, 191) states that "in the USA, the National Recreation Association (now National Recreation and Park Association, NRPA) [in the early years of the twentieth century recommended a] standard of 10 acres (4 ha) of open space per 1000 population." The ten acres were divided into neighborhood, district, and "large urban" parks and between children's play, sport, and informal recreation. The idea of fixed national or state open-space-planning standard declined dramatically in favor of the adoption of needs-based approaches to recreation planning. Veal also reports that the NRPA "in 1971 . . . confirmed and updated its standards, declaring needs-based modeling methods to be 'highly theoretical' and unsuitable for neighbourhood level planning (Buechner, 1971: 23); a 1983 report presented a needs-based methodology in addition to standards (Lancaster, 1983); [and] a 1996 report dropped standards altogether and advocated the use of a needs-based approach (Mertes and Hall, 1996: 7)" (Veal 2008, 3). Roger Lancaster (1990) provided some standard dimensions and suggestions for open spaces and recreational sport areas. The National Recreation and Park Association provided standards for parks for different purposes (see Table 3.1).

Parking is another facility that influences urban design projects. In the United States, no standard guidelines exist to provide an ideal number of car spaces for different land uses. The Pennsylvania Housing Research/Resource Center at the Pennsylvania State University produced *Pennsylvania Standards for Residential Site Development* (2007). Chapter 4 of that publication is on parking standards and serves as a good reference to dimension car spaces and their characteristics and position in residential areas. Another U.S. source for parking standards is *Shared Parking* (Smith 2005), provided by the Urban Land Institute (an American non-profit research and education organization founded in 1936). The book contains methods for calculating parking requirements for different areas, such as shopping centers, stadiums, hotels, residences, offices, medical clinics, and banks. Envision Central Texas (ECT 2003a, 2003c, 2003e, 2003g, 2003k) provides an example of such an application in design guidelines for demonstration sites. Peter Calthorpe developed these guidelines, and as a result, they embody a New Urbanist perspective.

London Bridge Tower

In urban design, consideration of the site specifics sometimes overwhelms the rigidity of facilities standards. For example, the London Bridge Tower (also known

Table 3.1 National Recreation and Park Association Standards for Park Acreage

Component	Use	Service Area	Desirable Size	Acres/1,000 Population	Desirable Size Characteristics
Mini-Park	Specialized facilities that serve a concentrated or limited population or specific group, such as children or senior citizens.	Less than 1/4-mile radius	1 acre or less	0.25 to 0.5	With neighborhoods and in close proximity to apartment complexes, townhouse development, or housing for elderly people.
Neighborhood Park or Playground	Area for intense recreational activities, such as field games, crafts, playground apparatus areas, skating, picnicking, and wading pools.	1/4- to 1/2-mile radius to serve a population of up to 5,000 (a neighborhood)	15+ acres	1 to 2	Suited for intense development. Easily accessible to neighborhood population (geographically centered for safe walking and biking access). May be developed as a school park facility.
Community Park	Area of diverse environmental quality. May include areas suited for intense recreation facilities, such as athletic complexes or large swimming pools. May be an area of natural quality for outdoor recreation, such as walking, viewing, sitting, or picnicking. May be any combination of the above, depending on site suitability and community needs.	1- to 2-mile radius (several neighborhoods)	25+ acres	5 to 8	May include natural features, such as bodies of water and areas suited for intense development. Easily accessible to neighborhood served.

Source: Municipal Research and Services Center of Washington 1994, 22.

as the "shard of glass"), designed by the Renzo Piano Building Workshop, does not provide car spaces. The site where the tower was erected is dense and well served by trains (six lines), metro (two lines), and buses (fifteen lines). To boost use of public transportation, the municipality of London asked the designer to provide ground space for the rail lines and no parking spaces, except for service vehicles and disabled people (Irace 2007). The project, as described on the Renzo Piano Building Workshop website (see Figure 3.13/Plate #6),

> includes the redevelopment of the train station concourse and bus station. The existing roof is to be removed and replaced with a glazed canopy, and retail units relocated to open up visual connections between the train station, bus station and taxi ranks. Two new 30 m by 30 m [98.5 feet by 98.5 feet] public squares will form the centre of the scheme. Such improvements to the public realm are vital to the regeneration of this congested and neglected part of the city and will hopefully provide the catalyst to further development in the area. (RPBW 2010)

Public City Spaces

Sometimes, a designer may need to plan a site within a historical texture or in a city full of many functions and may have to differentiate between public and private spaces. The term *public spaces* not only refers to parks and free access areas but also is used in a wider sense. This combination of spaces can be termed the *public city*. The term sums up the combination of physical and nonphysical elements that support a wide variety of social actions and urban activities.

In 1938, Lewis Mumford wrote the following plea for the social city:

> The city is . . . the physical form of the highest and most complex types of associative life. One further conclusion follows from this concept of the city: social facts are primary, and the physical organization of a city, its industries and its markets, its lines of communication and traffic, must be subservient to its social needs. Whereas in the development of the city during the last century [the nineteenth] we expanded the physical plant recklessly and treated the essential social nucleus, the organs of government and education and social service, as mere afterthoughts, today we must treat the social nucleus as the essential element in every valid city plan: the spotting and inter-relationship of schools, libraries, theaters, community centers, is the first task in defining the urban

Figure 3.13 (also Plate #6)
London Bridge Tower plan. (©Renzo Piano Building Workshop.)

> neighborhood and laying down the outlines of an integrated city. (Mumford 1938, 482)

It is almost impossible to precisely separate the "public" from the "private" parts of the city. These two parts act as overlapping layers that are often interconnected and sometimes blurred (occasionally, there are semipublic or semiprivate spaces), but the public city acts as the linking element of the different components. The public city can be divided, for the sake of this description, into three key components:

- *Infrastructures*—the physical components to move, to organize, or to deliver goods, supplies, commodities, and people: roads, rail networks, bridges, parking spaces, sidewalks, bike paths, sewer systems, water and electric supply, telephone lines, cables, and natural gas distribution
- *Public facilities*—hospitals, schools, theaters, sports amenities, libraries, places of worship, and cultural or entertainment centers
- *Public spaces*—the places where people interact with built elements, such as squares, gardens, parks, open spaces, pedestrian areas, streets, and paths

Increasingly, green spaces (greenways, parks, and so forth) are considered a form of green infrastructure for the ecosystem services they provide. Green infrastructure and public space can provide both environmental and social benefits. Public spaces provide places for the collective life. They supply the elements of the public city, and they "allow for shared experiences that can give rise to mutual respect—however grudgingly—that is the basis for a thriving metropolitan culture" (Gastil and Ryan 2004, 9).

John Sorrel, chairman of the English Commission for Architecture and the Built Environment, stated in a foreword to a publication by Sarah Gaventa on public spaces that "everyone in the world uses public space: as soon as you leave your home and walk into the street, or square, or path outside, you are in a public space. In this sense, the public realm is one of the few services that every single person benefits from: whether rich or poor, young or old" (Sorrel 2006, 7).

Jan Gehl, the "doyen of public-space design"—as he was called by Richard Rogers (2010)—dedicated forty years to research on urban public spaces. His research has many parallels with Kevin Lynch's first studies on urban spaces described in his "Travel Journal (1952–53)" (Lynch 1990). Gehl explored the quality of public realm in Denmark's cities and elsewhere, the reasons for their success or decline, and who were the users and how they used the space (Gehl 1987; Gehl and Gemzoe 1996, 2000). His books offer a wide range of examples and emphasize the role of the urban designer as a people observer who is able to interpret the habits and preferences of users and how the design of existing public spaces affects how people experience them. Gehl uses area pedestrian counts and stationary activity surveys to discover and to quantify where people walk and what people do in the central parts of cities. Gehl also analyzes the quality and condition of outdoor furniture, paving materials, and other urban features.

The intersection of public and private spaces is the focus of a study that Jerold Kayden (2000) conducted with the New York City Department of Planning and the Municipal Art Society of New York. Kayden focuses on a specific type of public space called "privately owned public space." His study provides a helpful guide for what to consider in studying open spaces, including their history and the laws that govern design, operation, and enforcement.

Matthew Carmona (2010) provided a classification of urban public spaces that shows the wide range of public space types an urban area would contain (see Table 3.2).

The Public Image

Kevin Lynch dedicated much of his life to studying the physical city and the urban experience as well as the interaction between physical space and its human use. He was especially curious "to know how the public, not the trained designer, saw and understood the everyday environment, what they valued in it, how it shaped their lives and activities, and how they in turn shaped the urban form" (Banerjee and Southworth 1990, 4).

In *The Image of the City* (1960, 2–3), Lynch described a study of three cities—Boston, Jersey City, and Los Angeles—considering

> the visual quality of the American city by studying the mental image of that city which is held by its citizens. It . . . [is concentrated] especially on one particular visual quality: the apparent clarity or "legibility" of the cityscape. By this we mean the ease with which its parts can be recognized and can be organized into a coherent pattern. . . . [The] book will assert that legibility is crucial in the city setting . . . and will try to show how this concept might be used today in rebuilding our cities.

The objective of Lynch's study, which became a seminal book in the field of urban design and planning, is to individuate "the public image," that is, "the

Table 3.2 Urban Contemporary Public Spaces

Space Type	Distinguishing Characteristics	Examples
	"Positive" Spaces	
1. Natural/seminatural urban space	Natural and seminatural features within urban areas, typically under state ownership	Rivers, natural features, beaches, canals
2. Civic space	The traditional forms of urban space, open and available to all and catering to a wide variety of functions	Streets, squares, promenades
3. Public open space	Managed open space, typically green and available and open to all, even if temporally controlled	Parks, gardens, commons, urban forests, cemeteries
	"Negative" Spaces	
4. Movement space	Space dominated by movement needs, largely for motorized transportation	Main roads, motorways, railways, underpasses
5. Service space	Space dominated by modern servicing requirement needs	Car parks, service yards
6. Leftover space	Space left over after development, often designed without function	"SLOAP" (space left over after planning), Modernist open space
7. Undefined space	Undeveloped space, either abandoned or awaiting redevelopment	Redevelopment space, abandoned space, transient space
	"Ambiguous" Spaces	
8. Interchange space	Transport stops and interchanges, whether inside or outside	Metros, bus interchanges, railway stations, bus/tram stops
9. Public "private" space	Seemingly public outside space, in fact privately owned and to greater or lesser degrees controlled	Privately owned "civic" space, business parks, church grounds
10. Conspicuous space	Public space designed to make strangers feel conspicuous and, potentially, unwelcome	Cul-de-sacs, dummy gates enclaves
11. Inside "public" space	Formally public and outside uses, inside and often privatized	Shopping/leisure malls, introspective megastructures
12. Retail space	Privately owned but publicly accessible exchange spaces	Shops, covered markets, gas stations
13. Third place space	Semipublic meeting and social places, public and private	Cafés, restaurants, libraries, town halls, religious buildings
14. Private "public" space	Publicly owned but functionally and user-determined space	Institutional grounds, housing estates, university campuses

continued

Table 3.2 *continued*

15. Visible private space	Physically private but visually public space	Front yards, allotments, gated squares
16. Interface space	Physically demarked but publicly accessible interfaces between public and private space	Street cafés, private pavement space
17. User selecting space	Space for selected groups, determined (and sometimes controlled) by age or activity	Skate parks, playgrounds, sport fields/grounds/courses
	Private Spaces	
18. Private open space	Physically private open space	Urban agricultural remnants, private woodlands
19. Outside private space	Physically private spaces, grounds, and gardens	Gated streets/enclaves, private gardens, private sport clubs, parking courts
20. Inside private space	Private or business space	Offices, houses, and so forth

Source: Carmona 2010, 169, 170.

common mental pictures carried by large numbers of a city's inhabitants: areas of agreement which might be expected to appear in the interaction of a single physical reality, a common culture, and a basic physiological nature" (Lynch 1960, 7).

His research aims at discovering the physical quality linked with the attributes of identity and mental image structure. According to Lynch: "This leads to the definition of what might be called *imageability*: that quality in a physical object which gives it a high probability of evoking a strong image in any given observer" (9).

Two basic analyses were carried out in each city:

- A systematic field reconnaissance of the area was made on foot by a trained observer, who mapped the presence of various elements, their visibility, their image strength or weakness, and their connections, disconnections, and other interrelations, and who noted any special successes or difficulties in the potential image structure. These were subjective judgments based on the immediate appearance of these elements in the field.
- A lengthy interview was held with a small sample of city residents to evoke their own image of their physical environment. The interview included

requests for descriptions, locations, and sketches, and for the performance of imaginary trips. The persons interviewed were people who were long resident or employed in the area, and whose residences or work places were distributed throughout the zone in question (Lynch 1960, 15).

An outcome of Lynch's analysis was that each city possesses a public image that overlaps with many individual images. In urban design, form should be used to reinforce meaning and not to negate it. Lynch found it convenient to classify the environmental images collected in his study into five recurrent elements:

- *Paths* are the channels along which the observer customarily, occasionally, or potentially moves. They include streets, walkways, transit lines, canals, and railroads. For many people, these elements dominate their images of places.
- *Edges* are the linear elements not used or considered as paths by the observer. They are the boundaries between two areas, linear breaks in continuity: shores, railroad cuts, edges of development, and walls. For many people, these elements are important organizing features, particularly for holding together generalized areas, as water or walls demarcate a city.
- *Districts* are the medium-to-large sections of the city, conceived as having a two-dimensional extent, which the observer mentally enters and which are recognized as having some common, identifying character.
- *Nodes* are strategic spots in a city where observers can enter and which are the intensive foci to and from which they are traveling. They may be primarily junctions, places of break in transportation, crossings, or convergences of paths, moments of shift from one structure to another. Or, nodes may be simply concentrations, a condensation of some use or physical character.
- *Landmarks* are another type of point reference, but the observer does not enter them; they are external. They are usually a simply defined physical object, such as a building, sign, store, or mountain.

Ecologists and landscape ecologists use similar terms to read landscapes: corridors, edges, patches, matrices, and mosaics. According to Cliff Moughtin and his colleagues (2004, 52–53):

Path, nodes, landmarks, districts and edges all have a significant role in determining the legibility of the city, but even at the smaller scale of the district or city quarter they have similar functions of giving identity to the place. Districts,

> too, have minor paths, nodes, landmarks, identifiable sub-areas with distinctive boundaries. These structuring ideas help the designer to focus on the kind of physical components which, if used sensitively, can make a district or city memorable and rich in perceptual detail for both the citizen and the visitor.

The public image and the recurrence of the elements in the mental maps of the interviewed people help the designer, according to Lynch, to create a visual plan. The method proposed by Lynch has been broadly applied. The approach is valid in urban design with some precautions. The image and the acknowledgment of five key elements for the study area need to be identified by the designer through consultation with the public. The recognition of the same elements by the designer may limit and even corrupt the analysis and the outcomes.

One of Lynch's most important lessons was to involve citizens, including children and elderly people, as protagonists of the analytical phase. Traditional Lynch analysis is undertaken by questionnaire or direct interview, often accompanied by "mental maps" drawn by actual or potential users of the site.

If the experience is to be repeated, the designer should consult with psychologists, human behavioral experts, or urban anthropologists to be able to direct the survey toward useful outcomes and not by misunderstanding the signals coming from the public. Kevin Lynch—generally in all his books, but in particular in *Site Planning* (Lynch and Hack, 1984), *The View from the Road* (Appleyard, Lynch, and Myer, 1964), and *Managing the Sense of a Region* (Lynch, 1976)—made wide use of graphic elaborations, which can be quite simple to reproduce and can provide great inspiration for urban designers during the analytical phase.

Nolli Maps

The *Nolli map* is a common technique used to display the fabric of urban areas. Such maps are also called "figure-ground" because they represent figures (buildings) in black and ground (open spaces) in white. The name comes from Giovanni Battista Nolli, a cartographer from the province of Como, Italy. In the first half of the eighteenth century, Nolli completed the first systematic relief map of the entire city of Rome and its antiquities with a new instrument: the *pretoriana* tablet. The meticulous relief of the urban texture inside the walls comprises the plans of the three hundred churches, the courtyards, and the stairways of the main palaces, the *chiostri* of all the convents, the vestigial of every monument, and ancient ruins. The original map (a large 69.29 by 81.89 inches, or 1,760 by 2,080 millimeters) is now conserved in the collections of the Library of Art History at Palazzo

Venezia in Rome. The map was published in 1748, two years before the 1750 Jubilee (Bevilacqua 2005).

According to Roger Trancik (1986, 98), Nolli's map is the best illustration of the figure-ground theory, in which "space is conceived as a positive entity in an integrated relationship with the surrounding solids." According to this theory, "the starting point for an understanding of urban form is the analysis of the relationship between building mass and open space. The figure-ground approach can be a powerful analysis tool for identifying the texture and patterns of the urban fabric as well as problems in its spatial order" (98). According to Robert Venturi, Denise Scott Brown, and Steven Izenour, in *Learning from Las Vegas* (1972, 18–19), the Nolli map "reveals the sensitive and complex connections between public and private space in Rome. Private building is shown in gray crosshatching that is carved into by the public spaces, exterior *and* interior. The spaces, open or roofed, are shown in minute detail through darker *poché* [a term used to describe solid design elements, such as walls or columns, that are indicated in black on architectural plans]. Interiors of churches read like piazzas and courtyards of palaces, yet a variety of qualities and scales is articulated." Such a map for Las Vegas helped reveal and clarify public and private spaces.

Venturi and his colleagues (1972) applied the Nolli map technique to the Las Vegas strip, substituting churches and *chiostris* with casino entrance halls and wedding chapels. In doing so, they revealed the structure of the city. This technique helped to show the value of public and semipublic spaces by revealing places of connection and distribution in a city or in its parts.

A recent use of the Nolli map applied to public domain in urban space is the "Heuristic Nolli Map," developed by Hwang and Koile (2005). This model evolved as a doctoral dissertation at the Harvard Graduate School of Design to help perceive the urban space. Form, function, and use pattern are used.

> The concept of the Heuristic Nolli Map encompasses the creation of a user's representation of the public domain and the subsequent modification of that representation during the design process. The representation includes a data model and a machine learning component that embodies a user's interpretation of what constitutes public domain. The result of the machine learning component is a classifier, which reports the "publicness" of an entity; and a user's customized typology of the public domain. The Heuristic Nolli Map thus provides a methodology that allows a designer to manage and use her [or his] knowledge in a systematic way. (Hwang and Koile 2005, 2–3)

The model demonstrates the potential for contemporary use of a tool that is more than four hundred years old. It is an elegant and fertile combination of a mature representational tool with advanced computer systems. However, University of Virginia landscape architecture professor Beth Meyer (1997, 57) cautions about the use of traditional figure-ground diagrams. She argues that their "value as an analytical tool is limited to a coarse grain of study. Regardless of whether the spatial model relies on object buildings or figural space, figure-ground diagrams fail to represent the spatiality of trees, landforms, and other 'in-between' conditions. They render the world in black or white, either-or."

Meyer advocated a figured ground instead, which she defines as "that undulating body between the figural object and neutral field, between mass and void. It finds structure in the ground, its topographic and geological structure" (1997, 52). For instance, a plan for an extension of green areas in Austin, Texas, used a figured-ground diagram to illustrate new green areas in relationship to built-up areas (see Figure 3.14) (Steiner and Almy 2010).

Figure 3.14 Walk-for-a-Day figured-ground diagram. (By Dean Almy and Li Hang.)

Think "Outside the Box" in Gathering Knowledge

An urban design, whether having started as a competition, from a direct assignment, or being carried out as a workshop task, is always defined by a border that delimits the study area. The border can correspond with a property limit or a zone established by local officials or an urban plan adopted by the local planning authority or through a historical or ecological framework. The designer will meet the client's demands, create the briefing, and address the prerequisites that come from participants. The designer needs to respect the physical limits of the area as well as the task assigned.

It is sometimes useful, when circumstances permit and opportunities inspire, to extend beyond the limits: to think "outside the box." "Outside the box" is an expression that describes nonconforming, creative thinking. The term is said to derive from a famous puzzle created by early twentieth-century British mathematician Henry Ernest Dudeney, in which someone is asked to interconnect nine dots in a three-by-three grid by using four straight lines drawn without the pencil leaving the paper. In order to be successful, the puzzle solver has to realize that the boundaries of the dot array are psychological. The only way to solve the puzzle is to extend the lines beyond the artificial boundary created by the nine dots (see Figure 3.15).

In urban design, to think "outside the box" can mean any of the following:

- *To expand* the borders of the analysis (no area is a island), to locate and quantify impacts beyond the site boundary yet part of the system set in place (e.g., where do materials come from, where does electricity come from, where does wastewater and stormwater go?)
- *To think beyond* the project and its prerequisites to suggest transformations outside the boundaries of the study area, such as connections with public transit and visual links with surrounding landscapes

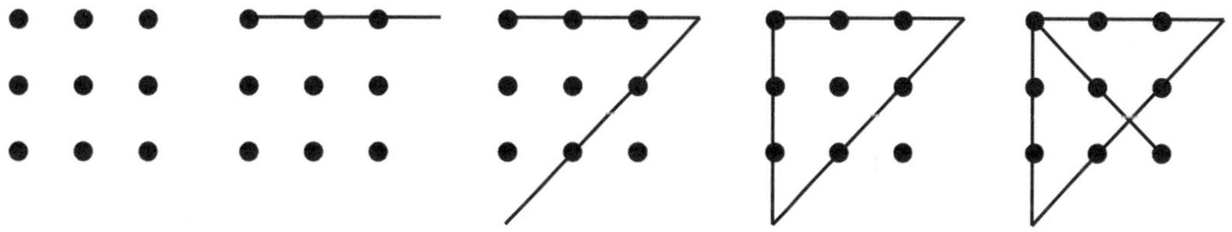

Figure 3.15 Interconnect nine dots in a three-by-three grid by using four straight lines drawn without the pencil leaving the paper. To solve problems it is useful to "think outside the box." (Drawing by Danilo Palazzo.)

- *To look* at the plan not with the eyes of a designer but to imagine how it could be seen and received by those who do not understand design jargon (This approach can help limit the damage caused by excessive and sophisticated graphic tricks that saturate design presentations and seem to show buildings as colorful candies placed on bright red backgrounds with small, extraterrestrial-looking beings.)
- *To widen* the design references to include nature and cultural traditions

To think outside the box implies designer imagination. Thought should not be limited to staying within the given borders. Operating outside the box also means abandoning the solitary presumptions of the technician and widening the knowledge base. It means knowing that there is not only one solution to a problem and that solutions are also determined by the program, to organize and to perform the analysis in an urban design process. In other words, urban design requires that creativity gets along with the abilities to organize urban design tasks and with the competence to use the collected data and knowledge as a steady base for the ensuing steps and the final project.

Summary

Ecology informs us about connections, about how everything is connected to everything else. At the scale of an urban design site, we must learn how to make and see these connections. How does sunshine cross the site throughout the day and create shadows in the process? How do these patterns of sunlight and shade vary across the site? How much rain or snow falls on the site? And, when? The answers to such questions help the designer to understand the potentials and limitations of the site.

The more the designer understands the site, the more strengths can be enhanced and the more weaknesses avoided or decreased. The designer needs to reveal the "genius of the place," as the English poet Alexander Pope advocated in the eighteenth century. After we survey the site through reports, maps, and visits, we need to pull the knowledge we have gained together through a synthesis.

4. Synthesis

The information collected by the urban design team creates a framework of knowledge from which the designer starts the preliminary design phase and concludes the analysis. Any further data collection and analytical investigation depends on such factors as the nature and dimension of the urban design task, the time and the information available, and the competencies of the design team.

To prepare for the design phase, the knowledge acquired must be summarized to be used effectively. There are many techniques for summarizing and analyzing the knowledge gathered about the site. Five techniques will be described in this chapter: (1) Strengths-Weaknesses-Opportunities-Threats (SWOT) analysis, (2) a constraints and opportunity map, (3) transects, (4) exploded axonometric drawings, and (5) suitability analysis. These tools have the advantage of being easy to arrange and rather effective.

Starting with an examination of the information collected in the *knowledge* phase of the process, the designer is able to offer a diagnosis of the site. This phase can be supported by the use of software able to model different phenomena (e.g., traffic, sunlight, or noise). Support can also come from the use of GIS to store and to process mapped data. In the *synthesis* phase, the designer can use other techniques to increase or consolidate knowledge of the place and understanding of the design task. Comparison of scale and realization of physical models are two techniques that help the designer to be aware of both spatial dimensions and the interactions of different spaces at the site. Collecting analogous case studies allows designers to compare their task with precedents urban design has accrued through past practice.

This stage involves connecting all of the outcomes from the surveys conducted in the knowledge stage into a comprehensive portrait of the site to gain a broad perspective and holistic view. Ideally, this synthesis of the information will lead the urban designer down the best road for the project.

Synthesis Techniques

How the collected information is synthesized depends on the time and resources available and on the techniques the designer decides to use. Time is influenced by the type of design. In the case of a competition or a workshop, time is usually at a premium, and fast techniques are typically necessary. Resources not only are economic in nature but also relate to professional specialties on the design team. In general, three types of relationships emerge between the experts and disciplinary knowledge, described here through graphic diagrams (see Figures 4.1/Plate #7, 4.2/Plate #8, and 4.3/Plate #9) and musical metaphors:

- The designer acts as a *one-man band*, playing all instruments. Or, rather, the designer personally explores the different competencies, with the risk of not fully appreciating its contents.
- The designer plays the role of an *orchestra conductor*. Experts do not interact with one another but instead relate their studies to the designer, who coordinates a multidisciplinary approach in which the designer "asks questions" of the experts.
- The designer is part of a team of experts, as in a *musical ensemble*, where the hierarchy between the different players is hidden but all work together toward the goal. In an interdisciplinary relationship such as this one, the designer participates with other experts in defining the project (Palazzo 1993).

SWOT Analysis

SWOT analysis is a technique developed more than fifty years ago to help with decision making in business ventures. Since the 1980s, it has been applied to support decision making and policy making in public administration and in design. Some European Union programs require the use of SWOT analysis to evaluate plans and policies. The goal of this analysis is to define the opportunities of the area under study and the elements and conditions that represent limitations. The area involved in the design can be described and concisely analyzed using this technique. The SWOT analysis is intended to highlight the key issues and the links among

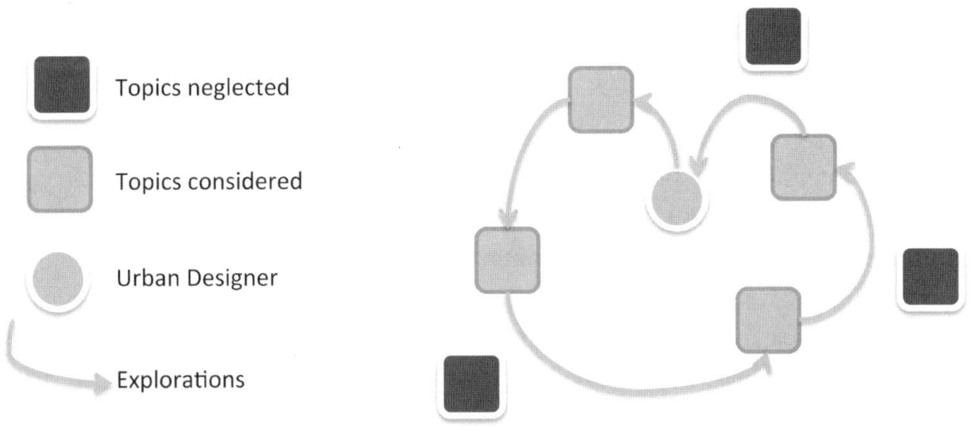

Figure 4.1 (also Plate #7) The designer as a "one-man band." (By Danilo Palazzo.)

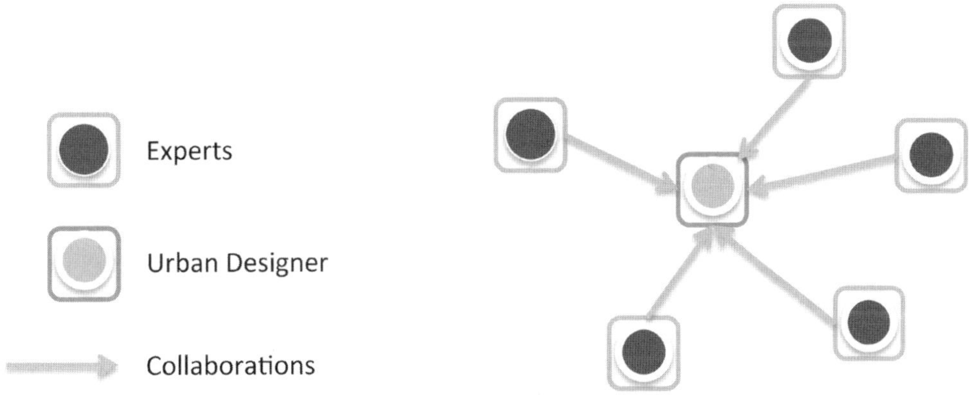

Figure 4.2 (also Plate #8) The designer as an "orchestra conductor." (By Danilo Palazzo.)

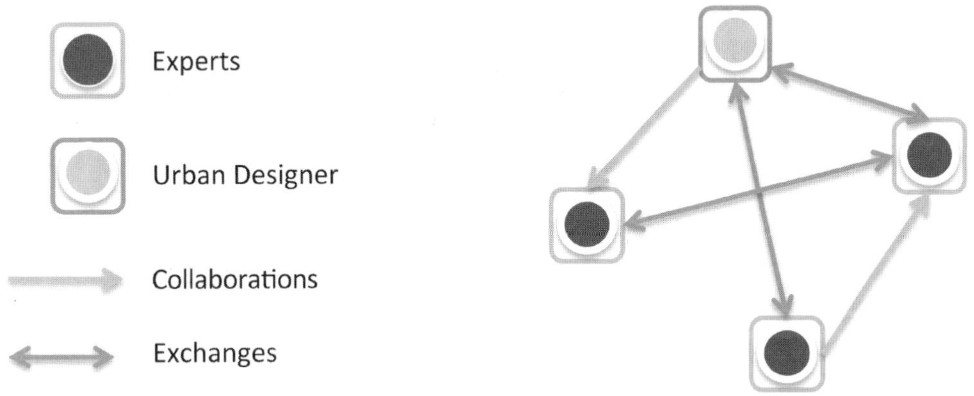

Figure 4.3 (also Plate #9) The designer as part of an ensemble. (By Danilo Palazzo.)

existing issues. Strengths and weaknesses relate to the area's own characteristics and are interpreted as internal factors. Opportunities and threats deal with the area's competitive environment (external factors) (see Figure 4.4).

SWOT analysis can be compiled from the outcomes of the analysis and surveys developed during the previous stage. The SWOT analysis would work as a synthesis of the research conducted to enhance the designer's knowledge of the place. A designer can carry out a SWOT analysis with some typical questions, such as those posed in Box 4.1.

Urban design can emphasize strengths and offer proposals to mitigate and adapt to weaknesses. SWOT analysis can be used in different steps during the design process: *ex-ante* to define the actual state of the site, *during* the design process to evaluate the benefits of the project in the different steps, and *ex-post*, after the implementation, to assess the goals achieved.

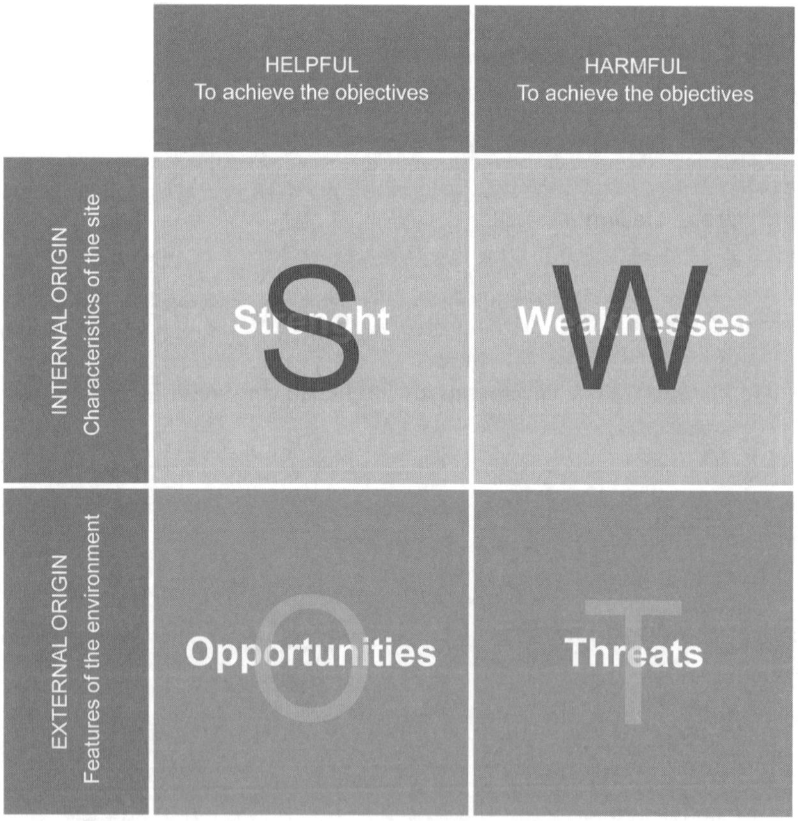

Figure 4.4 The Strengths-Weaknesses-Opportunities-Threats (SWOT) scheme. (By Danilo Palazzo.)

Box 4.1 Typical Questions to Start a SWOT Analysis

Strengths

What are the advantages intrinsic to the area in its actual state?
What differentiates it from its surroundings?
What is well organized?
What is doing well?
What are the good characteristics?
What are the ecosystem services already provided?

Weaknesses

What can be improved?
What is done poorly or inconsistently?
What should be avoided?
What intrinsic ecosystem services have been compromised by current or past uses?

Opportunities

What are the interesting trends and favorable possibilities?
What are the changes in urban or regional government policy related to the study area or to the greater area?
What are the changes in cultural and social trends?
What are the changes in markets and local events?
How might the health and ecology be restored?
What ecosystem services can be created?

Threats

What are the obstacles the area faces?
The most significant problems of the site and the surrounding area are related to

- environment: pollution, water quality, green spaces, urban heating, criminality, social perception, urban landscape
- land- or building-use conflicts: uncontrolled development around the area
- urbanization: what indications of the city plan or what urban policies that are going to be implemented will negatively affect the study area
- transport and communication infrastructure: connection of the area with other parts of the city; parking places, sidewalks, bicycle lanes, public transportation
- public spaces and infrastructure: social and cultural facilities, places to walk or stand safely, lighting
- management issues: lack of image or negative perception, prescriptive regulations
- demographic issues: population income, age profile, professional base, workforce

What natural phenomena (floods, earthquakes, hurricanes) pose a danger to human health, safety, or welfare?

SWOT analysis can also be applied to a geographically defined area (a portion of the site or an area wider than the site) or to a set of issues (such as transportation, public spaces, and social perception). It can also be applied to different scales (the site, the city, the region) as necessary. SWOT analysis can be arranged by the designer, as part of a public process, or by seeking neutral and objective expertise. The realization of a SWOT analysis can be divided into four general phases:

- selection of the context (or of the issues) to which to apply the analysis
- identification of strengths, weaknesses, opportunities, and threats
- classification of the outcomes in a list: from the most important to the least
- rendering of the SWOT analysis in a matrix, a diagram, or a map

Although SWOT analysis is flexible and easy to compile, it might describe reality in too simplistic of terms and should be considered subjective and unscientific. During the compilation of a SWOT analysis, it is important to set clear rules for determining whether a factor will be considered endogenous or exogenous. It is also crucial not to anticipate the designer's project hypothesis in the analysis. To overcome subjectivity, or to at least minimize it, the designer can describe the factors utilized and the sources for the factors.

Opportunities and Constraints Map

An opportunities (or possibilities) and constraints (or restrictions) map is a useful tool to summarize collected information. Constraints are generally elements that limit future development, such as the location of roads and public transportation, the existence of nuisances (e.g., noises or smells), existing uses, and historic structures. This mapping may be viewed as the visualization of weaknesses and threats from the SWOT analysis. Opportunities generally advance the design and can be seen as a visual representation of strengths and opportunities from the SWOT analysis.

The map can help to guide, for example, the most suitable positions for community services, buildings, or paths. This may reduce negative environmental impacts and development costs. The opportunities and constraints map can also be used as a communication tool to present clients with what should be done and what should not (see Chapter 8, Presentation). To be most effective, cool colors (from blue green through blue violet, most grays included) are suggested for map constraints and warmer hues (from red through yellow, browns and tans included) for opportunities.

Typical constraints include the following:

floodplains
slopes greater than a certain angle
landslides
places of seismic activity
subsidence areas
wetlands and endangered species habitats
culturally sensitive locations
prime agricultural lands
historic sites or districts
archaeological sites or districts
buildings or sites protected by law for their historical, cultural, landscape, or architectural values
road widening or new road projects (when they could negatively influence or limit the development)
land-use restrictions
environmental restoration sites
ecological networks or corridors (when they enforce limits or distances to development)
natural and industrial hazard areas
underground facilities of higher interest and areas with enforced regulations

Typical areas of opportunities include the following:

land ownership (availability of public or private lands)
accessibility
current land uses
provisions for services (such as hospitals, schools, and museums)
proximity to facilities and points of interest (airports, train stations, cinemas, and community services)
environmental and historical points of interest
landmarks
linkages with adjacent areas in the city or in the nearness of particular interest (e.g., environmental restoration sites or ecological networks and corridors)
misused buildings of architectural significance that can be renovated and utilized for new functions

projects planned for the surroundings that can add value to the site under transformation

Constraints and opportunities can be recorded on a map with symbols and colors. Such maps can help the urban designer to better interpret the place and its context. This lays the groundwork for subsequent design decisions.

Opportunities and Constraints in the Leamouth Peninsula, London

London Thames Gateway presents a key development focus area for London and for England's national government. It is the venue of the Olympic and Paralympics games in 2012. The London Thames Gateway boundary is defined in a United Kingdom Government document, *RPG9a—The Thames Gateway Planning Framework* (UK Government 1995). The framework establishes a set of principles; agreed-upon strategic objectives for economic and housing development, transportation, and the environment; and an outline of the land-use vision for a subregion. Using many drawings and maps, the RPG (Regional Planning Guidance) defines the Gateway area and shows how partnership and regeneration will be key aspects of the development (UK Government 1995).

Development of such a large area takes time. London Thames Gateway will probably still be a key element of the mayor's agenda in 2050 (New London Architecture 2006). Several projects are being designed in the area, including one by Skidmore, Owings & Merrill (SOM), who designed the Leamouth Peninsula for the developers Ballymore Properties.

Situated where the Lea River meets the Thames River, the Leamouth Peninsula has a special character because of its waterfront location. The area presents a significant opportunity, not least because of its excellent location across from the Millennium Dome and the availability of development sites. While the properties are in a variety of ownerships, a draft development framework proposes a comprehensive redevelopment of the peninsula in a way that will bring maximum regeneration benefits to the wider area.

The vision for the peninsula is based on the principles of sustainable mixed-use development. It builds on the Leamouth Regeneration Framework, which was produced by WS Atkins Planning Consultants, an English environmental consultancy, to guide future planning and development of the larger Leamouth area. The framework was created by a large steering group and with the input of key interested parties.

The SOM design of the Leamouth Peninsula aims to transform underutilized land at the gateway to the Lower Lea Valley. The plan is for a 17-acre (6.91-hectare) site at a bend in the Thames River north of the Dome and Greenwich Peninsulas. The scheme includes new housing (about three thousand units), offices, shops, cafés, and cultural and educational facilities in buildings from three to twenty-seven stories tall, along with public spaces designed by Martha Schwartz, parking, and extensive riverfront access. The core of activities will extend across the river via a landmark pedestrian linkage designed by Thomas Heatherwick, which will be supported from nearby buildings. The project will contribute a crucial link among a group of isolated and underserved Docklands neighborhoods.

During the design process, SOM produced one map for the constraints and one for the opportunities to show the relevant elements for the final proposal. According to the designers, the main opportunities were the city's plan to create a new bridge to connect the site to the neighborhoods, the open views, the possibility of creating two distinct identities with a common language (Leamouth North and Leamouth South), and the role of the place as a missing link between the Lower Lea Valley (Olympics) and the Millennium Dome. The major constraints were the lack of connectivity to the neighborhoods, the setback from the river due to flood risk, the height restriction due to the airport's flight path, and the noise pollution (see Figures 4.5/Plate #10, 4.6/Plate #11, and 4.7/Plate #12).

Transects

A *transect* is a line across the landscape through which the designer records the relevant phenomena for the study, such as bedrock, plants, buildings, and roads. Transects furnish a cross section of a place. Patrick Geddes first proposed the application of transects in planning at the beginning of the twentieth century in the famous 1905 Geddes Valley section (see Figure 4.8), "whereby places within each geographic region were evaluated and described according to their location on a scale from mountain to sea" (Walters 2007, 110). Many planners, urban designers, and landscape architects followed Geddes's lead, including Ian McHarg, who found transects an especially helpful device for displaying and analyzing the natural and cultural factors of a place. For instance, one can see how bedrock relates to the surface terrain of a place and, in turn, to its vegetation and land use. More recently, New Urbanist architects, led by Andrés Duany and Elizabeth Plater-Zyberk, have applied transects to their design and planning practices.

For their design of Brooklyn Bridge Park, Michael Van Valkenburgh Associates used an effective section showing the relationship between the Brooklyn Heights neighborhood and the East River (Berrizbeitia 2009; see Figure 4.9/Plate #13).

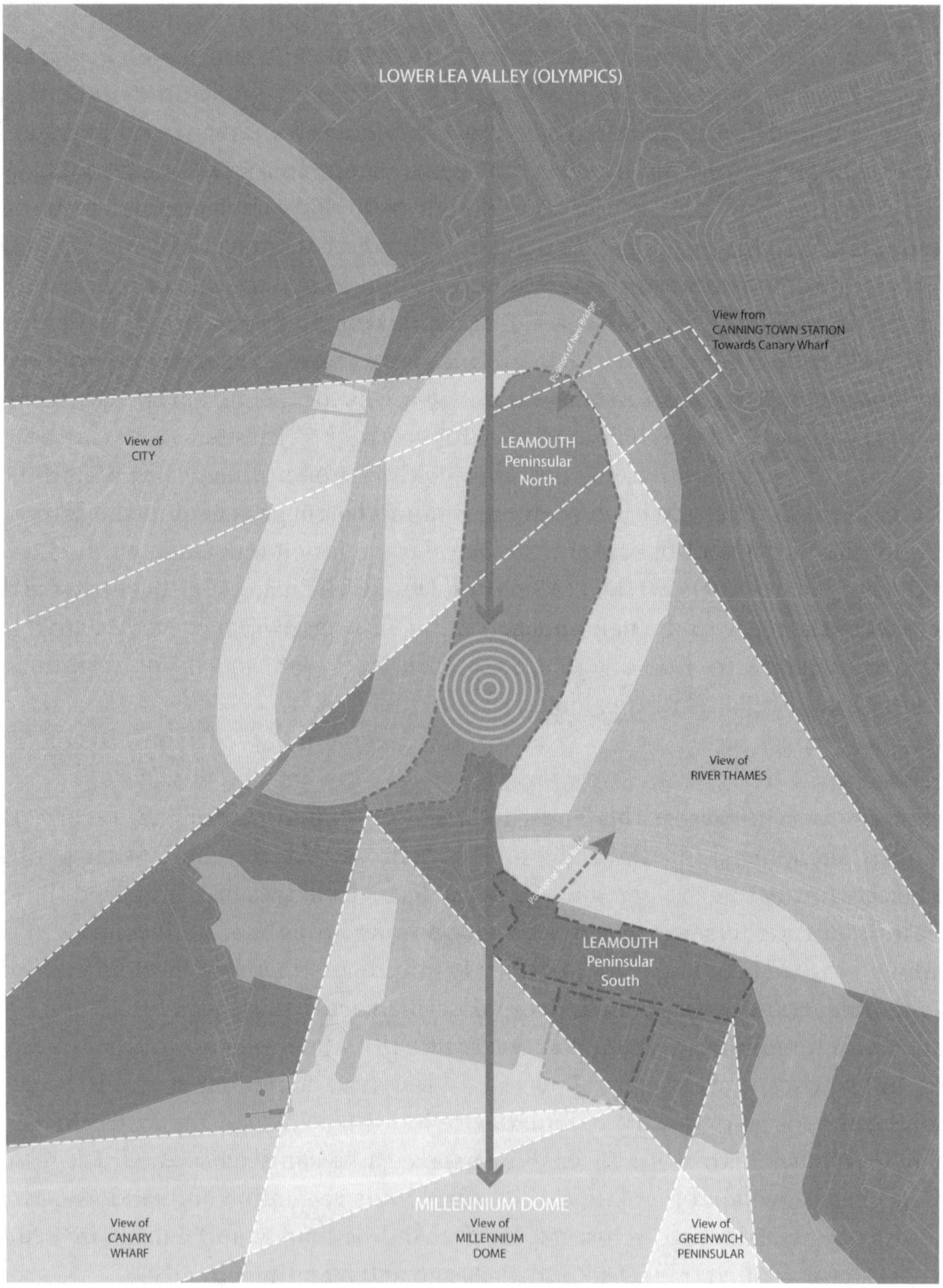

Figure 4.5 (also Plate #10) The opportunities map for the Leamouth Peninsula, London. (Courtesy Skidmore, Owings & Merrill, London office.)

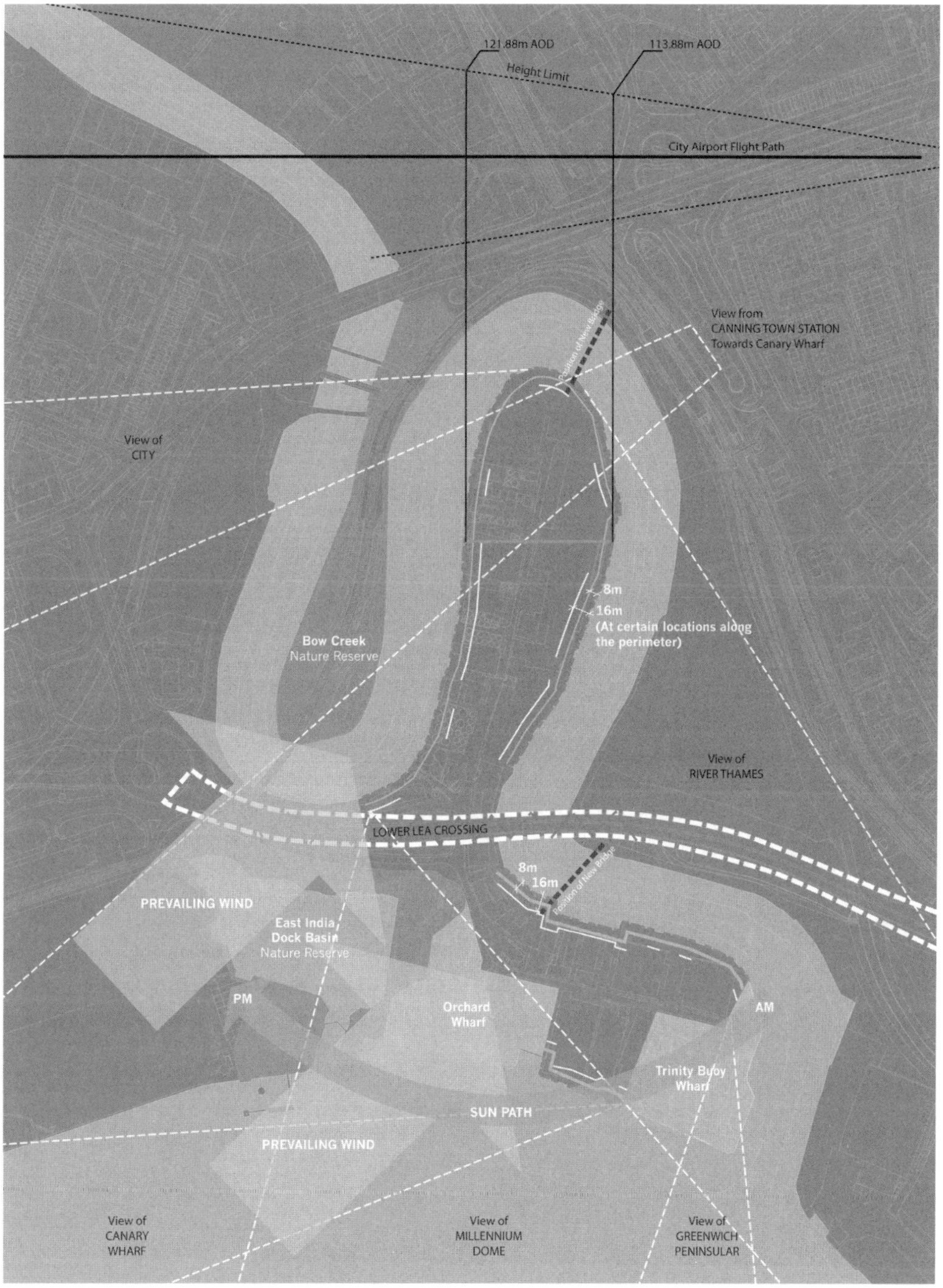

Figure 4.6 (also Plate #11) The constraints map for the Leamouth Peninsula, London. (Courtesy Skidmore, Owings & Merrill, London office.)

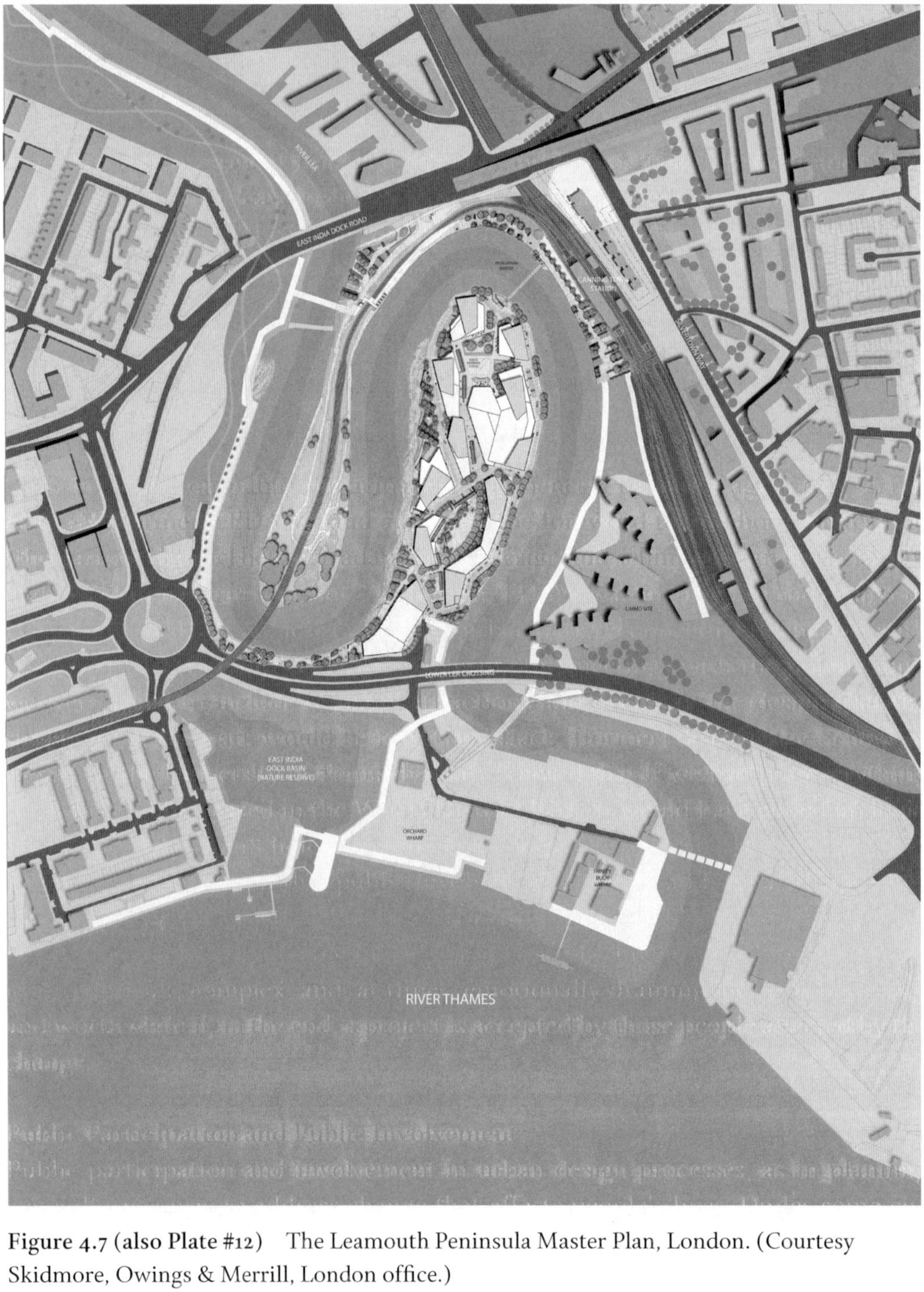

Figure 4.7 (also Plate #12) The Leamouth Peninsula Master Plan, London. (Courtesy Skidmore, Owings & Merrill, London office.)

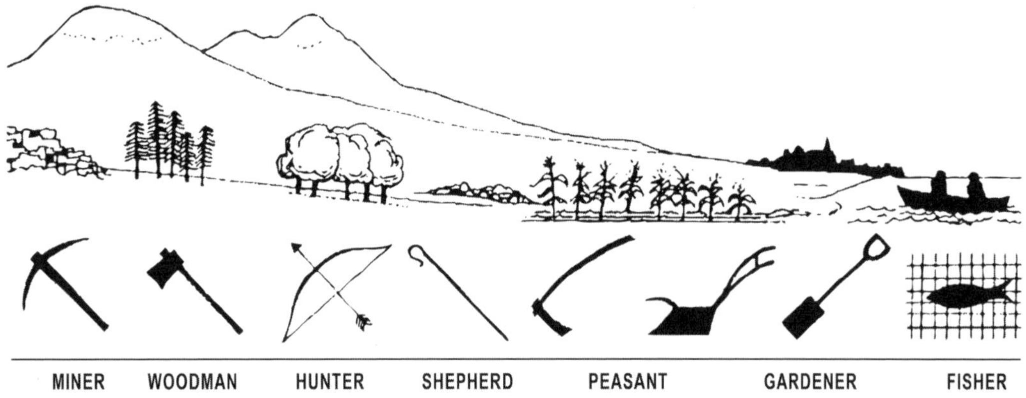

Figure 4.8 Geddes Valley section, from ridgeline to shoreline, nineteenth century: the first transect to show natural conditions with associated human presence. (Courtesy Center for Applied Transect Studies, http://www.transect.org/natural_img.html.)

This transect illustrates the interrelationships among a noisy expressway, a famous promenade, and a new park that creates opportunities for recreation and connections with urban nature.

The transect synthesizes information from different areas of a site. Frequently, the designer will make several transects across the site—for example, from east to west and from north to south. This helps reveal specific characteristics, such as microclimate. For instance, shade and shadows will differ east to west and north to south. This information is important to help the urban designer determine ideal building heights and the location of trees. Transects can also help the designer better understand site drainage. As gravity pulls water downhill, drainage systems can be designed to take advantage of natural elevations and to identify where interventions to the current system are necessary. Transects can also reveal the relationship of bedrock and underground utilities, which has important implications for building location and height.

Exploded Axonometric Drawings

Exploded axonometric drawings "show multiple layers of information and how they relate to one another spatially" (Cantrell and Michaels 2010, 134). These drawings are a series of plans stacked on top of one another. In this way, floorplans for buildings can be displayed in relationship with one another as well as other factors, such as plumbing and electrical systems and external conditions.

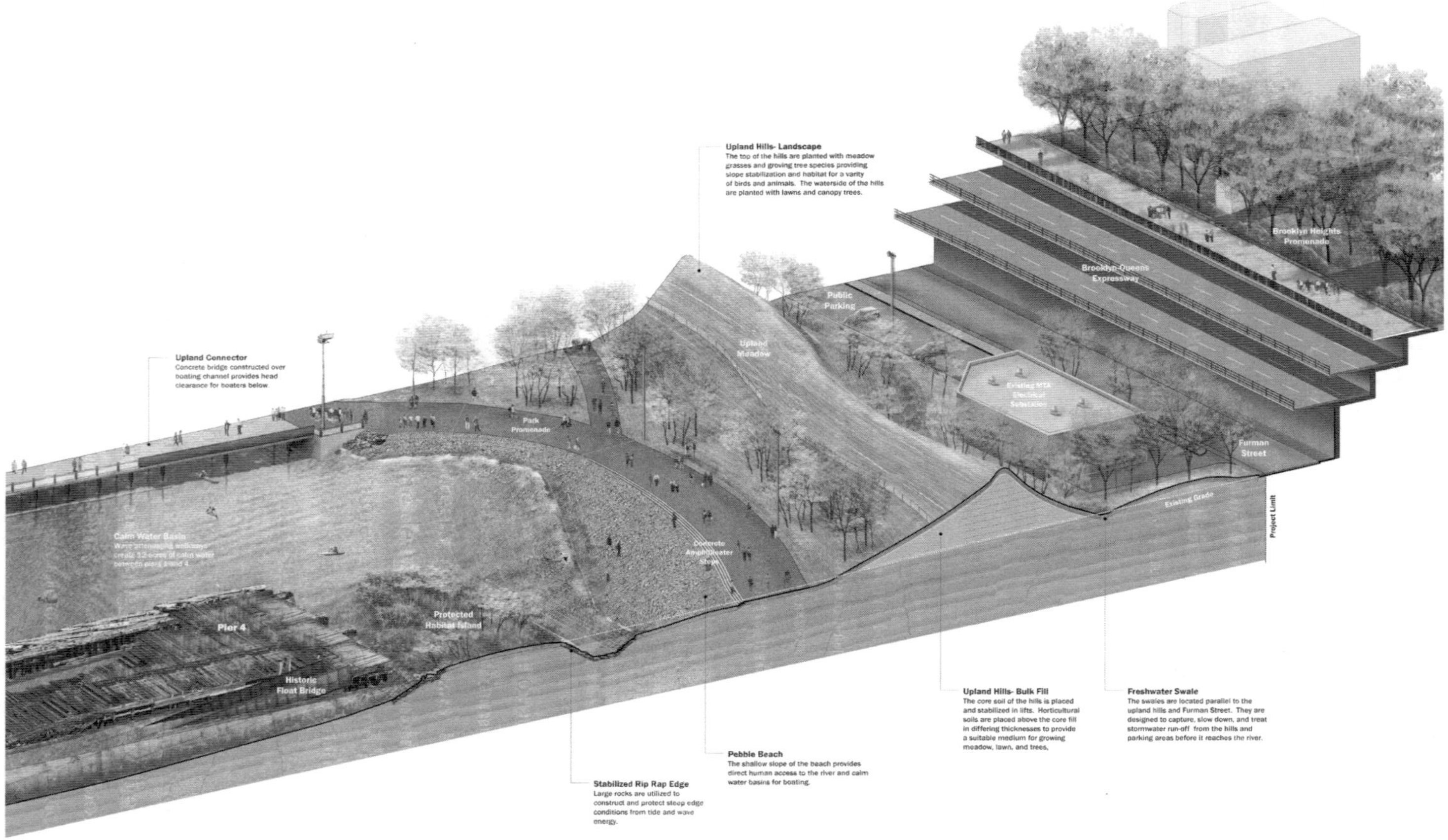

Figure 4.9 (also Plate #13) Brooklyn Bridge Park section, New York, 2008. (Courtesy Michael Van Valkenburgh Associates.)

For example, StossLU employed an exploded axonometric drawing for the Nankang Depot Stormwater Park, which was a proposal for a new landscape infrastructure on the site of an existing rail yard in a redeveloping area of Taipei, Taiwan (Figure 4.10). As proposed, the park would function socially and recreationally as a highly programmed neighborhood open space, with play courts and surfaces alternating with undulating, planted landforms. The park is designed to capture, infiltrate, and hold an enormous quantity of seasonal rainfall from the site and adjacent areas, in order to alleviate flooding that has plagued this part of Taipei. It accomplishes this in recessed areas of the park's surface as well as in a large holding tank beneath the site. The park's linear landforms, set perpendicular to the flow of traffic along the boulevard, also activate the park as an important experiential element for vehicular users of the boulevard and mark a new gateway for the city of Taipei.

Such drawings have communication and analytical benefits. For communication, the exploded axonometric drawing is a tool that illustrates and displays to the client or to the public how a site, and its context, is composed of different elements frequently perceived as an indistinct and blurred unity. For analysis, the separation of different layers of the landscape components helps the urban designer understand the importance of individual parts and their interaction. The exploded axonometric drawing is a useful tool to organize the different information collected during surveys and to show the relations between the existing parts and to evaluate the effects on those parts for the future transformation.

Suitability Analysis

Suitability analysis is one of the best known and most effective methods to synthesize the collected information. This method became well known around the world thanks to Ian McHarg (1969). McHarg suggested designing with rather than against nature by analyzing the role played by each part of the site in the natural ecosystem and building only on land that can sustain development without broad negative effects.

The original method consisted of producing maps on transparent paper, one for every element inventoried, in which "social values" were divided in three different shades of gray (the lighter represents the most suitable area for every factor considered). Then the maps were laid over one another on a backlit table. Scrutinizing the collective maps determined the final result: "one after another [the transparent maps] were laid down, layer after layer . . . , an elaborate representation . . . like a complex X-ray photograph with dark and light tones. Yet in the

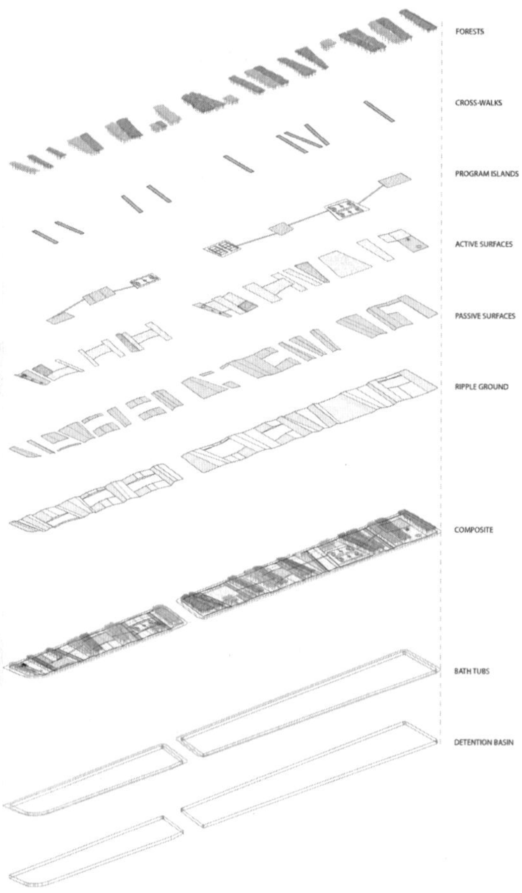

Figure 4.10 Exploded axonometric drawing for the Nankang Depot Stormwater Park, Taipei, Taiwan, 2010. (Courtesy StossLU.)

increasing opacity there were always lighter areas and we can see their conclusion. . . . The darker the tone the greater the social cost . . . , the lighter the tone the less the social cost" (McHarg 1969, 35, 40). The lighter spots on the map, showing the areas where the concurrence of propitious factors combined with the absence of any detrimental ones, constitutes the highest fit for the specific land use. The overlay of physical maps was eventually replaced by GIS technologies, and this method is now applied all over the world (Treu 2004). Ecological analysis has continued to inform urban design theories and processes, such as those developed by Ken Yeang (1995, 2006), Charles Waldheim (2006), Richard Weller (2009), and Mohsen Mostafavi (2010).

Geographic Information System Technology

In addition to physical models, computer technology can also be employed to represent site characteristics. One of the more widespread methods for processing, synthesizing, and combining land data—especially in planning and management of land uses—is using GIS software for storage, retrieval, mapping, and analysis of geographic data. Spatial features are stored in a coordinated system that refers to a particular place on the earth. The spatial features are associated with descriptive attributes in tabular form. Data and associated attributes in the same coordinate system can then be layered for mapping and analysis (see Figure 4.11).

GIS differs from computer-aided design (CAD) and other graphical computer applications in that all data are geographically referenced to a map projection in an earth-coordinate system. Data from various sources can be brought together into a common database.

Another property of a GIS database is *topology*, which defines the spatial relationships among different elements. The fundamental components of spatial data in a GIS are points, lines (arcs), and polygons. Using GIS technology, it is possible to perform analyses, such as modeling the flow through connecting lines in a network, combining adjacent polygons with similar characteristics and overlaying geographic features.

GIS technology may be used in many phases of urban design processes, from

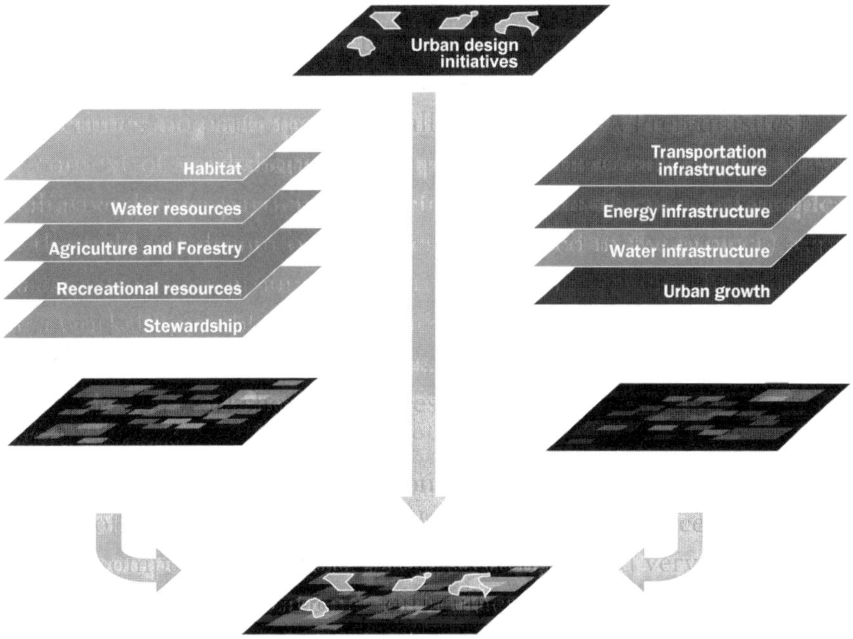

Figure 4.11 Overlay of mapped data through GIS. (Based on a diagram by the Regional Plan Association.)

analysis to design to communication. Batty and colleagues (1998) provided a scheme that connects data representation with a generic urban design process (see Figure 4.12). The rationale behind the representation assumes that an urban design task "involves a very wide range of issues from the socio-economic, to the functional and the behavioral, to the aesthetics as well as to the constructional and the environmental [and also] that the designer has complete control over the process, taking account of these various factors by dipping into the GIS tool kit as and when required" (Batty et al. 1998, 8). GIS helps to connect data and to define the relationship among them. Gathering different urban and design site spatial features can be the starting point for multilayered analysis and creating thematic maps. Data stored in a GIS can be called up through queries. A suitability analysis can benefit from the use of GIS. The combination of natural features—such as slopes, physiographic elements, risk and hazardous areas, and threatened natural areas or habitats—can lead to a constraints map that will influence design opportunities.

Although GIS technologies have been employed mostly in urban, landscape, and regional planning, some examples and experimental uses in urban design are

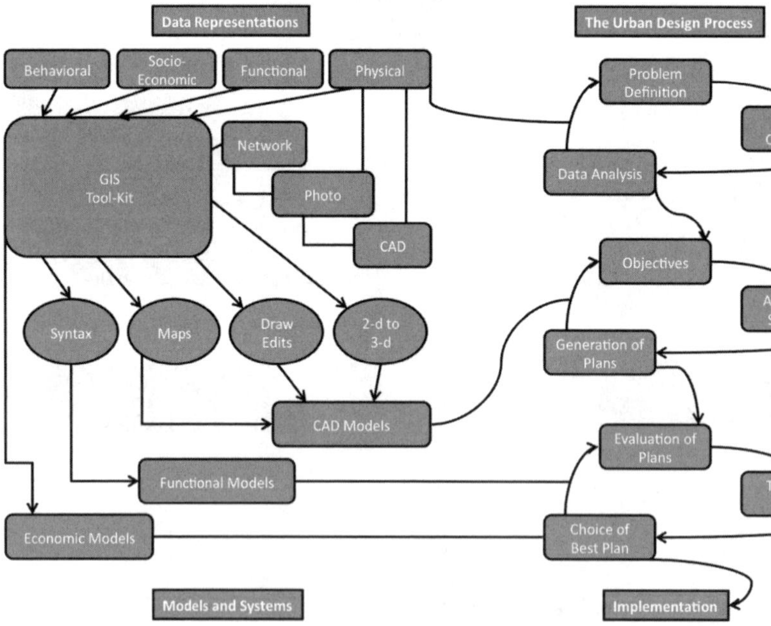

Figure 4.12 New computer technologies in the process of urban design. (Adapted from Batty et al. 1998, 7.)

provided in literature. "Multiple Centrality Assessment" offers a GIS application with the aim to map centrality in different cities to understand their potentialities of becoming public spaces and attracting people and new functions (Porta, Latora, and Crucitti 2006). Fisher-Gewirtzman et al. (2005) presented a model, "Spatial Openness Index," that expresses the volume of free spaces potentially seen from a given point in terms of three-dimensional visual spatial information. The model enables the simulation of landscapes for a more realistic estimation of the view.

GIS technology can also be used to compare redesigned urban maps over time to interpret the morphology and evolution of urban forms and tissues (Oliveira and Pinho 2006). The "Metric Axial Model" has been proposed by Mohamed Salheen and Leslie Forsyth (2001) to predict pedestrian movement using attributes suggested by transportation planning literature. GIS-based visual analysis was applied on different urban fabrics in Singapore to measure the urban visibility (Yang, Putra, and Chaerani 2007). GIS can also be used to facilitate public participation and to increase community understanding and participation in the design and revitalization of neighborhoods (Al-Kodmany 2000).

Awareness of the Space and the Design Task

The designer, at this particular moment of the process, might feel the need to get a wider awareness and familiarity with the project space. Scale comparisons and physical models can help deepen awareness of the space and the design task.

Scale Comparison

Scale comparison helps the designer understand the site's size by comparing it with known dimensions of other places. It is used in design and communication activities. In the design phase, scale comparisons help the designer to become familiar with the site, especially when it is not known or is almost impossible to visit or access directly, typically with international competitions. In the communication phase, scale comparison is especially useful in facilitating spatial thought, which it is not particularly widespread among the public and is one of the most difficult skills to acquire (see Chapter 8, Presentation).

Many techniques can be used to generate a scale comparison. One that is particularly well suited to a teaching environment or to when the area is not very large consists of understanding the dimension of the site (or its parts) by comparing shapes of known spaces with the site at the same scale. For example, the size of an official soccer field (344 by 223 feet, 105 by 68 meters, 1.763 acres, 0.714 hectares) or the size of an official football field (120 by 53 yards, 109 by 48 meters, 1.292

acres, 0.523 hectares) can be used, or even a well-known public square or city park. To know that the 10 acres (4.05 hectares) of a site area can contain nearly six soccer fields or about eight football fields can represent an effective reference for the designer and for those who participate in a public presentation. Moreover, this spatial process avoids, or at least limits, scale errors typical of first design-process steps. An area can be overfilled or, on the contrary, left too empty.

Another way to proceed in a scale comparison is to show the design site juxtaposed with known urban spaces. For example, New York New Visions (2002a) compared the 16 acres (6.5 hectares) of Ground Zero with commonly known spaces, including Grand Central Station, Rockefeller Center, Bryant Park, and Gramercy Park (see Figure 4.13). Or, in the example above, the site size is almost four and a half times the size of Milan's Piazza Duomo, or the site is almost 1/80th of New York City's Central Park (843 acres, 341.4 hectares).

The area of the airport of Vatnsmýri, south of Reykjavík, covering 370.5 acres (150 hectares), was considered for transformation and enhancement in a 2007 international competition (see Chapter 2, Prerequisites). The appropriation of the study area spatiality was obtained through the comparison of the site with known city portions (see Figure 4.14).

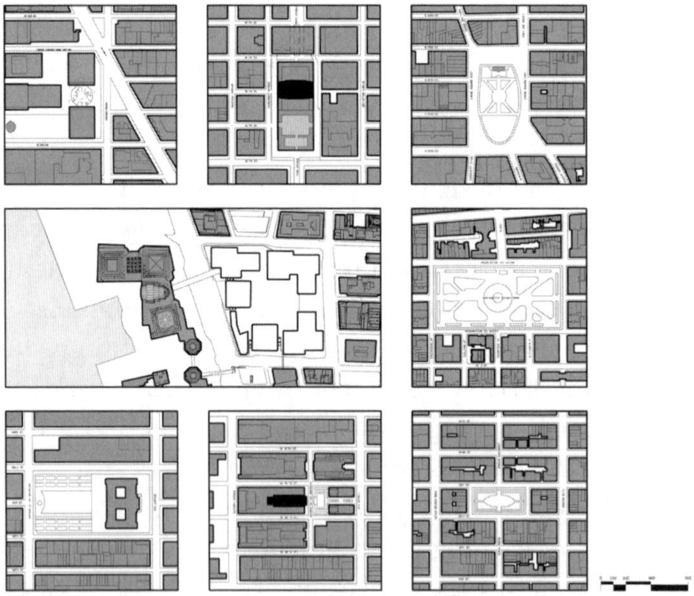

Figure 4.13 The area of the World Trade Center (middle) compared with seven popular places in New York City at the same scale. (From New York New Visions 2002b. Courtesy of New York New Visions.)

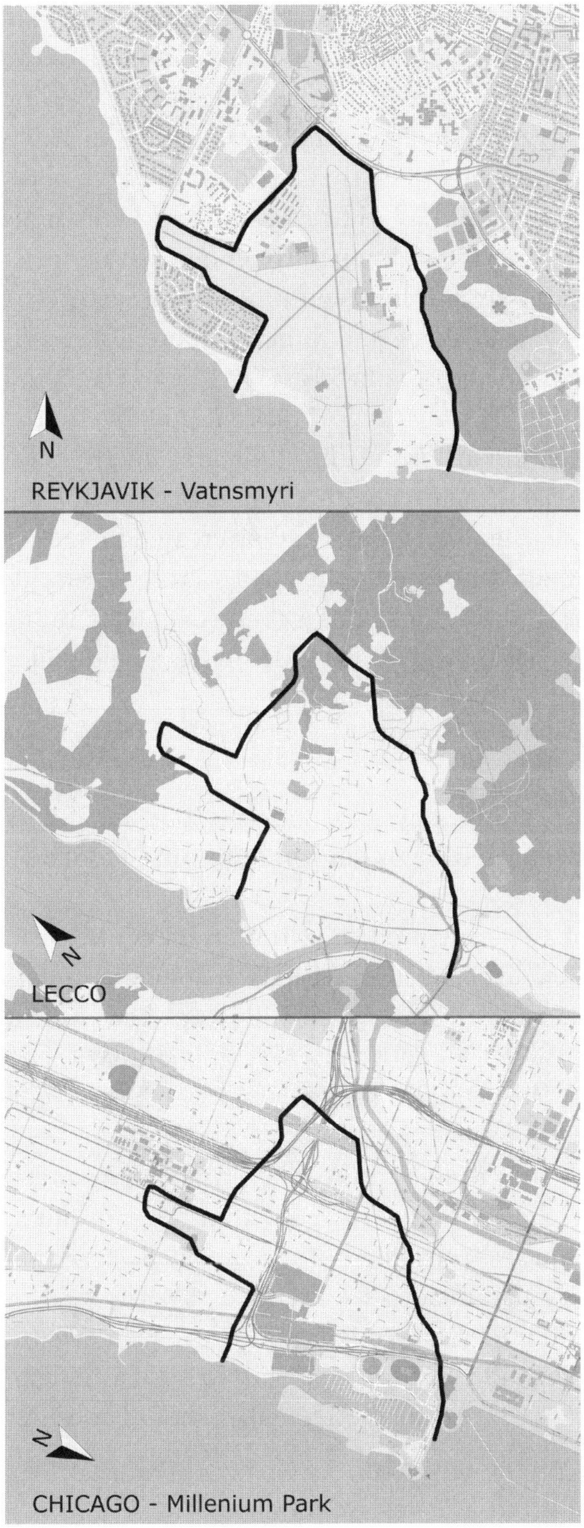

Figure 4.14 The competition area of the airport of Vatnsmýri, Iceland (top), overlapped on a map of Lecco, Italy (middle), and Chicago, Illinois (bottom). (Adapted by Ramon Busi on OpenStreetMap. ©OpenStreetMap contributors.)

In other circumstances, the designer may discover that the site is a nearly exact reproduction in real scale of another place. In Milan, during the first phase of the competition for the historical neighborhood of Milan's Fair (eventually won by a team composed of Daniel Libeskind, Zaha Hadid, Arata Isozaki, and Pier Paolo Maggiora), a strong resemblance between the square that enclosed the 63.01 acres (25.5 hectares) of the transformation area and another close-by area, known as Selinunte quarter, was noted. The quarter is predominantly composed of social housing built between the end of the 1930s and the beginning of the 1940s. The area resembles the square of Milan's Fair in shape and dimension but not in orientation. Both are nearly regular squares of approximately 1,640 to 1,804 feet (500 to 550 meters) per side (see Figure 4.15). This "discovery" made it possible for the designers to become familiar with the dimensions of the study area and to compare the densities of the existing housing quarter with those envisaged for the Fair area. A comparison enables simulating, through virtual or created images of real pictures, the effects of different building heights, the change in road widths, and the relationships between facades and sidewalks and walking distances. In the communication phase, the scale comparison can be extended from single buildings to the space relationships created by the entire plan.

Physical Models

Throughout the process, the designer can use physical models of the site and its surrounding context. A physical model presents a useful communication tool during public dialogues.

During the preliminary design phase, scale models of the urban context can play relevant roles. A reproduction of an urban district with its major components (roads, public space, green areas, and built volumes) helps illustrate the context for the plan. A physical, three-dimensional model has a concision and synthesis impossible to find in aerial photos or through bird's-eye-view drawings (see Figure 4.16).

A model can accommodate the various design trials. In the final communication stages, budget permitting, a model can be constructed with more substantial materials and with different techniques—from computer-controlled laser machines (see Figure 4.17) to completely handmade (see Figure 4.18). The goal of using a model is to provide a clear and understandable vision of the plan even to those without a design background. The model needs to be built to scale using materials and means best suited for the site size. The model maker should consider

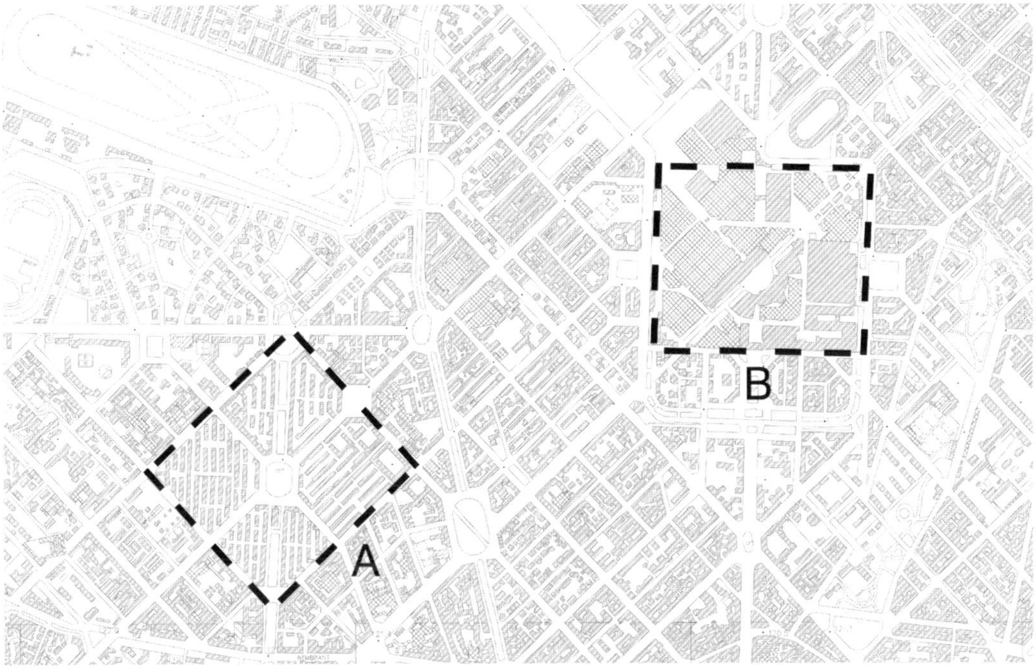

Figure 4.15 Comparison between the Selinunte neighborhood (A) and the Milan's Fair site (B), Milan, Italy. (Drawing by Ramon Busi.)

the design mission, the purpose the designer has in mind, and the space available to process simulations and conduct trials.

The Rapid Model in the International Workshop on Timişoara, Romania

A rapid model was used in an international workshop held in Lecco in 2005 for the city of Timişoara, Romania (Tadi 2007). The multinational team consisted of professors from the Milan Polytechnic and urban designers from the London and San Francisco SOM offices as well as from the Arep Groupe of Paris (a French firm working on train stations, moving systems, urbanism, and architecture). The participants had to redefine functions and shapes of an area between the city's north and east rail stations. "Therefore the workshop topics involved the [issue] of redrawing an important part of the city . . . to propose an urban image and a new lifestyle for the prominent future, acting simultaneously at local and global scale" (Tadi 2007, 40). The goal was to come up with convincing and realistic schemes that, in the form of urban and architectural projects, would be able to highlight

a

b

c

Figure 4.16 Phases of construction of the model for an urban design studio on the requalification of a central part of Milan, Italy: (a) modeling the buildings, (b) the base map, (c) the model. (By Danilo Palazzo.)

Figure 4.17 A model made with a Rapid 3D printer. (Courtesy Prototypes Lab–Milan Polytechnic, Lecco's campus. Scientific leader: Maria Pignataro. Technical staff: Monica Pozzi.)

potentials and to select long-term planning strategies for the study area itself and for the whole city of Timişoara.

During the two-week workshop, several models were produced. The aim of the very first models, made quickly, was to help designers understand the place and the relationship between the site and the urban districts around it during the

Figure 4.18 Students preparing a cardboard rapid model. (Photograph by Danilo Palazzo.)

synthesis phase. The models were used as a base for the very first design ideas. A 1:1000 scale model was produced (approximately 16 by 7 feet, or 5 by 2 meters). The base map was a scale blow-up of an aerial photo printed on paper (see Figure 4.19/Plate #17), glued on a rigid paper support, and bearing a transparent Plexiglas slab to help protect and hold the aerial photo reproduction firm. Over this layered base, the existing and proposed buildings, made to scale with expanded

Figure 4.19 (also Plate #17) The Timişoara (Romania) workshop model. The quick model was prepared to understand the place and the relationship between the site and the city. (By Massimo Tadi.)

polyurethane, were pasted. After the workshop, a final physical model, which included some details of the urban and architectonic design, was sent to Timişoara.

Case Studies

Searching for precedent case studies is a widespread custom in design (see Francis 2001). Case studies suggest potentials, risks, and cautions that need to be considered (Yin 2003, 2009). Jon Lang (2005, xxiii) argues that

> case studies represent the accumulated history of many fields of human endeavour. . . . When designing we rely heavily on the knowledge developed through individual cases being cumulatively converted into prescriptive theories or paradigms. . . . What we designers call "case studies" tends to be descriptive statements of the geometric qualities of specific designs. The way the schemes were brought into existence (if they have been), the dynamics of the political forces that shaped them, their cost, and modes of financing, even the way they function, all fall outside the realm of such studies. If done thoroughly, however, case studies can provide empirical evidence of the processes and methods used to achieve specific design ends.

Mark Francis identified the critical dimensions of case studies (see Box 4.2) and suggested a framework for them (see Box 4.3).

Architecture, urban design, landscape architecture, and planning can benefit from the accumulation of wisdom from past projects implemented in previous centuries as well as those of our contemporaries. Building on Francis's model (2001), the Landscape Architecture Foundation sponsored a series of case study books with relevance to urban design. Francis himself published case studies on urban open space (2003a) and the Village Homes community in California (2003b). Meanwhile, Jack Ahern and colleagues have published case studies on biodiversity design and planning (Ahern, Leduc, and York 2007); Jeffrey Hou and colleagues, on greening cities (Hou, Johnson, and Lawson 2009); and Krista Schneider, on context-sensitive highway design (2003).

Various examples of urban design plans and implementation are reported in specialized journals. Reading these publications, it is possible to follow the design evolution from the first interpretative sketches through to every technological detail. Monographs dedicated to architects, urban designers, or city planners allow us, also through critical contributions, to know nearly everything we want to know about the authors, the projects, and the contexts of the designs. Thematic books on different subjects, such as city parks, residential quarters, squares, public spaces, and sport facilities, propose a wide variety of solutions already adopted for problems similar to those the designer is addressing. The Internet has significantly expanded this already immense mass of information.

To this almost endless range of information, projects processed by the designers themselves need to be added. In a large firm, many cases may be available. Beyond large firms, public squares, districts, street portions, parks, and gardens planned by anonymous designers can frequently mean as much as any famous architect's project.

Box 4.2 Critical Dimensions of Case Studies

Baseline information/context—List the location, size, client, designer(s), consultant(s), density, and land use type.

Roles of the key participants—What are the roles of the urban designer and other professionals? Clients? Users? What is the nature of the team? Who leads the team? What is their role in the beginning of the project? How does this change during the course of project?

Financial—List the initial budget and the final costs. What are the reasons for any difference?

Process—What is the political process? Decision-making process? Design process? Implementation process? Who influences a project's decisions and outcomes? Why? How does the project come together?

Definitions of and responses to problems—What problem(s) is the project trying to solve? Was it solved? If so, how? If not, why not? Were other problems solved?

Goals—What are the key goals (social, ecological, aesthetic)? How were they set? Who defined them? Did the goals change during the course of the project? Is so, how?

Program—How was the program developed? Who developed it? Was it modified during the course of the project?

Design—What are the key design concepts? What is the inspiration for form? How did the designer translate goals into form?

Site visit(s)—What does the project look like? How does it work? How does it feel?

Use—How is the place used? Who uses it? Who does not use it?

Maintenance and management—What are the problems of management and maintenance? What are the maintenance costs? How is the project perceived by space managers?

Perception and meaning—Describe how the place is perceived and valued.

Scale—What is the size of the project? Dimensions of key elements? Amount of site coverage and impervious surface?

Time—How well does the place fare over time? How does the project age incrementally?

Unique constraints—How were the constraints addressed in the process?

Community—How is the community served by this project? What is its social impact? What is its meaning?

Environmental sensitivity and impact—How is the environment served by this project? What is its contribution to sustainability?

Impact on profession—How is the profession served by this project? What does the project contribute to the professional knowledge base?

Infrastructure—What are the underlying challenges of the site? What are the technological constraints?

Lessons learned—Describe the site-specific lessons learned in comparison to the more general lessons?

continued

continued

Theoretical underpinning—Why was the project done? What is the question (or questions) it is trying to answer? What is the problem (or problems) it is trying to solve?

Outside critiques—Include critiques by awards jury, experts, users, review committees, design critics, and journalists. Has there been any controversy associated with the project? If so, has this been resolved? How?

Source: Adapted from Francis 2001, 20.

The challenge is how to choose from this vast and expanding mass of possible cases the ones most relevant for the design at hand. One possible tactic is to select a case study based on a list of criteria that could contain the following items:

- *Similarity.* The functions, dimensions, climatic and cultural site characteristics, budget, and available competencies of the case study should have similarities with the urban design project.
- *Documentation availability.* Information should be available beyond short descriptions and photos in trendy journals. For example, the designers' reports, the cost of the initiative, and the conditions through which they have been realized and the partnership roles can be helpful.
- *Direct knowledge and/or the opportunity to visit and investigate the precedent.* For realized projects, it may be worthwhile to apply methods generally employed in a site visit: take pictures, sketch, speak with people, observe, and record.
- *Designers' statements.* Sometimes, papers in journals or in monographs contain considerations about the project by its author—for example, about the prerequisites that have been respected, on what the author would have done but was prevented from doing and why, or on the judgment of the project years after its completion.
- *Visitors' declarations.* One the most important opinions on urban design comes from those who use it. Some analytical methods, such as Kevin Lynch's mental maps or the behavioral analyses, can be applied to existing urban design to understand how the project works from the perspective of its inhabitants and users.
- *Critical literature on the project.* In some circumstances, it is possible to find critiques of the project and of how it took root (or not, and why not) in its social context.

Box 4.3 A Suggested Format for Case Studies

Abstract/Fact Sheet

Photo(s)
Project background
Project significance and impact
Lessons learned
Contacts
Keywords

Full Case Study

Project name
Location
Date designed/planned
Construction completed
Cost
Size
Urban designer(s)
Client
Consultants
Managed by
Context
Site analysis
Project background and history
Genesis of project
Design, development, and decision-making processes
Role of urban designer(s)
Program elements
Maintenance and management
Photograph(s)
Site plan(s) to scale
User/use analysis
Peer reviews
Criticism
Significance and uniqueness of the project
Limitations
General features and lessons
Future issues/plans
Bibliography of project citations/related references
Websites/links
Contacts for further information

In-Depth Analysis

Archival research (e.g., project records, newspaper articles, photographs, drawings, and correspondence)
Awards or special recognition for the project
Copies of articles or reports on the project
Interviews with client
Interviews with managers and maintenance people
Interviews with users
Interviews with nonusers
Longitudinal studies of the place over time

Source: Adapted from Francis 2001, 21.

In *Urban Design,* Jon Lang (2005) furnishes fifty case studies with different typologies. The typological classification was adopted using three categories:

firstly according to the process by which they were generated and built [Lang uses such categories as "total urban design," where a team has control of the whole process, or "plug-in urban design," in which infrastructure elements are

> used as catalysts for development], secondly according to the type of product they are [new towns, urban precincts, elements of infrastructure, and individual items such as monuments] and thirdly, according to the urban design paradigm [e.g., the City Beautiful, the Rationalist City, the Garden City, New Urbanism, Landscape Urbanism, the city of commercial pragmatism], within which they were designed. (43)

Lang adds that the designer needs to look at each case study and consider the political, market, legal, and social contexts in which they occurred.

Case study–based learning is a disciplinary practice that urban design shares with other fields, both those that overlap (architecture, landscape architecture, urban planning) and those more distant (medicine, law, business) (see Francis 2001; Yin, 2003). As a teaching tool for students and practitioners alike, it can be useful to choose an urban design case study within reach and analyze its components and parts: who promoted the project and who commissioned the design, how much did it cost, who designed it, how much time was involved in the process, what were the implementation challenges, does it work, does it generate value, which modifications were made to the original design, and who used it and how and when (see Box 4.2). Learning from past case studies, including more obscure projects, helps to expand design awareness.

Sometimes, it can even be advantageous to choose precedents with flaws or to choose designs that are well known because they failed. Not only positive examples can help advance a design. Why do some projects not generate the "urbanity" they tried to accomplish? Why have public spaces been rejected by inhabitants? Has a plan failed to produce its projected economic value? If so, why?

The literature provides examples of great urban design failures. For instance, Robert Saliba (1997) analyzed the case of the Prince of Wales' Urban Design Task Force in Lebanon. The goal of the task force was to tackle the postwar issue of "reconnecting the city," using community participation, neo-rational urbanism, and process-orientated urban design, which ended up not being applicable in the postwar Lebanese context of top-down corporate planning and patron-client relationships. Kenneth Kolson's *Big Plans* (2003) as well as Peter Hall's *Cities of Tomorrow* (2002) and *Great Planning Disasters* (1982) recount many failed cases at the city and metropolitan scales. Lang, in *Urban Design* (2005), also presents genuine urban design failures.

Diagnosis

After the synthesis phase is largely completed, the designer can determine how to proceed with the design. The synthesis of information essentially has two motivations: the first for design diagnosis and the second for communication.

The first corresponds to the need to recognize the project prerequisites and the client's demands. Summarizing the collected information presents a rigorous undertaking, necessary to identify what is important and relevant for the subsequent design steps. The second motivation regards the relationship with the public and/or with the client. For reasons of terminology and time, it is hardly appropriate to display, to the client or to the public, the entire analytical process in detail, especially when this process has been extensive and laborious. Summarizing the elements through diagnosis also allows for more effective representation and easier communication with the affected population.

The word *diagnosis*, adopted from the medical field, here means the examination of phenomena based on the characteristics of the place and the task. The examination can be done directly on-site or through laboratory investigations. The goal is to understand a place in order to improve it, to transform it, to correct it, or to protect it.

Physical models and GIS technology can be used to synthesize information to arrive at a diagnosis. Specialized software can be used to analyze data in depth for specific reasons. For instance, vehicular traffic data collected, however broad and extensive, may not be enough to reach a diagnosis. There could be the need to develop a model to elaborate the extent of vehicular flows, their origins and their destinations, traffic composition, and traffic jam locations. Familiarity with these simulations gives the designer a deeper knowledge from which to start—for example, to propose modifications to roadways, improvements to pedestrian crossings, and roundabouts or crossroads.

Software applications can process or simulate solar brightness, or *albedo*, produced by specific pavings or the shadows generated by existing or designed buildings. Software can map the site to show which areas are more or less subject to noise pollution and should be considered during the design process. There is even software that can simulate the behaviors of a crowd in a public space and patterns of human behavior and movement in dense urban areas (Arizona State University 2007).

Frequently, the diagnosis is summarized in a site analysis map or diagram. A site analysis map can build on an opportunities and constraints map but also go further by diagnosing the phenomena that require intervention. Sometimes, a diagram may be better than a map to summarize the diagnosis.

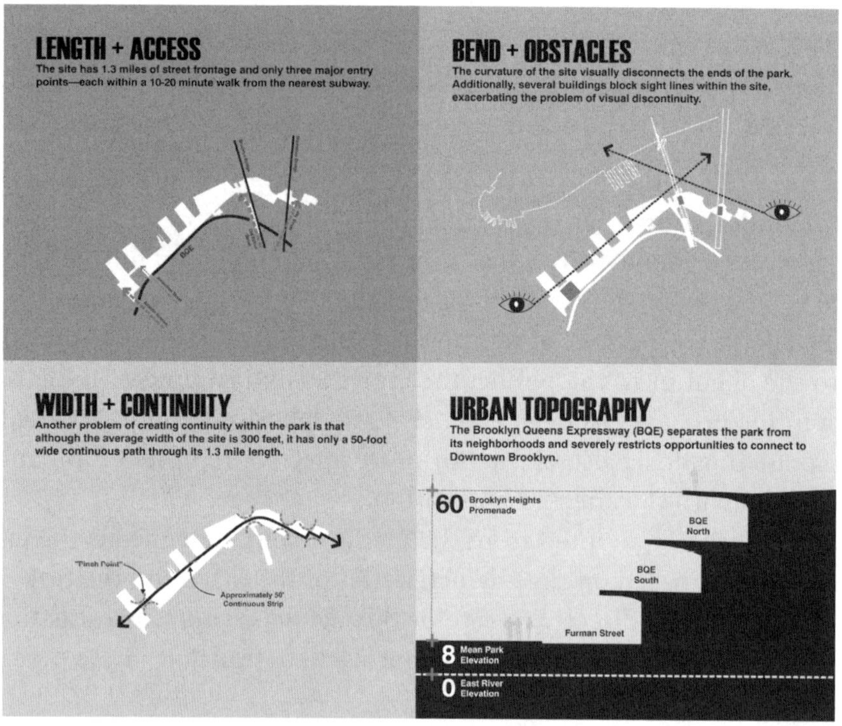
LENGTH + ACCESS
The site has 1.3 miles of street frontage and only three major entry points—each within a 10-20 minute walk from the nearest subway.
BQE
BEND + OBSTACLES
The curvature of the site visually disconnects the ends of the park. Additionally, several buildings block sight lines within the site, exacerbating the problem of visual discontinuity.
WIDTH + CONTINUITY
Another problem of creating continuity within the park is that although the average width of the site is 300 feet, it has only a 50-foot wide continuous path through its 1.3 mile length.
"Pinch Point"
Approximately 50' Continuous Strip
URBAN TOPOGRAPHY
The Brooklyn Queens Expressway (BQE) separates the park from its neighborhoods and severely restricts opportunities to connect to Downtown Brooklyn.
60 Brooklyn Heights Promenade
BQE North
BQE South
Furman Street
8 Mean Park Elevation
0 East River Elevation

a

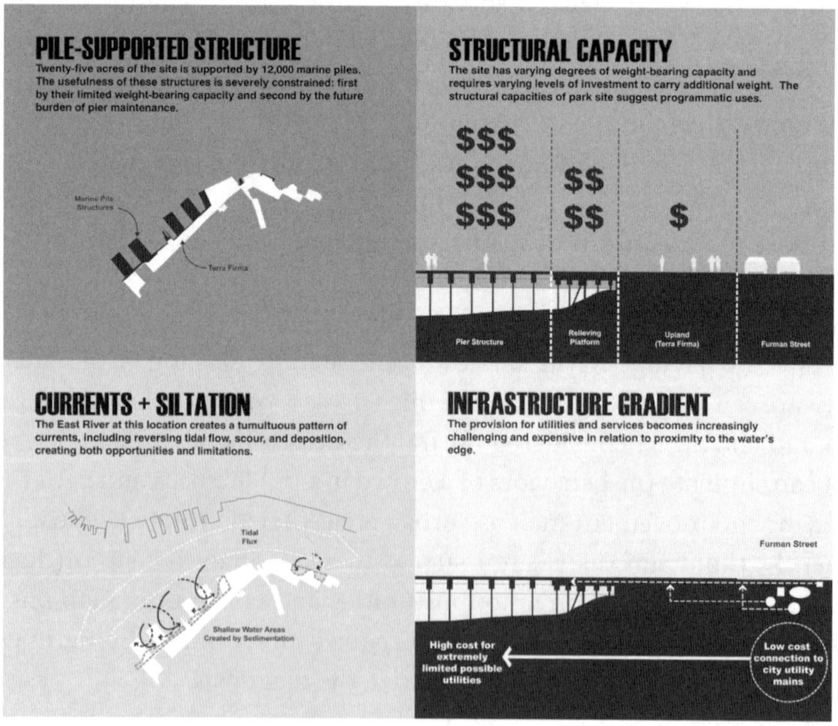
PILE-SUPPORTED STRUCTURE
Twenty-five acres of the site is supported by 12,000 marine piles. The usefulness of these structures is severely constrained: first by their limited weight-bearing capacity and second by the future burden of pier maintenance.
Marine Pile Structures
Terra Firma
STRUCTURAL CAPACITY
The site has varying degrees of weight-bearing capacity and requires varying levels of investment to carry additional weight. The structural capacities of park site suggest programmatic uses.
$$$
$$$
$$$
$$
$$
$
Pier Structure
Relieving Platform
Upland (Terra Firma)
Furman Street
CURRENTS + SILTATION
The East River at this location creates a tumultuous pattern of currents, including reversing tidal flow, scour, and deposition, creating both opportunities and limitations.
Tidal Flux
Shallow Water Areas Created by Sedimentation
INFRASTRUCTURE GRADIENT
The provision for utilities and services becomes increasingly challenging and expensive in relation to proximity to the water's edge.
Furman Street
High cost for extremely limited possible utilities
Low cost connection to city utility mains

b

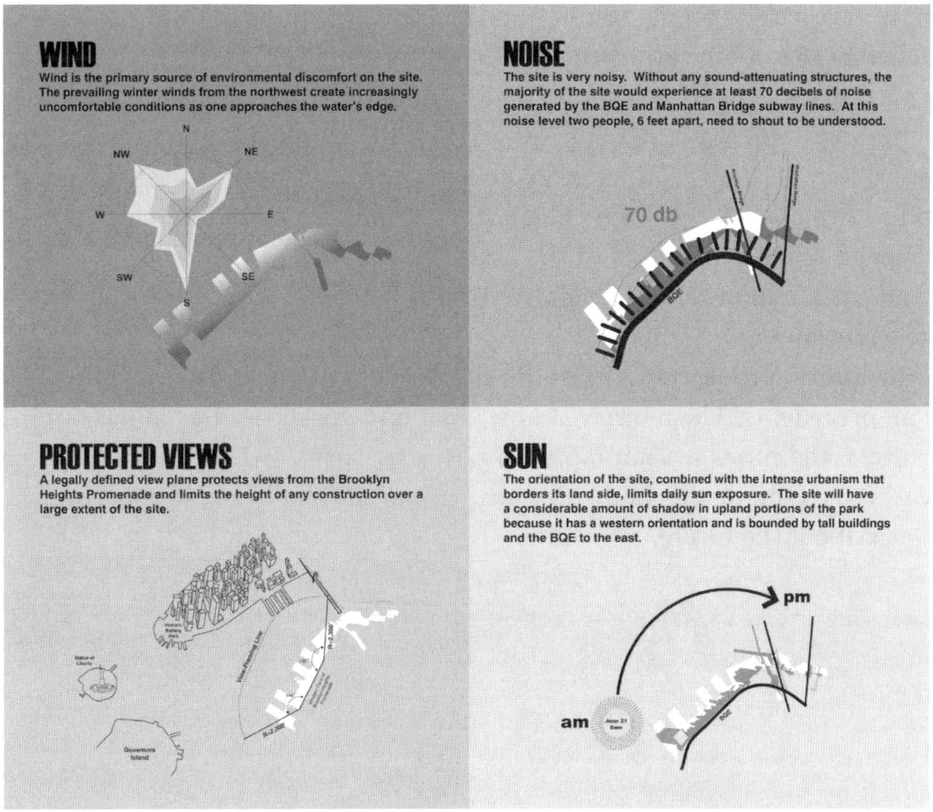

c

Figure 4.20 (also Plate #14) Site analysis and project criteria (a, b, and c) for Brooklyn Bridge Park, Brooklyn, New York, 2008. (Courtesy Michael Van Valkenburgh Associates.)

In their Brooklyn Bridge Park design, Michael Van Valkenburgh Associates combine maps and diagrams to summarize their site diagnosis (Berrizbeitia 2009) (see Figure 4.20/Plate #14). They illustrated such factors as access, visual connections, wind, noise, and solar orientation.

Michael Van Valkenburgh Associates' site diagnosis revealed several helpful factors. For instance, the Brooklyn riverfront site had varying degrees of weight-bearing capacity that required different levels of investment to carry additional weight. This helped direct uses away from the most costly areas. In addition, the designers analyzed how views of Manhattan from the Brooklyn Heights Promenade could be protected and where the highest levels of noise were on the site.

Summary

Urban design involves pulling together considerable information about a place, as discussed in Chapter 3 (Knowledge). SWOT analyses, opportunities and constraints maps, transects, exploded axonometric drawings, and suitability analyses are five tools that can aid in the synthesis of such information. Design requires an awareness of space, which involves an understanding of scale. Physical models and GIS technology help the designer synthesize complex information about a site. In this way, urban design is similar to ecology: both connect information to understand and to explain relationships. The analyses, models, and GIS maps enable the designer to make a diagnosis of the site. The purpose of this diagnosis is to understand a place in order to transform it for the benefit of people, other species, and the environment.

In addition to learning from the site, urban designers use case studies to learn from precedents. The more we know what has worked and what has not in similar projects, the more we can build on past experience. After information has been synthesized about the study area, the urban designer is ready to enter into dialogues about the future.

5. Options

At this point in the process, the urban designer can define the project goals and strategies with considerably more precision and thus can arrive at the preliminary draft plan for the study area. Such a concept plan may be viewed as a sketch of possible futures. The designer works with the client to select an option from these possibilities or to create a new option. The designer, in this phase, must characterize preferences and priorities. The outcomes of the environmental context analyses, as well as the assumptions and results from the synthesis, have to be considered. The options the designer develops should be based on clear reasons that can be communicated to the client so that the options can easily be amended, enhanced, or rejected.

The goals identified by the designer consider the client's requirements, the prerequisites, and the environmental characteristics. For a better understanding, we can draw a parallel to a generic architectural design process. In a hypothetical, but common, situation, the client formulates some requirements about a house to be designed:

- its specific use (e.g., vacation home)
- its inner characterization (how distinct spaces will be used by each family member)
- any particular requirements (e.g., a large kitchen, a library, or a swimming pool)

Prerequisites depend on the following:

- the natural conditions of the site (e.g., geological features of the subsoil, water flows, native plants, indigenous wildlife, physiography)
- the history of the place
- comparisons with surrounding buildings, urban context, and landscape
- the capacity to adapt to change with future transformations of the current uses

Design constraints derive from existing rules, such as building codes, an official plan, or a zoning ordinance that defines cover ratio, maximum height, or distance from other buildings. With client requirements, prerequisites, and constraints in mind, the designer establishes *goals*, suggests strategies to reach them, and selects preferred options in cooperation with the design team and/or the client. Starting with these options, the designer should be able to establish how to orient the requested building, giving preference to solar exposure, to geographic position, or to views on the landscape. The designer will determine if it is advantageous to approach the maximums permitted by local ordinances for height and surface cover. The designer will select specific technologies to reduce energy consumption, even if this means reducing the extent of glass surface. The designer will also provide ideas regarding energy production, such as the use of wind or solar power to produce energy or to heat water, taking advantage of the temperature difference between underground water and the air by selecting a geothermal heating pump, or considering a green roof to provide insulation and absorb rainwater. The designer will integrate the selected system (photovoltaic modules, solar thermal collectors, heating pump) into the design and will offer interior layout proposals. The designer, therefore, will establish the design conditions that respond to the prerequisites.

In much the same way, the urban designer will gather requests and demands for a site, combined with the acquired knowledge and summarized to produce a preliminary sketch for an urban design.

Tools for Making Choices

To clearly present the options, designers come up with a combination of oral representations, written and graphic images, and design outlines, which are sometimes described with the terms *meta-project* or *preliminary design*. The meta-project, a composed term that means "project of a project," describes the content, objectives, and strategy to be adopted in order to fulfill a certain combination of design goals. In other words, the preliminary design is like the plot of a movie or of a novel: it describes a rough pattern of events and the links between them that will be used to write the entire work.

Preliminary design is a term that might be efficient in some circumstances, but it does not adequately convey the sketchy nature of the options at this stage. The word *concept* better communicates this cursory stage. A concept suggests an opinion or an idea. A concept plan anticipates the final plan and includes draft contents. It helps to define the basis for creating and evaluating potential options. A good description for a concept is provided by Bernard Leupen and colleagues (1997, 13, 16):

> Designers [on the basis of their considerations, conclusions, and viewpoints] must interpret the task and adjust the relative importance of the various requirements and expectations. This act of *interpreting* is a preliminary step when embarking on a design. Next the designer's view of the task leads to a *concept*. A concept need say nothing about the form the design is to adopt.
>
> Above all, it expresses the idea underlying a design and gives direction to design decisions, organizing them and excluding variants. . . . Thus, developing a concept is the first step towards making a design.

There are various forms a concept can take. Rough goals and visions help define a concept plan.

Lists of General Goals

To draw a concept plan, the designer needs to define a goal or, better, a list of goals. "A goal is a statement that describes, usually in general terms, a desired future condition" (Anderson, Klein, and Meck 2007, in Steiner and Butler 2007, 4). Goals are usually defined in objectives (measurable results), policies (ways to achieve the goals), and programs or actions (the system of projects or intervention to achieve design goals, objectives, and policies) (see Box 5.1).

Objectives follow from goals and take the form of measurable outcomes. Apart from specific project goals, it might be useful to consider some more general and common lists of goals and performance dimensions taken from the urban design literature to help the designer address the project.

A Project for Public Spaces (PPS) handbook on the management of downtown public spaces (1984) offers four categories to consider, which can be extended to

Box 5.1 An Excerpt of Objectives and Policies about Campus Design Element's Goals in the University of South Florida Polytechnic Master Plan by Santiago Calatrava

Goal: The USF Polytechnic Campus Master Plan Update will establish an integrated and coherent order of campus open spaces defined by a unified architectural framework.

Objective 3.1: Locate the building program identified on USF Polytechnic's Ten Year Capital Improvements Plan, as well as other near term projects identified by USF Polytechnic, in order to define: (i) the campus core; (ii) the iconic symbol of the university; (iii) the campus entries and system of peripheral vehicular circulation and parking; (iv) a network of pedestrian circulation; and (v) a hierarchy of open space culminating with a consistent campus edge.

Policy 3.1.1: *USF Polytechnic* shall give priority to siting the buildings identified on the Ten Year Capital Improvements Plan and other near term projects identified by *USF Polytechnic* in positions indicated herein. These locations will provide the spatial definition of the central lake, pedestrian walkways and paths, and wooded lawns and parks within the campus.

Policy 3.1.2: Construct campus academic buildings consistent with the criteria defined in the 15.0 Architectural Design Guidelines Element in order to provide definition of open spaces and preserve land resources.

Policy 3.1.3: *USF Polytechnic* shall initiate land use and design review processes established for the purpose of reviewing and ensuring compliance with master plan goals, objectives, and policies in accordance with the 15.0 Architectural Design Guidelines Element.

Policy 3.1.4: *USF Polytechnic* will identify where implementation of City of Lakeland and/or Williams SPI Overlay District design standards are appropriate related to the campus design character of *USF Polytechnic*/host community context area described in 12.0 Intergovernmental Coordination Element.

Policy 3.1.5: The timing and phasing requirements and priorities for the development of buildings, facilities, and open spaces shall be consistent with the principles established are listed in the 14.0 Capital Improvements Element.

Policy 3.1.6: In all building designs, *USF Polytechnic* shall seek to control the massing and height of buildings, within the context of the campus design and architectural guidelines, in order to maintain the character and expression of the existing landscape and secure the future development potential of the existing campus lands.

Policy 3.1.7: *USF Polytechnic* shall use the USF System Campus Development Committee (CDC) established for the purpose of reviewing and ensuring land use compliance with goals, objectives, and policies in accordance with the *USF Polytechnic* Campus Master Plan. Design review shall continue to be performed by the President, appropriate Vice President, and Executive Vice President.

Objective 3.2: Establish a hierarchy of campus open spaces including the central lake, pedestrian walkways and paths, open lawns and parks, and natural wooded areas.

Policy 3.2.1: *USF Polytechnic* shall position future buildings as shown on the 10-year plan

continued

continued

so that their *massing* contributes to the definition of public space. Facades and entries shall facilitate public use. Mechanical or service areas shall be separated from the public entries and placed away from the public spaces.

Policy 3.2.2: *USF Polytechnic* shall utilize future buildings and additions as described on pages herein in Objective 3.2 and in the 4.0 Future Land Use Element to shape a coherent set of public open spaces.

Policy 3.2.3: *USF Polytechnic* shall establish a hierarchy of campus open spaces accentuating the preservation and enhancement of the existing landscape. The establishment of a clear circulation system, including implementation of new pedestrian walkways and paths as described herein in Objective 3.2, shall articulate a variety of scale and detail.

Policy 3.2.4: Buildings shall be set back from the adjacent roadway center line as indicated in the 15.0 Architectural Design Guidelines Element.

Policy 3.2.5: Future buildings shall be carefully sited to minimize impacts to existing trees. At the time of construction, trees shall be protected from damage through the use of perimeter barricades placed at the tree drip lines or critical root zones (whichever is greater), both during and after construction.

Policy 3.2.6: *USF Polytechnic* shall explore procedures for funding campus landscape improvements independent of individual building construction projects. Site design that is funded through new building project budgets shall be monitored for consistency with the overall campus landscape design intent. Funds should be distributed in a targeted manner, prioritized for funding development deemed to have the greatest potential for impact on and improvement of the campus. The intent shall be to implement a campus landscape framework that is visibly composed as a whole rather than a collection of individual, unrelated small landscape pieces. *USF Polytechnic* recognizes the value of landscape development as infrastructure of the built environment that is integral to the process of campus development for the use of students, faculty, staff and visitors.

Objective 3.5: Enhance functional linkages between campus facilities.

Policy 3.5.1: *USF Polytechnic* shall establish functional linkages between campus facilities by initiating systematic implementation of pedestrian circulation and wayfinding demarcation. *USF Polytechnic* shall encourage tree planting, appropriately scaled pedestrian lighting, signage and installation of amenities such as benches and bike racks; and by systematic phasing of new building projects provide programmatic activity linkages and reinforcement of pedestrian movement patterns.

Objective 3.6: Decrease energy consumption on campus as measured per capita and per building.

Policy 3.6.1: *USF Polytechnic* shall encourage compactness in the development of the campus in order to increase efficiency of utility line services, to encourage pedestrian movement over vehicular movement on campus, and to preserve land resources.

Policy 3.6.2: *USF Polytechnic* shall require new building design to respond to the particular

continued

continued

climatic conditions of Central Florida and shall require issues of energy conservation including building orientation and siting, massing, shading and shape to be addressed during the design. *USF Polytechnic* shall encourage climatic responses such as; walkways, breezeways, shaded courts, solar screens and operable windows.

Policy 3.6.3: *USF Polytechnic* will endeavor to support the use of the United States Green Building Council's Leadership in Energy and Environmental Design (LEED) Green Building Rating System principles in the design and construction of facilities in the interest of sustainability.

An excerpt of objectives and policies about Campus Design Elements Goal in the University of South Florida Polytechnic Master Plan by Santiago Calatrava.

Source: Calatrava 2009, 3-1, 3-3.

urban design projects more generally and broadened to include other aspects. The categories suggested from PPS are comfort, accessibility, vitality, and image.

- *Comfort* is obtained through amenities, such as places to sit, protection from the sun, and pleasant places to wait for the bus.
- *Accessibility* is created by making spaces easy to use for pedestrians as well as vehicles.
- *Vitality* is enhanced through the design by making a space more active with cafés, vendors, and other street-oriented activities.
- *Image* is the quality of a place resulting from a changed appearance that can attract people.

Apart from the above list, we suggest to consider more categories to complete the set of general goals. These categories include the followings:

- *Security.* People need to feel comfortable to walk, spend their spare time, shop, and work, both day and night.
- *Maintenance.* A well-designed space with little maintenance can deteriorate very quickly.
- *Sense of place.* Specificity of a place (introduced in Chapter 3 as the *genius loci*), including its climate, should be considered (Spirn 1984; Givoni 1998).

- *Sustainability.* A design should consider and conserve the natural amenities of the site (see, for instance, http://www.sustainablesites.org).
- *Implementation.* "The process should begin with implementation in mind. Develop a plan that is tied to the realities of receiving funding, obtaining approval and getting the project built" (Carter 2007, in Steiner and Butler 2007, 11).

Jan Gehl (2010, 232) has suggested five planning principles to assemble people and events in new urban areas that can be considered as general goals in urban design projects:

- Carefully locate the city's functions to ensure shorter distances between them and a critical mass of people and events.
- Integrate various functions in cities to ensure versatility, wealth of experience, social sustainability, and a feeling of security in individual city districts.
- Design city space so it is inviting and safe for pedestrian and bicycling traffic.
- Open up the edges between the city and buildings so that life inside buildings and outside in city spaces can work together.
- Work to strengthen the invitation to invite longer stays in city spaces.

Matthew Carmona and his colleagues (2002, 66), discussing the economic, social, and environmental values of good urban design, propose seven goals to be supported in generic site projects:

1. *Character*—to promote character in townscape and landscape by responding to and reinforcing locally distinctive patterns of development and culture
2. *Continuity and enclosure*—to promote the continuity of street frontages and the enclosure of space by development, which clearly defines private and public areas
3. *Quality of the public realm*—to promote public spaces and routes that are attractive, safe, and uncluttered and that work effectively for all in society, including disabled and elderly people
4. *Ease of movement*—to promote accessibility and local permeability by making places that connect with one another and are easy to move through, putting people before traffic and integrating land uses and transport
5. *Legibility*—to promote legibility through development that provides recognizable routes, intersections, and landmarks to help people find their way around
6. *Adaptability*—to promote adaptability through development that can respond to changing social, technological, and economic conditions

7. *Diversity*—to promote variety and choice through a mix of compatible developments and uses that work together to create viable places that respond to local needs

Toward an Urban Renaissance, the final report of the Urban Task Force (1999), chaired by Lord Richard Rogers, defined a framework of key principles of urban design, which can also be considered as general project goals. This framework was designed to "guarantee successful places," but as the same authors observe, "they cannot even ensure good design, but they can provide a set of ground rules for starting to think about a site or area—whether an empty brownfield or greenfield site, or the refurbishment of an existing housing estate or urban area. As such, they can provide the basis for criteria for assessing plans and proposals" (70–71). Some of these framework criteria also could be goals for urban design projects:

- *Public realm.* Priority should be given to the design of the public realm. Public spaces should elicit a sense of safety and community.
- *Access and permeability.* A user-friendly public realm should make walking and cycling easy. Car dependency should be minimized and public transportation maximized.
- *Mixed activities.* Diversity of activities and uses should be encouraged—within buildings, streets, urban blocks, and neighborhoods.
- *Sustainable buildings.* Buildings, landscapes, and public spaces should be designed and built with a high aesthetic and structural standard.
- *Environmental responsibility.* Land should be regarded as a scarce and finite resource. Development should enhance the environment, not just limit the damage to it, by respecting biodiversity, harnessing natural resources, and reducing use of nonrenewable resources.

The five *basic* "performance dimensions" of urban design identified by Kevin Lynch in *Good City Form* (1984, 118) provide another list of possible general objectives. These performance dimensions can be considered in the general design phase:

1. *Vitality*—the degree to which the form of settlement supports the vital functions, the biological requirements and capabilities of human beings—above all, how it protects the survival of the species.

2. *Sense*—the degree to which the settlement can be clearly perceived and mentally differentiated and structured in time and space by its residents and the degree to which that mental structure connects with their values and concepts; the match between environments, our sensory and mental capabilities, and our cultural constructs
3. *Fit*—the degree to which the form and capacity of spaces, channels, and equipment in a settlement match the pattern and quantity of actions that people customarily engage in, or want to engage in—that is the adequacy of the behavior settings, including their adaptability to future action
4. *Access*—the ability to reach other persons, activities, resources, services, information, or places, including the quantity and diversity of elements that can be reached.
5. *Control*—the degree to which the use and access to spaces and activities and their creation, repair, modification, and management are controlled by those who use, work, or reside in them

Some leading New Urbanists compiled a list of community and regional planning principles that can help inform goal setting (Box 5.2). Their list of Ahwahnee Principles is especially helpful because it includes implementation strategies.

Ideally, one of the project goals will be to create a more sustainable space or community. Table 5.1 was developed for the U.S. Environmental Protection Agency Sustainable Development Demonstration Project. Subsequently, it was used in Enric Miralles/Benedetta Tagliabue and EDAW's design of Parc de Diagonal Mar in Barcelona (see Figure 5.1/Plate #18). Tim Beatley (2011) has carried this concept even further in his ideas for biophilic urban design. He builds on Janine Benyus's (2002) urban biomimicry strategies (see Box 5.3). Beatley goes on, using a base provided by Cynthia Girling and Ronald Kellett (2005), to list biophilic urban design elements at various scales (see Box 5.4).

In some circumstances, goals benefit from opportunities that are developed during the design process but outside the control of the urban design project. A new public transportation line or civic center close to the project area, envisaged by an administrative body, can support the plan. This way of thinking can be intro duced into the process using "if . . . then logic" and puts the potential for changing conditions, given and controlled by design, in perspective.

Our suggested goals are general and might inspire the urban designer, but they cannot take the place of site- or project-specific goals. The general goals are, for

Box 5.2 The Ahwahnee Principles

Preamble:

Existing patterns of urban and suburban development seriously impair our quality of life. The symptoms are: more congestion and air pollution resulting from our increased dependence on automobiles, the loss of precious open space, the need for costly improvements to roads and public services, the inequitable distribution of economic resources, and the loss of a sense of community. By drawing upon the best from the past and the present, we can plan communities that will more successfully serve the needs of those who live and work within them. Such planning should adhere to certain fundamental principles.

Community Principles:

1. All planning should be in the form of complete and integrated communities containing housing, shops, work places, schools, parks, and civic facilities essential to the daily life of the residents.
2. Community size should be designed so that housing, jobs, daily needs, and other activities are within easy walking distance of each other.
3. As many activities as possible should be located within easy walking distance of transit stops.
4. A community should contain a diversity of housing types to enable citizens from a wide range of economic levels and age groups to live within its boundaries.
5. Businesses within the community should provide a range of job types for the community's residents.
6. The location and character of the community should be consistent with a larger transit network.
7. The community should have a center focus that combines commercial, civic, cultural, and recreational uses.
8. The community should contain an ample supply of specialized open space in the form of squares, greens, and parks whose frequent use is encouraged through placement and design.
9. Public spaces should be designed to encourage the attention and presence of people at all hours of the day and night.
10. Each community or cluster of communities should have a well-defined edge, such as agricultural greenbelts or wildlife corridors, permanently protected from development.
11. Streets, pedestrian paths, and bike paths should contribute to a system of fully connected and interesting routes to all destinations. Their design should encourage pedestrian and bicycle use by being small and spatially defined by buildings, trees and lighting; and by discouraging high-speed traffic.

Regional Principles:

1. The regional structure should be integrated within a larger transportation network built around transit rather than freeways.

continued

continued

2. Regions should be bounded by and provide a continuous system of greenbelt/wildlife corridors to be determined by natural conditions.
3. Regional institutions and services (government, stadiums, museums, etc.) should be located within the urban core.

Implementation Strategies:

1. The general plan should be updated to incorporate the above principles.
2. Rather than allowing for developer-initiated, piecemeal development, a local government should initiate the planning of new and changing communities within its jurisdiction through an open planning process.
3. Prior to any development, a specific plan should be used to define communities where new growth, infill or redevelopment would be allowed to occur. With the adoption of specific plans, complying projects can proceed with minimal delay.
4. Plans should be developed through an open process and in the process should be provided illustrated models of the proposed design.

Source: Local Government Commission 1991; Calthorpe et al. 1998.

Figure 5.1 (also Plate #18) Parc Diagonal Mar, Barcelona. Design by EMBT Architects and EDAW (now AECOM). (Photograph by Dixi Carrillo. Courtesy AECOM.)

Table 5.1 Sustainable Design Evaluation Checklist

SUSTAINABLE	Completely	Partly	Neither	Partly	Completely	NOT SUSTAINABLE
Creates new jobs						Reduces employment opportunities
Buildings and spaces are adaptable						Buildings and spaces are not adaptable
Provides educational opportunities						Reduces educational opportunities
Creates affordable human habitat						Destroys affordable human habitat
Reduces health risks						Increases health risks
Diminishes inequities						Increases inequities
Increases opportunities for social interaction						Reduces opportunities for social interaction
Enhances safety						Creates unsafe environments
Maximizes open space provision						Minimizes open space provision
Builds on local context						Disregards local context
Reduces stress (physical and psychological)						Increases stress
Beautiful						Destroys beauty
Diverse						Homogenous
Remediates natural landscape						Degrades natural landscape
Creates purer air						Destroys pure air
Creates purer water						Destroys pure water
Uses rainwater						Wastes rainwater
Replenishes groundwater						Depletes groundwater
Produces its own food						Produces no food
Creates richer soil						Destroys rich soil
Uses solar energy						Wastes solar energy
Stores solar energy						Consumes fossil fuels
Creates silence						Destroys silence
Consumes its own wastes						Dumps waste unused
Maintains itself						Needs repair/cleaning
Matches nature's pace						Disregards nature's pace
Provides wildlife habitat						Destroys wildlife habitat
Moderates climate and weather						Intensifies climate
Increases use of renewable resources						Increases use of nonrenewable resources
Uses local resources						Imports resources
Self-sufficient						Relies on imports
Encourages walking/biking						Encourages automobile use
Encourages transit use						Encourages private automobile use
Reduces length of daily automobile trips						Increases length of daily automobile trips

Sources: Steiner et al. 1998; Steiner 2008.

Box 5.3 Biomimicry Strategies for Cities

1. Use waste as a resource.
2. Diversify and cooperate to fully use the habitat.
3. Gather and use energy efficiently.
4. Optimize rather than maximize.
5. Use materials sparingly.
6. Don't foul their nests.
7. Don't draw down resources.
8. Remain in balance with the biosphere.
9. Run on information.
10. Shop locally.

Source: Benyus 2002; Beatley 2011.

Box 5.4 Biophilic Urban Design Elements across Scales

Scale	*Biophilic Design Elements*
Building	Green rooftops
	Sky gardens and green atria
	Rooftop garden
	Green walls
	Daylit interior spaces
Block	Green courtyards
	Clustered housing around green areas
	Native species yards and spaces
Street	Green streets
	Sidewalk gardens
	Urban trees
	Low-impact development
	Vegetated swales and skinny streets
	Edible landscaping
	High degree of permeability
Neighborhood	Stream daylighting, stream restoration
	Urban forests
	Ecology parks
	Community gardens
	Neighborhood parks and pocket parks
	Greening grayfields and brownfields
Community	Urban creeks and riparian areas
	Urban ecological networks
	Green schools
	City tree canopy
	Community forest and community orchards
	Greening utility corridors
Region	River systems and floodplains
	Riparian systems
	Regional greenspace systems
	Greening major transport corridors

Source: Modified from Girling and Kellett 2005, first appeared in Beatley and Newman 2008, and reused in Beatley 2011.

the most part, valid everywhere and in most circumstances. Who can deny the importance of accessibility, quality of the public realm, or diversity from our list? It is important that the urban designer, in cooperation with the client, defines a task-specific list of goals.

Visioning

An urban design project can provide communities with a vision to attract investment; to coordinate often discordant interests; to address critical environmental, cultural, and social issues; and if possible, to inspire future users, keeping in mind Daniel Burnham's well-known declaration: "Make no little plans: they have no magic to stir men's blood."

A vision adds inspiration to a project, which helps people understand what a place can become. Vision involves imagining what a city or a community could look like after years or decades in the future. *To imagine* derives from values expressed in social context that can be translated to a written or visual description of a viable situation starting from the recognized potentiality of the place. The imagined vision helps direct governments and other interested parties in such a way as to achieve the vision represented.

For example, Martin Luther King proclaimed a vision for the future of civil rights in his "I Have a Dream" speech. Similarly, President John F. Kennedy presented a vision in 1961: "We choose to go to the moon" by the end of the decade. As the declarations of King and Kennedy illustrate, visions need to be pursued. American planner John Fregonese notes: "Vision without action is hallucination."

At least two dimensions are implied in the creation of an image or images: a technical one and a social one. The technical dimension helps to recognize the potentialities and to orient the vision toward viable prospects. It defines limits and circumscribes conditions and ways through which images can come true. The social dimension occurs as different groups of people are engaged in formulating the vision. In democracies, visions for public spaces are impossible to construct without public participation.

A Visioning Process: Envision Central Texas

Envision Central Texas (ECT) is an example of a vision that started with a broad scope but then went into detail at the urban design scale (Steiner 2011). ECT developed cartographic documentation, with considerable detail, that exhibits a regional and urban vision. The ECT vision does not merely offer written descriptions of possible futures but also proposes the tools, resources, and projects in critical issue areas, such as transportation, land use, and the environment, to address the significant growth pressures experienced by the metropolitan region. ECT's aim is to create a common vision to help guide actions and innovative steps to manage growth in a positive way. "A Vision for Central Texas" was designed to become and to reinforce the identity of "a vibrant, economically powerful, globally connected, locally led community that absorbs and tames its growth by becoming taller and denser in places, greener throughout, more connected—while keeping its unique sense of place and soul" (ECT 2004, 5).

ECT began in 2001 when business, civic, and government leaders from five counties in metropolitan Austin (Bastrop, Caldwell, Hays, Travis, and Williamson) organized meetings to propose the initiative. An eight-person committee established a nonprofit organization with a governing board of directors and an executive committee. This committee sought to include representatives from every county, constituency, and vested interest group in the region. ECT is a private, nonprofit organization that receives funding from several local governments and businesses. Apart from the central city (which is also home to the University of Texas and the state capital), the metropolitan Austin area incorporates five surrounding counties. The total population of the metropolitan region was approximately 1.25 million inhabitants when the visioning process began in 2002. The region's population had grown by 47 percent in the 1990s and is expected to double in the next twenty to thirty years. The region covers 3,980 square miles (10,308 square kilometers), of which approximately 1,157 square miles (2,997 square kilometers) were developed in 2000.

Regionally, the population density is very low, only 318 people per square mile (113 persons/square kilometer), but it is expected to increase during the next twenty to thirty years. In the urbanized areas, the density in 2000 was 1,080 people per square mile (417 persons/square kilometer) (Steiner 2011).

To manage the visioning process, the board of directors selected Fregonese Calthorpe Associates, a regional planning consulting firm based in Oregon and California. John Fregonese was previously the planning manager of Metro, the Portland, Oregon, metropolitan area's regional government. Peter Calthorpe is one of the most significant architects of the New Urbanism movement (Calthorpe 1993; Calthorpe and Fulton 2001). The University of Texas at Austin acted as an *honest broker* of information that helped inform and guide the process.

ECT is a growth management program for the Austin metropolitan area that demonstrates how a regional approach to sustainable planning can accommodate a doubling of population while protecting environment and quality of life. ECT engaged extensive public participation to produce four scenarios, which led to a preferred scenario for future growth. The initiative has also featured spatial design concepts and the application of sustainability indicators (Steiner 2011; http://www.envisioncentraltexas.org).

To create a shared vision that joins the whole metropolitan area around common strategies to resolve disputes and to address the resolution of critical issues, a public process of participation was organized, which included workshops involving hundreds of people. The workshops helped generate four growth scenarios, which considered the available land to direct future growth and the integration of transportation and land use. Scenarios may be viewed as stories, or histories, of the future. To elaborate trends and projections to address the realization of the scenarios, economic models of land uses and transportation were employed while considering environmental concerns, such as the protection of aquifers and prime agricultural lands.

The scenarios highlighted the differences between various growth policies and subsequent development patterns:

- *Scenario A* supplies the "business-as-usual" projection. This scheme spreads another 1.25 million people across the landscape in patterns similar to recent low-density developments, using transportation systems already in place or approved. The scenario results in an increment of density (1,323 people per square mile, or 511 persons/square kilometer) in urbanized areas. People would continue to commute long distances to work by car because of the concentration of jobs in the urban core (see Figure 5.2).
- *Scenario B* foresees that most of the new growth would surround major roadways, both new and existing. Housing and job growth would occur throughout the five counties. Some redevelopment would occur in existing neighborhoods. Overall, most residents would still live in single-family houses. Regional transportation options would include toll roads, new express bus routes, a commuter-rail system and a central light-rail system. Density in urbanized areas would reach 1,714 people per square mile (662 persons/square kilometer) (see Figure 5.3).
- With *Scenario C*, growth would occur in both existing communities and emerging new towns. Current towns and cities would gain jobs and residents, but even more mixed-use development would result in fewer residents in single-family houses. New towns would be built along major roads and railways, preserving open space and undeveloped land between communities. Regional

transportation options would be similar to those of Scenario B. Density would be around 1,756 people per square mile (678 persons/square kilometer) (see Figure 5.4).

- In *Scenario D,* most growth would occur in existing towns and communities. More land would remain undeveloped than in the other scenarios. Regional transportation options would be similar to those of Scenario B. Density would reach 1,939 people per square mile (749 persons/square kilometer) (see Figure 5.5) (Steiner 2011; ECT 2003a, 2003b, 2003m).

Figure 5.2 Envision Central Texas, Scenario A. (Courtesy Envision Central Texas.)

Figure 5.3 Envision Central Texas, Scenario B. (Courtesy Envision Central Texas.)

The four scenarios were presented to the public, and a questionnaire was distributed to Central Texas residents in the fall of 2003. Over twelve thousand questionnaires were returned—half through the Internet and half by mail. Residents of all five counties responded to the survey in proportion to the actual population distribution in the region. This survey, according to Fregonese Calthorpe Associates (2003), represented a significant portion of the population—about one in one

Figure 5.4 Envision Central Texas, Scenario C. (Courtesy Envision Central Texas.)

hundred residents. More than 50 percent of the respondents preferred Scenario D, which received a large positive vote across the region. Using knowledge gained from the initial public workshops, ECT, together with Fregonese Calthorpe Associates, developed a preferred scenario and also conducted a series of community test-site planning workshops throughout the five counties. Peter Calthorpe's architecture firm, Calthorpe Associates, led the test-site workshop, which served

Figure 5.5 Envision Central Texas, Scenario D. (Courtesy Envision Central Texas.)

as a pilot project to examine different planning tools for addressing typical issues within the Central Texas region and to provide opportunities to explore solutions at the local level (see Chapter 9, Details). The vision proposed development patterns that emphasized new forms of local urban design with marked differences from the past.

The concept plans provided design visions for the evolution of the different sites into mixed-use, walkable districts by creating a mixture of housing options, retail and office uses, civic functions, recreational areas, and community gathering places with greater density than in existing neighborhoods. Several design visions, with different mixtures and functions were provided for the test sites (ECT 2003b, 2003d, 2003f, 2003h, 2003l) (see Figures 5.6 and 5.7).

The concept plans involved design guidelines that specify placement, orientation, and massing of new buildings (see Chapter 10, Implementation). The guidelines also contain proposals on permitted uses, building design (street orientation, transparency, materials, and climate-oriented design), examples for different building types and functions, parking requirements and street sections (ECT 2003a, 2003c, 2003e, 2003g, 2003k).

Concept Plan

A concept plan is an instrument that graphically transforms the ideas and goals that the designer and the client want to pursue. The plan identifies nonnegotiable factors that bind the plan and that must be considered. A SWOT analysis, an opportunities and constraints map, a transect, an exploded axonometric drawing, or a suitability analysis (see Chapter 4, Synthesis) can become the departure point of the concept plan. The concept plan should contain a graphic description of the "strong idea" (or ideas) the designers advocate to pursue. The design takes its definitive shape and direction around a strong idea, which can be an orientation that prevails over the entire spatial order, such as the concentration of green and open spaces instead of their diffusion. The concept plan is not the design; it would not have to contain the final shapes of buildings but just the building footprints. The concept plan may be viewed as a sketch rather than a final drawing and will show, through universal and easily comprehensible symbols, the preliminary relationship of spaces and uses.

Graphic design software can be used to illustrate ideas and concepts. In addition to showing how concepts relate to natural factors, such as underlying bedrock, the urban designer can map existing and proposed buildings. Such maps can display possible uses within buildings, how inside spaces are related to the outdoors, emergency exit routes, the proximity of transit routes, and the location of infrastructure.

A Proposal for the Recovery of the Gonzaga Axis in Mantua

Mantua (Mantova) is a northern Italian city of great artistic and architectural interest. Its historical center was built over several periods. Between the eleventh and the twelfth century AD, the *civitas vetus* (the old town) was developed in the

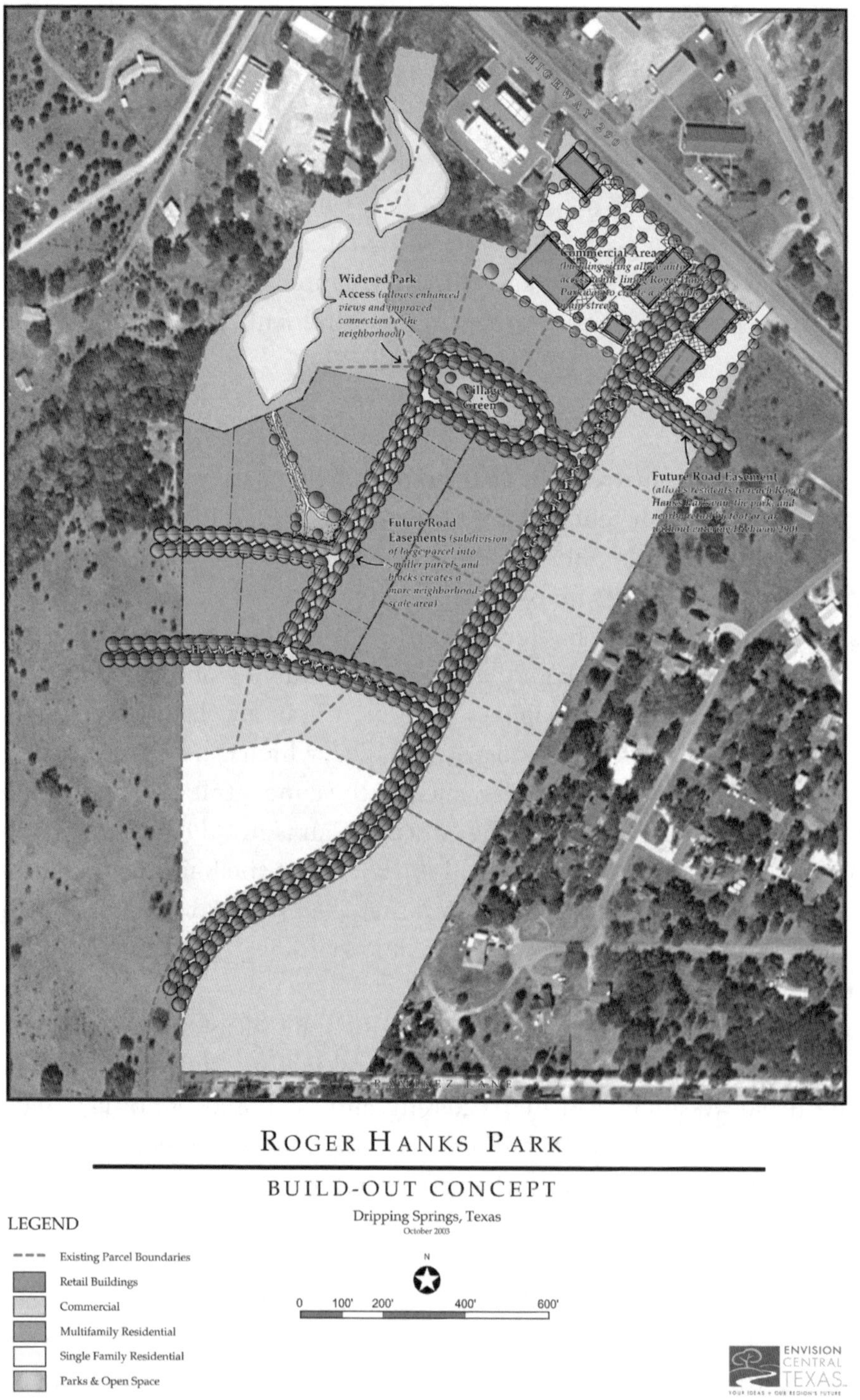

Figure 5.6 Roger Hanks Park, Build-Out Concept. (Courtesy Envision Central Texas.)

Figure 5.7 Roger Hanks Park, Urban Design Framework Map. (Courtesy Envision Central Texas.)

northern part of the city (see Figure 5.8/Plate #19). The most recent urban expansion, with railroad and automobile development, took place throughout the twentieth century. During the preparation of a strategic document (Treu 2001) for the whole city, the municipality suggested the improvement of legibility and pedestrian accessibility starting from a historical pathway, the Gonzaga Axis (named after the Gonzaga family who reigned there from the mid-fourteenth to the early eighteenth century). The axis connects the two main tourist attractions of Mantua's historical center, Palazzo Ducale and Palazzo Te. Along its route of approximately 5,600 feet (1,700 meters), some of the most important architectural monuments of the city can be found.

The Gonzaga Axis is walked daily by thousands of Italian and foreign visitors to Mantua. The site analysis showed some weaknesses concerning seating, sign posting, maintenance of some existing spaces, paving, and legibility for inhabitants and tourists.

The Gonzaga Axis, however, offers many opportunities to develop and improve tourism and the overall historical center as well as to enhance local business opportunities. The axis has become the most important commercial strip of the entire city. After a preliminary survey of the route, a list of goals was developed in accordance with the city government. The main goals were as follows:

- To facilitate the orientation legibility from one end of the route to the other
- To use graphic images rather than multilingual signs to guarantee legibility for tourists coming from other nations
- To make the route suitable for citizens of all ages and abilities
- To define options from the main route where there are accessibility problems caused by private cars
- To improve urban conditions along the axis
- To supply guidelines for the next steps

The design began by identifying those places that could be included in the restoration of the axis. Specific concept plans were developed for each such place. The designers studied five specific places: the Palazzo Te Park, the Piazza Porta Cerese, the Via Nazario Sauro, the Via Torquato Tasso, and the Piazza Martiri di Belfiore. The concept plans were preliminary proposals to suggest strong ideas for a more detailed project in the future (see Figure 5.9/Plate #20).

Legibility and pedestrian accessibility improvements were achieved with new paving that improved, while still respecting, the historical character of the city's

Figure 5.8 (also Plate #19) Historical map of Mantua, Italy. (From Treu 2001.)

original paving (see Chapter 9, Details). A colored and easily recognizable line (based on the model of Boston's Freedom Trail) was proposed. Any pedestrian, by following the line, could find the way to the other end of the axis. To obtain this solution, possibilities were studied in collaboration with pedestrian-use experts, who gave advice on the preference between different options. The several options considered were reduced to two. The pedestrian-use experts helped focus the implicit and explicit needs of any and all potential users of all ages, abilities, and sexes.

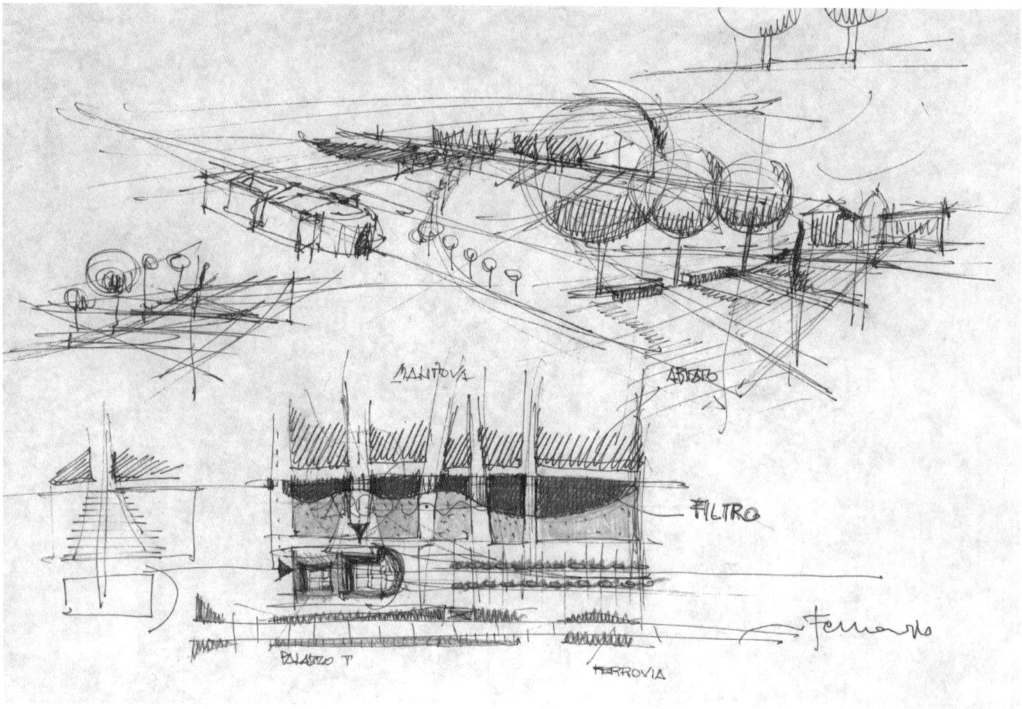

Figure 5.9 (also Plate #20) The concept plan for Palazzo Te, Mantua, Italy. (Drawing by Elena Stevanato.)

Choices

The identification of goals, the definition of a vision, and the production of a concept plan can stimulate the designer to assess how different options might affect the final configuration of the master plan. Producing and considering options and weighing their advantages and disadvantages is a useful exercise toward reaching a final proposal. The evaluation of various options should be part of the dialogue. This stage, more than any other, demonstrates that there is not only one solution to a design problem.

Civic Alliance and New York New Visions: A Vision and Three Scenarios for Lower Manhattan and Five Strategies for Ground Zero

On October 1, 2001, seventy-five civic leaders began a process that led to the founding of the Civic Alliance to Rebuild Downtown New York. These leaders had many different ideas on how to rebuild "but were united behind one goal: to transcend business-as-usual in support of an open, inclusive rebuilding process that would stand as a monument to democracy" (Civic Alliance and Regional Plan Association 2002, 1). The Civic Alliance formed working groups in eight subject areas: economic development; transportation and mobility; social, economic, and environmental justice; the memorial process; green buildings and sustainable systems; civic amenities; urban design; and the regulatory framework. For the next ten months, Civic Alliance general meetings focused on the work of each of these groups. In September 2002, the Civic Alliance published a report on the findings and recommendations on all eight subjects: *A Planning Framework to Rebuild Downtown New York* (Civic Alliance and Regional Plan Association 2002).

The report incorporated a vision for the whole Lower Manhattan area, not just the famous 16-acre (6.5-hectare) World Trade Center site:

> Lower Manhattan can become the world's first 21st century city, incorporating the best practices in urban design, green buildings and technology, transportation, and economic development. . . . We envision a new Downtown that is alive 24 hours a day . . . while simultaneously serving as a home to diverse and economically integrated residential communities, to shops and restaurants, schools, universities and to new industries. . . . This is a regional and global center of culture, and a place with a remarkable number of high quality public parks and spaces for both residents and visitors. It is a place that draws on the latest innovations in sustainable city design practices from all over the world to craft a beautiful and prosperous place to live and work. Above all, it is a place that honors those who died in a terrible act of war on Sept. 11, 2001. (Civic Alliance and Regional Plan Association 2002, 4).

The vision was based on six guiding principles:

- Focus public funds on infrastructure and civic amenities.
- Integrate the memorial design process with planning for Lower Manhattan and the World Trade Center site.
- Plan for all of Lower Manhattan, not just the World Trade Center site.
- Make it fair.
- Develop all plans in an open, inclusive process.
- Adopt "green" building and sustainable development principles.

The section of the document dedicated to urban design "emphasizes the importance of the public realm's services and buildings, the need to create a complete network of well-designed streets and linked open spaces, and continuous waterfront access opportunities" (Civic Alliance and Regional Plan Association 2002, 38). In December 2002, the Civic Alliance organized a planning and design workshop (Civic Alliance 2002a). As with the Envision Central Texas example, scenarios were used to develop visions for the future of Lower Manhattan. The workshop's mandate was to test implications for different planning priorities for Lower Manhattan. In particular, three scenarios were formulated:

- *Global Office*—emphasized a revitalized office economy
- *Residential Neighborhood*—emphasized a strong growth in residential population
- *Creative Hub*—emphasized the diversification of Lower Manhattan's economy

Three teams defined ideas, proposals, and recommendations for the three scenarios. Each scenario had a different set of investments and policies based on alternative visions, but all of the scenarios

- assumed mixed use for Lower Manhattan;
- were infrastructure and amenity driven; and
- considered three scales: the region, Lower Manhattan, and the World Trade Center site (Lane and Pirani 2003).

The three scenarios that emerged from the workshop recognized "shared vision of 'world trade' applying not just to goods and finance, but also to the new economy, education, language, sharing of ideas and a priority on world peace. At the World Trade Center site, 'sacred ground' was merged with 'meeting ground' to properly honor Ground Zero" (Civic Alliance and Regional Plan Association 2002, 3). Divergences were relatively few, since each scenario was based on the success of a mixed-use district.

New York New Visions (NYNV) is a pro bono coalition of architecture, landscape architecture, engineering, planning, and design organizations that came together immediately following the September 11 terrorist attacks on the World Trade Center. The coalition was engaged in Civic Alliance activities and included many groups, such as the American Institute of Architects, the American Planning Association, the American Society of Landscape Architects, the Regional Plan Association, and the Civic Alliance. In February 2002, NYNV prepared a document, *Principles for the Rebuilding of Lower Manhattan* (NYNV 2002b), which offers a series of principles and recommendations for the planning and rebuilding of Lower Manhattan.

In May 2002, NYNV presented the report *Possible Futures* (NYNV 2002a) to provide additional background for, and to discuss in more detail the implications of, planning guidelines presented in the earlier principles report. *Possible Futures* is urban design oriented. To better understand the future of the World Trade Center site, the "Growth Strategies Team," the report's collective author, produced a matrix of the relationship between a memorial and possible development for the site; "the matrix . . . organizes a variety of different site plans according to the approach each embodies toward the footprints of the World Trade Center towers" (NYNV 2002a, 6).

Five site strategies were considered (NYNV 2002a, 6):

1. The entire World Trade Center site remains open space.
2. New development is limited to areas mostly east of Greenwich Street and north of Fulton Street, leaving a large open space that includes the footprints of the towers.

3 and 4. The footprints of the towers are acknowledged, either as open spaces (Strategy 3) or as built memorial structures (Strategy 4), with the remainder of the site either fully developed or partially developed around contiguous open space.

5. The entire site is available for development on a new street and block system.

The five site strategies produced different variations (see Figure 5.10) that took many of the design opportunities for the site into consideration. The five strategies engaged, in different ways, the entire site and the twin towers' footprints: from a proposal that leaves the 16 acres (6.5 hectares) totally open and free of buildings, to new buildings on the towers' footprints. The matrix was a helpful tool to evaluate different design options. The combined activities of the Civic Alliance and NYNV represent an extraordinary example of creating choices for rebuilding an urban place after disaster.

Using Green Buildings, Neighborhood, and Site Rating Systems

The U.S. Green Building Council (USGBC) developed Leadership in Energy and Environmental Design (LEED) standards that can help urban designers to advance environmental concerns in individual buildings or at the community level (LEED ND) (http://www.usgbc.org). In addition, the Sustainable Sites Initiative (SITES)

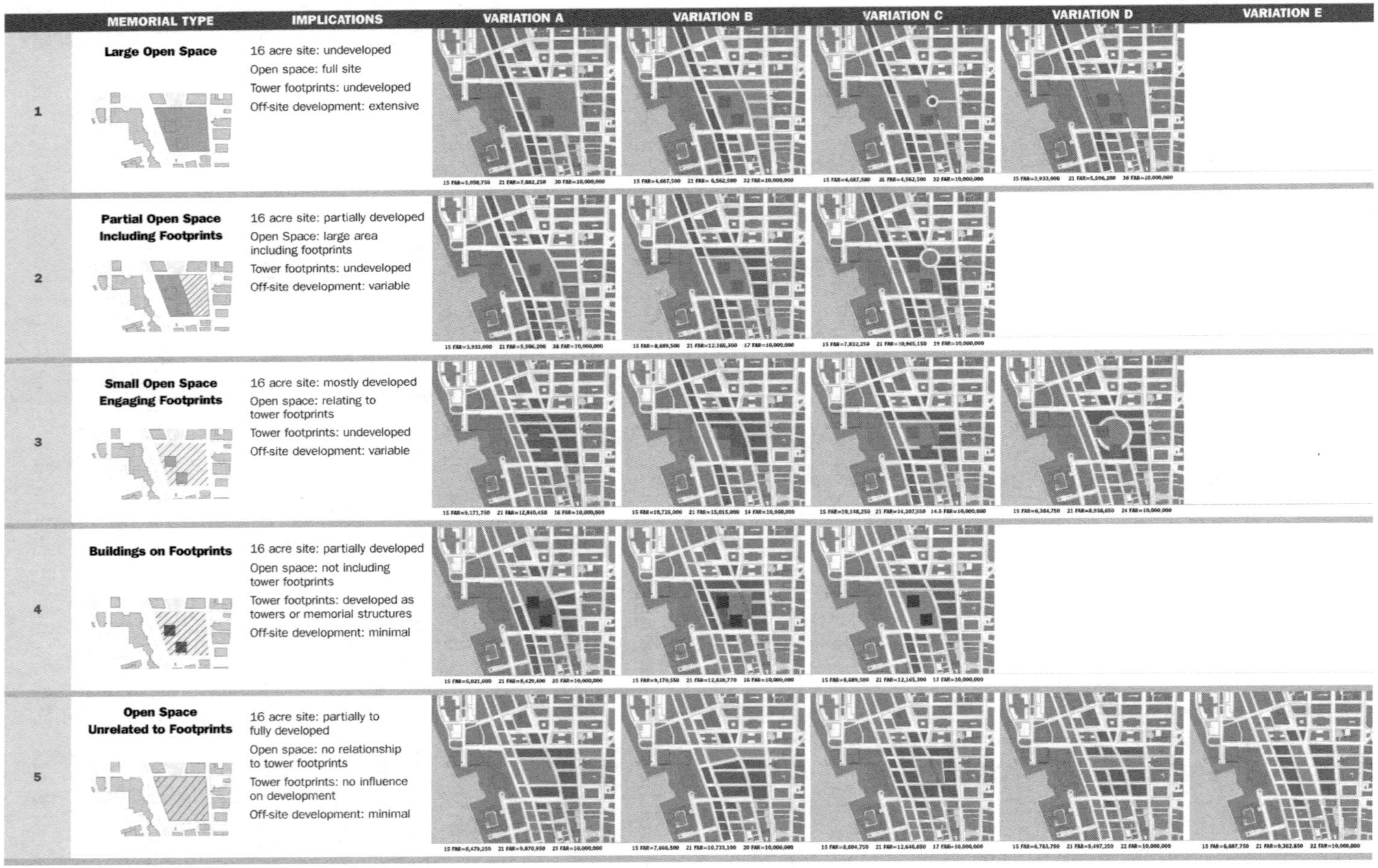

Figure 5.10 Matrix of diagrams of the World Trade Center memorial site, open space, circulation, and building site alternatives. (By New York New Visions. Courtesy Hutton Associates Inc.)

(2009, http://www.sustainablesites.org) developed guidelines for "sustainable land design, construction and maintenance practices." The SITES standards will be integrated into LEED and will be a stand-alone program. Already, SITES has been incorporated into New York City's High Performance Landscape Guidelines (Design Trust for Public Space and City of New York Parks & Recreation 2010). The LEED and SITES systems embody considerable knowledge about how buildings, communities, and landscapes may be constructed in a more environmentally responsible and energy-conserving manner. These systems can also be used through the design process in order to select how options differ in terms of LEED and SITES prerequisites and credits in order to assess choices considered.

Prerequisites are required for a project to be certified; credits provide bonus points. Box 5.5 provides examples for SITES credits relevant to urban design.

Many developers seek LEED and SITES certifications. As a result, urban designers need to incorporate prerequisites and credits into the process early. In addition, LEED and SITES can help designers develop wedge strategies to help their projects reduce greenhouse gas production and energy use. Developed through Princeton University's Carbon Mitigation Initiative, the wedges represent strategies to reduce global carbon dioxide emissions. The strategies focus on efficiency, decarbonization of power, decarbonization of fuel, and forest and agricultural soils. The first three areas can be addressed directly through urban design. If cities are made more livable, then suburban sprawl can be reduced, and then forest and agricultural areas can be protected and their soils used for carbon storage, the fourth strategic area identified through the Princeton initiative.

Another program is being led by the International Council for Local Environmental Initiatives—Local Governments for Sustainability (ICLEI), an international membership organization of local governments, including more than six hundred in the United States. ICLEI USA is working with the USGBC and the Center for American Progress on the development of the STAR Community Index. It seeks to become the definitive means by which local governments can measure and certify their sustainability (http://www.icleiusa.org/star).

High Point Case Study[1]

Environmental knowledge and rating systems can be used in design to produce more ecologically sensitive projects, as the High Point project by Mithūn helps to illustrate. Used as a precedent in the development of SITES, High Point is a

1 Adapted from Steiner et al. 2010. See also SITES 2009. Danielle Pieranunzi of the Lady Bird Johnson Wildflower Center was responsible for compiling this case study.

Box 5.5 Examples of SITES Credits

Select brownfields or grayfields for redevelopment.

Channel development to urban areas to reduce pressure on undeveloped land, reduce resource consumption, and restore ecosystem services to damaged sites.

Select sites within existing communities.

Encourage site development within existing communities to reduce pollution and development impacts, support the local economy, and improve human health.

Select sites that encourage nonmotorized transportation and use of public transit.

Encourage site development that is accessible by pedestrians and bicyclists and near public transit to reduce pollution and improve human health.

Reduce potable water use for landscape irrigation by 75 percent or more.

Limit or eliminate the use of potable water, natural surface water (such as lakes, rivers, and streams) and groundwater withdrawals for landscape irrigation. Encourage alternative irrigation methods and water conservation strategies.

Manage stormwater on-site.

Replicate the hydrologic condition (infiltration, runoff, and evapotranspiration) of the site based on historic, natural, and undeveloped ecosystems in the region.

Protect and enhance on-site water resources and receiving water quality.

Prevent or minimize generation, mobilization, and transport of common stormwater pollutants and watershed-specific pollutants of concern to receiving waters, including surface water and groundwater, and combined sewers or stormwater systems.

Design rainwater/stormwater features to provide a landscape amenity.

Integrate visually and physically accessible rainwater/stormwater features into the site in an aesthetically pleasing way.

Minimize soil disturbance in design and construction.

Limit disturbance of healthy soil to protect soil horizons and maintain soil structure, existing hydrology, organic matter, and nutrients stored in soil.

Identify and preserve all vegetation designated as special status by local, state, or federal entities.

Use native plants.

Plant appropriate vegetation that is native to the ecoregion of the site.

Use vegetation to minimize building heating requirements.

Place vegetation in strategic locations around buildings to reduce energy consumption and costs associated with indoor climate control for heating.

Use vegetation to minimize building cooling requirements.

Place vegetation and/or vegetated structures in strategic locations around buildings to reduce energy consumption and costs associated with indoor climate control.

Reduce urban heat island effects.

Use vegetation and reflective materials to reduce heat islands and minimize effects on microclimate and on human and wildlife habitat.

Use recycled content materials.

Use materials with recycled content to reduce the use of virgin materials and avoid sending useful materials to the landfill.

continued

continued

Use regional materials.

Reduce energy use for transportation; increase demand for materials, plants, and soils that are extracted, manufactured, or grown within the region to support the use of local resources; and promote a regional identity.

Protect and maintain unique cultural and historical places.

Protect and maintain cultural and historical location, attributes, and artifacts to enhance a site's sense of place and meaning.

Provide for optimum site accessibility, safety, and wayfinding.

Promote site use by increasing users' ability to understand and safely access outdoor spaces.

Provide opportunities for outdoor physical activity.

Provide on-site opportunities that encourage outdoor physical activity to improve human health.

Provide outdoor spaces for social interaction.

Provide outdoor gathering spaces of various sizes and orientations to accommodate groups, for the purpose of building community and improving social ties.

Reduce outdoor energy consumption for all landscape and exterior operations.

Select energy-efficient outdoor fixtures and equipment to reduce energy consumption and costs associated with site use and operations.

Use renewable sources for landscape electricity needs.

Use electricity from renewable sources to reduce the greenhouse gas emissions associated with site operations and to minimize air pollution, habitat destruction, and pollution from fossil fuel–based energy production.

Source: Adapted from http://www.sustainablesites.org.

34-block (120-acre, or 49-hectare) mixed-income, mixed-race residential neighborhood in Seattle, Washington. It is in the Central Puget Lowland (or Puget Trough) ecoregion, has a mild climate, and is classified as Marine West Coast with dry summers and cool, wet weather the rest of the year (http://www.seattlehousing.org/redevelopment/high-point/plan).

Responding to the community's request to reknit the neighborhood with the surrounding urban context, the Seattle Housing Authority started redevelopment activities, with the first phase completed in 2006 and the second in 2009. The project occupies roughly 8 percent of Seattle's Longfellow Creek watershed, an urban, salmon-bearing stream that is one of only four remaining in the city. Seattle Public Utilities realized that the redevelopment of the 1940s-era site mitigates a significant source of contaminated urban runoff. Creative, site-specific, low-impact development strategies were utilized for each urban block, and a natural drainage system was employed for the whole neighborhood.

Natural riparian corridors are an integral part of Seattle's drainage system, with more than 20 percent of the city's runoff flowing into local creeks. The project team focused on restoring and protecting the salmon habitat with systems to preserve and clean the watershed. Although the site is a grayfield developed in the 1940s, the design allows the site to process stormwater as effectively as the pastures presumed to have existed prior to the original development.

Roof runoff is directed to splash blocks that drain to furrows, dispersion trenches, raingardens, and pervious pavements. Stormwater that does not infiltrate on housing sites is directed to a 22,001-foot (6,706-meter) system, in which swales constructed with gravel and compost are graded with periodic berms to allow water to pond and filter into the soil (see Figure 5.11/Plate #21).

Figure 5.11 (also Plate #21) A vegetated median strip collects and absorbs rainwater from the street, keeping it out of city storm sewers in High Point, Seattle. Overall master planning, architecture, site design, and landscape architecture: Mithūn; civil engineers and right-of-way natural systems and landscape: SvR Design Company. (©Roger Williams. Courtesy Mithūn.)

Overflow from the system during extraordinary storm events is piped to a single stormwater pond for detention (see Figure 5.12/Plate #22), which is in contrast to a typical development in the Pacific Northwest, which requires up to 20 acres (8 hectares) to meet flow control for twenty-five- and one-hundred-year storm events. The result for High Point was a net gain in the project's development potential.

Native and adapted plants were used to reflect the local ecosystem and to minimize maintenance needs. More than eighty thousand ground covers were placed in the streetscape, and the addition of more than three thousand trees effectively tripled the number of trees on the site. Swale plantings vary to create an interesting year-round experience for residents.

Figure 5.12 (also Plate #22) High Point's natural drainage system provides clean water for 8 percent of the salmon-bearing Longfellow Creek watershed, a 1-mile-long (0.62-kilometer-long) urban creek system running through the heart of West Seattle. Overflow during extraordinary storm events is piped to an attractive detention pond. Overall master planning, architecture, site design, and landscape architecture: Mithūn; civil engineers and right-of-way natural systems and landscape: SvR Design Company. (©Roger Williams. Courtesy Mithūn.)

Native, drought-tolerant, and site-suitable plants were used to minimize the need for irrigation and pesticides. Amended soils improve water retention, while a computerized irrigation management system adjusts water supply based on plant need, solar orientation, and local weather information.

More than a thousand existing trees were evaluated and rated by an arborist with the design team; the team then optimized street and block layout to retain trees across the site. The arborist estimated each tree's financial value and posted the estimate near the tree so that construction crews would know exactly how much they would owe the Seattle Housing Authority if any trees were damaged. The value of the trees saved by this approach was estimated at $1.5 million.

Working with permitting agencies, interdisciplinary planning, collaboration, contractor education, public communication, and community celebrations was key to the High Point project's success. Protection of the natural drainage system during construction needs to be emphasized for the contractor, as the whole system needs to be functioning successfully prior to issuance of the certificate of occupancy. This requirement has schedule implications for the contractor, who must plan ahead.

Summary

At this stage in the urban design process, options for the future are created. These options provide many choices for the designer, the client, and any interested party. The designer uses options to illustrate how project goals may be achieved. Options should inspire the client and the public. A concept plan brings all possibilities together in a rough, incomplete, imperfect, preliminary manner. In doing so, the stage is set to begin dialogues about the future of the site.

6 ■ Dialogues

In the process of urban design, the term *dialogue* refers to the opportunities for a rapport between the designer and the client as well as between the designer and the public. The term is inspired by Edmund Bacon, who, in *Design of Cities* (1974), described how Market Street in Philadelphia was transformed. As a participant in the process, Bacon used the word *dialogue* to describe the complex ways planners and designers present ideas, communicate, receive feedback, and restructure their proposals.

Such relationships may occur throughout the design process and can either be scheduled or happen by chance. Two motivations stimulate a dialogue between designer and client: to inform and to involve. The resulting activities can be called "public information" and "public participation." According to James Creighton (1981, 4): "The difference is that the purpose of public information is *to inform the public* while the purpose of public involvement is not only to *inform the public* but also to *solicit public response* regarding the public's needs, values, and evaluations of proposed solutions." Participation implies an especially deep form of involvement, through which citizens become engaged in directing the outcome. The level of information, involvement, and participation depends on the circumstances.

Under certain circumstances, public participation is a form of protest. Urban transformations, as Eleanor Smith Morris (1997, 209) described about the 1980s battles over urban design projects in Great Britain, "tend to spark off a range of battles on multiple fronts—battles in front of planning committees . . . ; battles in front of commissions . . . ; battles in front of community groups, hastily put together to prevent the destruction of 'our neighbourhood'—'not in my back yard' (NIMBY-ism). Architecture and urban design became the focus for an increasingly divided taste in society because architecture and urban design are the most public of the arts. Everyone can see them." People often become involved to stop a project. Planners and designers should strive to engage and inspire people. Designers should encourage people to be open-minded, and conversely, designers should listen to the concerns expressed by the public.

One role of urban design is to make connections between global concerns and local issues. For example, an urban design might propose greater density. However, local groups may be weary of greater density in their neighborhood. The designer might illustrate how density can contribute to the reduction of greenhouse gases and conserve energy (see, for example, Owen 2009).

Dialogues can be used to connect local actions to regional and even global environmental consequences. Designers can engage ecologists in dialogues to increase the environmental literacy of all involved. Connections between humans and other species in the web of life may be abstract to the designer, the client, and the public. Ecologists can help reveal those connections and illustrate how a design can reinforce or damage these relationships.

Dialogue Comparison Characteristics and Risks

Dialogues with the public need to positively affect the design and the next steps of the process. The most important aspect is the attitude with which the designer approaches the dialogue. Designers should feel comfortable expressing their own ideas but also be equally open to revising and even changing them. Creighton (1981, 4) writes: "The final measure of the effectiveness of a public involvement program is not just that the public has been informed, but that the public comment has been solicited in a manner such that it has contributed to making a decision that is technically and economically feasible, environmentally sound, and supported by a large segment of the public."

Dialogue with the public provides a decisive moment and, in some cases, determinant, in a design process that enhances its democratic dimension. In a democratic dialogue, a proposal can be accepted, amended, modified, sent back, or refused. Designers must be ready to accept other ideas, proposals, and contributions, but they must also be ready to defend their own proposals with conviction and confidence. Designers should be open to change and not be arrogant.

However, Renzo Piano, regarding the role of participation in the design process, said that

Plate #1 (also Figure 0.4) Millennium Park, Chicago. This 24.5-acre (9.9-hectare) park transformed an area of rail yards and parking lots into a prominent civic center near the Lake Michigan shoreline. The park features the work of prominent artists, architects, and landscape architects, including Frank Gehry, Anish Kapoor, Kathryn Gustafson, Piet Oudolf, and Jaume Plensa.

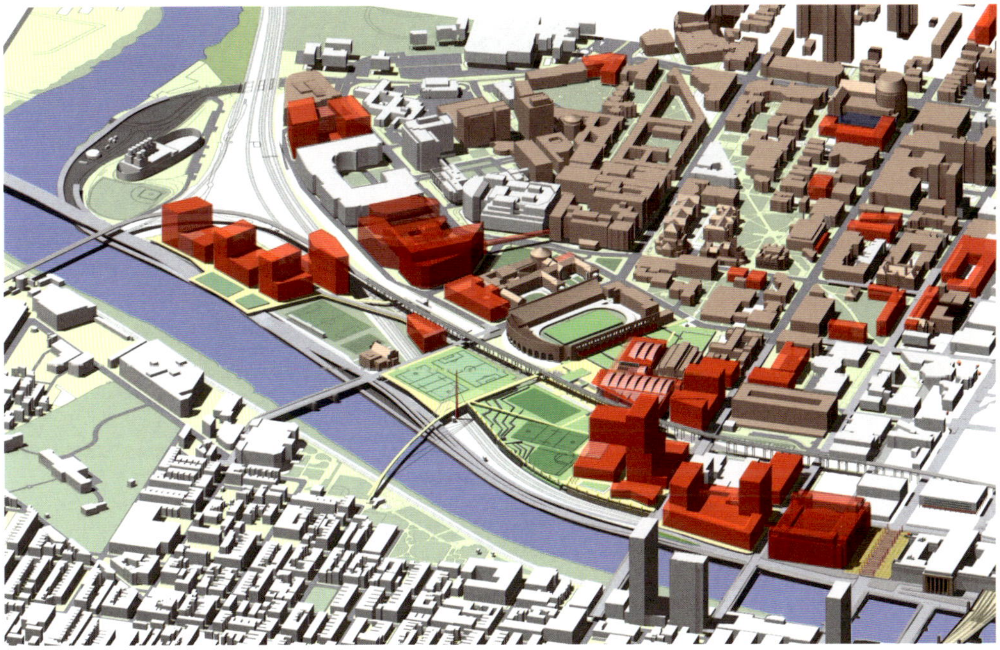

Plate #2 (also Figure 10.9) Penn Connects, a vision plan for the University of Pennsylvania: a regeneration of brownfield sites within the campus district.

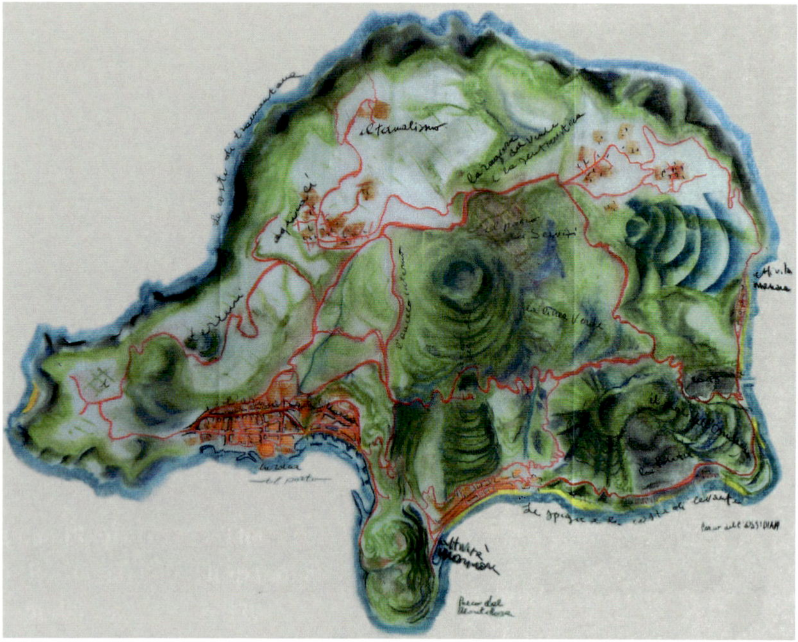

Plate #3 (also Figure 3.3) Isola di Lipari, Messina, Italy: the natural and human-made environments.

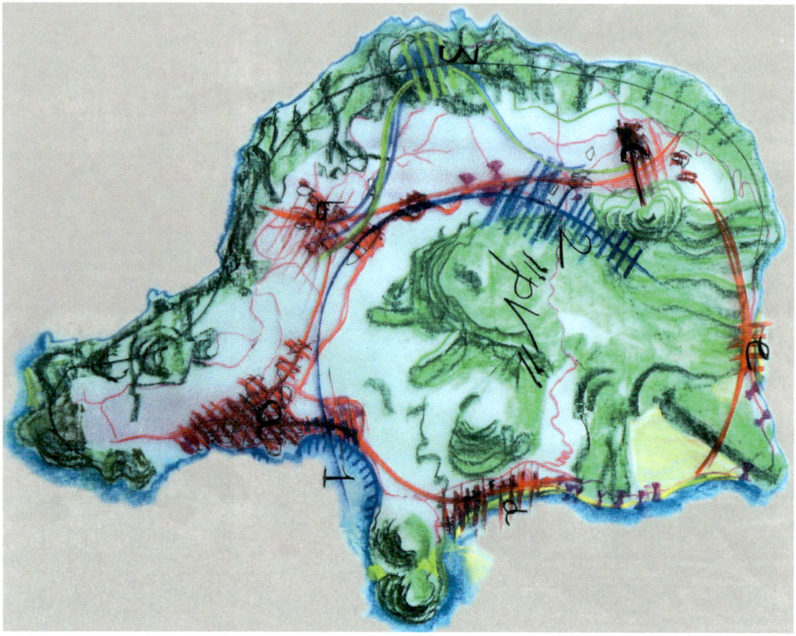

Plate #4 (also Figure 3.4) Isola di Lipari, Messina, Italy: ideograms to interpret the natural and human-made environments.

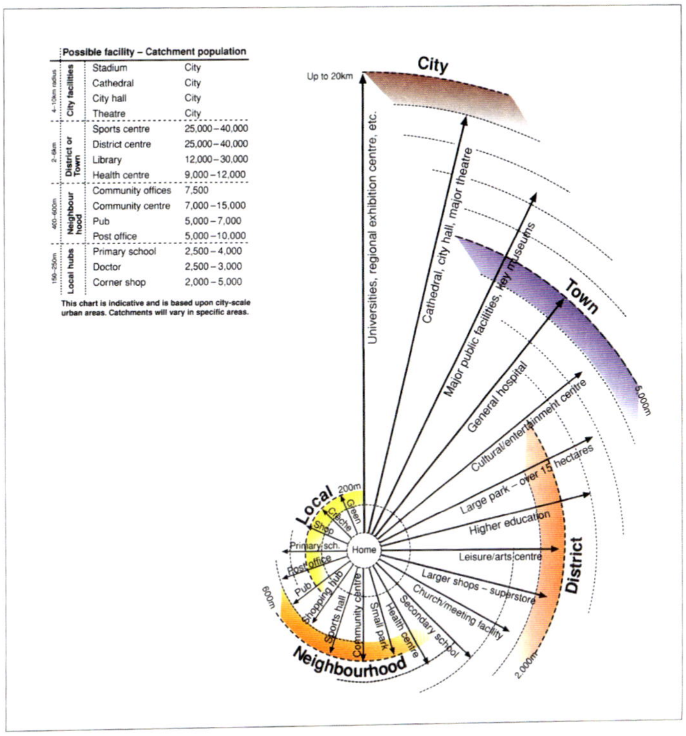

Plate #5 (also Figure 3.12) The city provides the framework for core institutions.

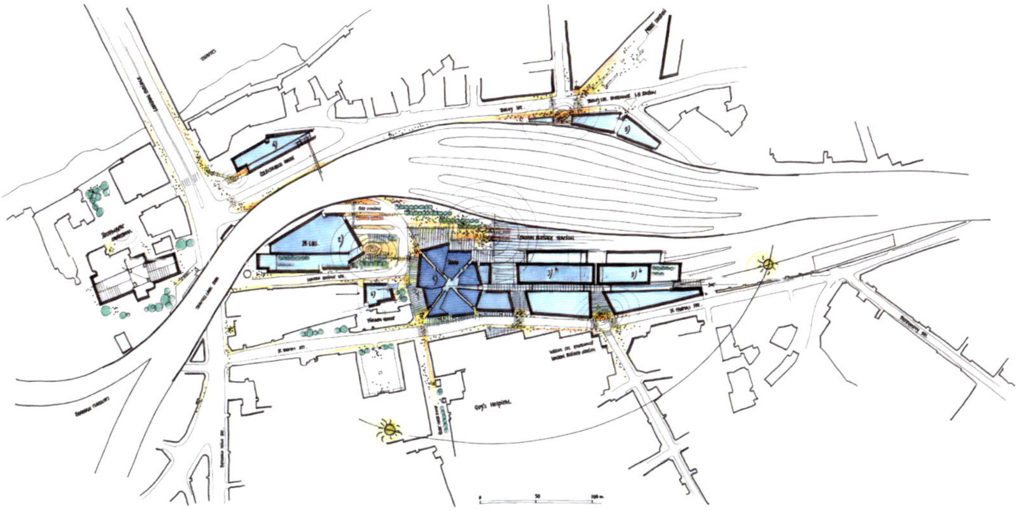

Plate #6 (also Figure 3.13) London Bridge Tower plan.

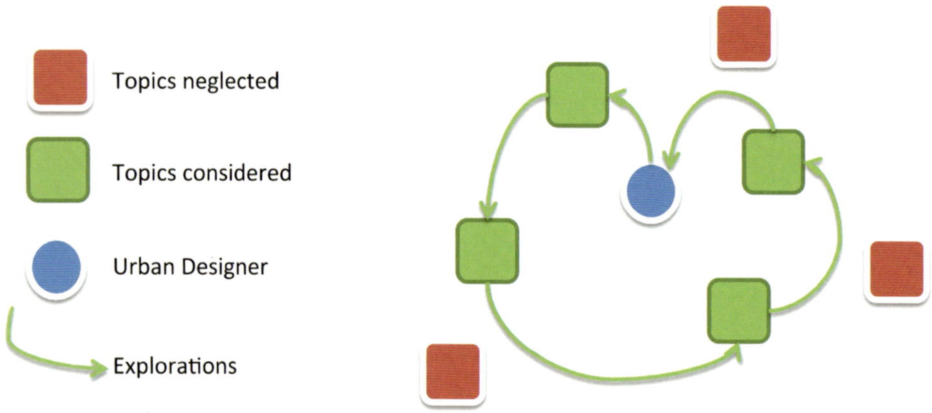

Plate #7 (also Figure 4.1) The designer as a "one-man band."

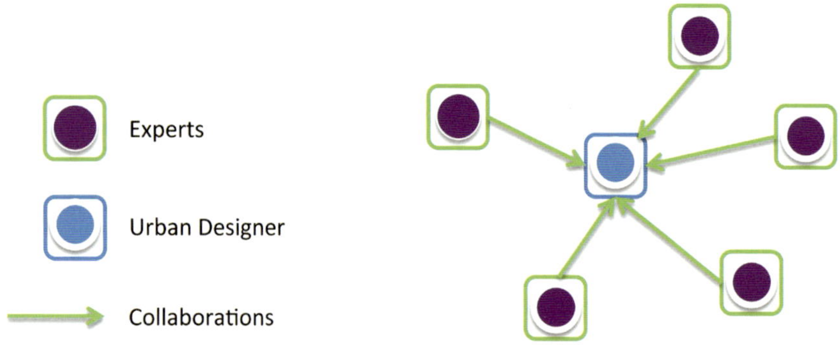

Plate #8 (also Figure 4.2) The designer as an "orchestra conductor."

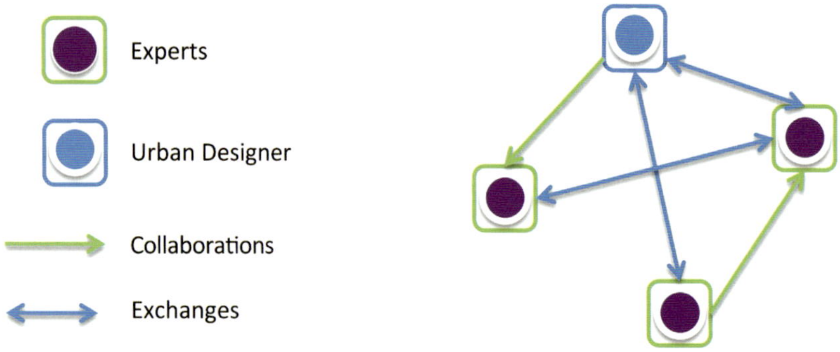

Plate #9 (also Figure 4.3) The designer as part of an ensemble.

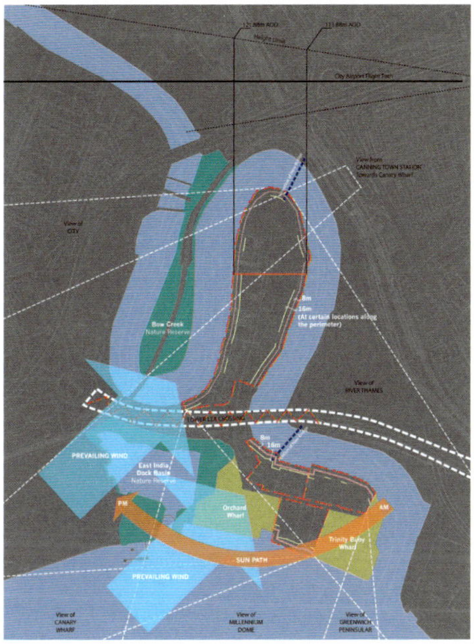

Plate #10 (also Figure 4.5) The opportunities map for the Leamouth Peninsula, London.

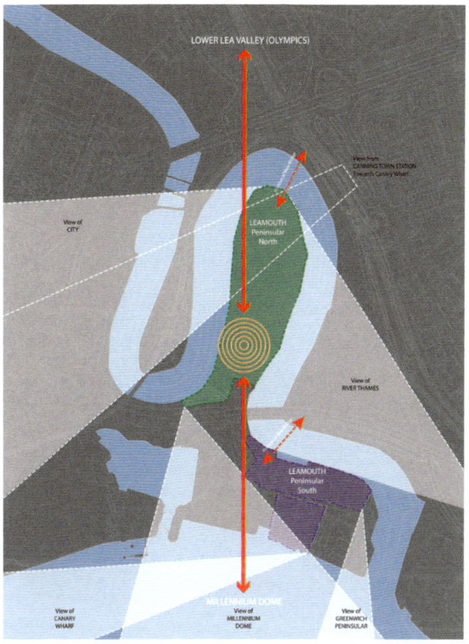

Plate #11 (also Figure 4.6) The constraints map for the Leamouth Peninsula, London.

Plate #12 (also Figure 4.7) The Leamouth Peninsula Master Plan, London.

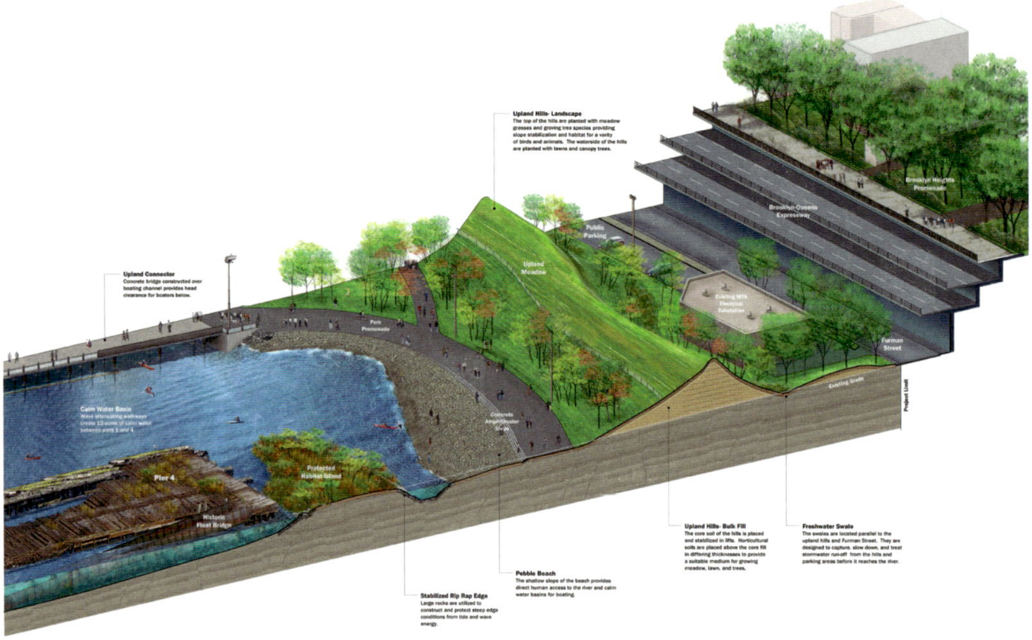

Plate #13 (also Figure 4.9) Brooklyn Bridge Park section, New York, 2008.

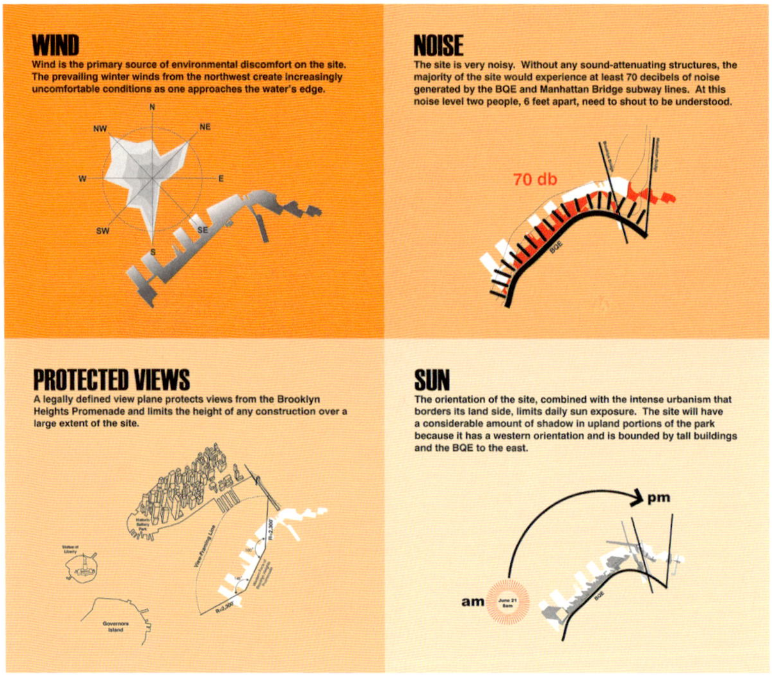

Plate #14 (also Figure 4.20) Portion of site analysis and project criteria for Brooklyn Bridge Park, Brooklyn, New York, 2008.

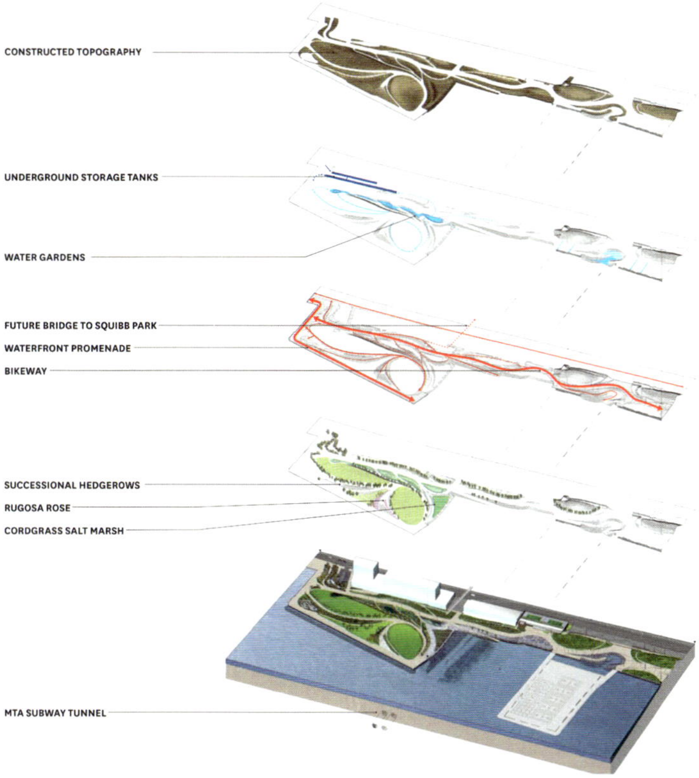

Plate #15 (also Figure 11.1) Axonometric drawing of Brooklyn Bridge Park systems at Pier 1, Pier 2, salt marsh, spiral pool, and upland areas, 2008.

Plate #16 (also Figure 11.2) Spring in Brooklyn Bridge Park.

Plate #17 (also Figure 4.19) The Timişoara (Romania) workshop model. The quick model was prepared to understand the place and the relationship between the site and the city.

Plate #18 (also Figure 5.1) Parc Diagonal Mar, Barcelona. Design by EMBT Architects and EDAW (now AECOM).

Plate #19 (also Figure 5.8) Historical map of Mantua, Italy.

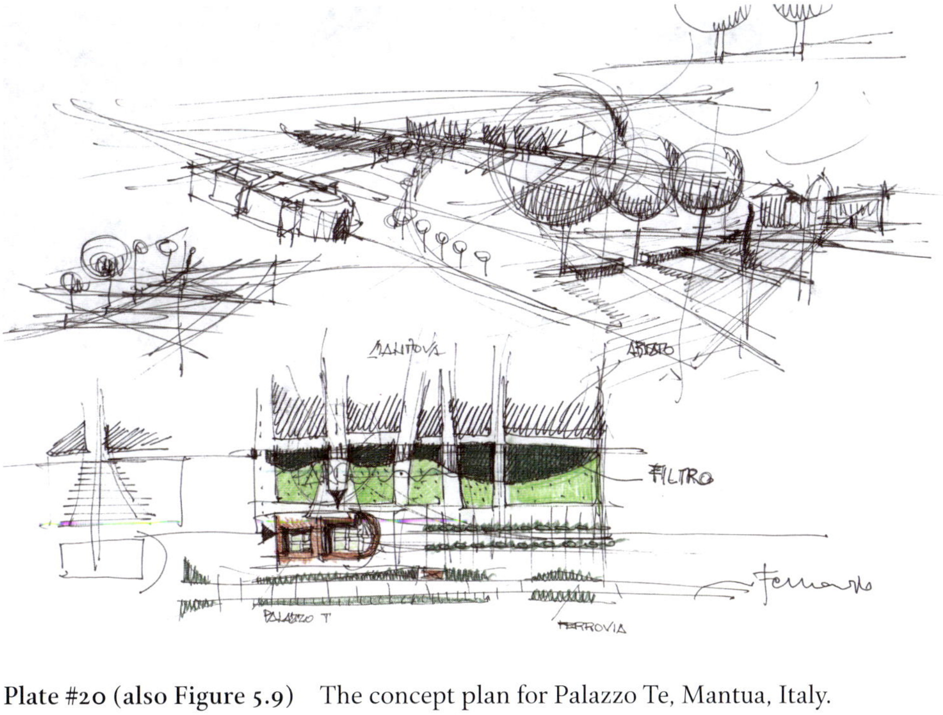

Plate #20 (also Figure 5.9) The concept plan for Palazzo Te, Mantua, Italy.

Plate #21 (also Figure 5.11) A vegetated median strip collects and absorbs rainwater from the street, keeping it out of city storm sewers in High Point, Seattle. Overall master planning, architecture, site design, and landscape architecture: Mithūn; civil engineers and right-of-way natural systems and landscape: SvR Design Company.

Plate #22 (also Figure 5.12) High Point's natural drainage system provides clean water for 8 percent of the salmon-bearing Longfellow Creek watershed, a 1-mile-long (0.62-kilometer-long) urban creek system running through the heart of West Seattle. Overflow during extraordinary storm events is piped to an attractive detention pond. Overall master planning, architecture, site design, and landscape architecture: Mithūn; civil engineers and right-of-way natural systems and landscape: SvR Design Company.

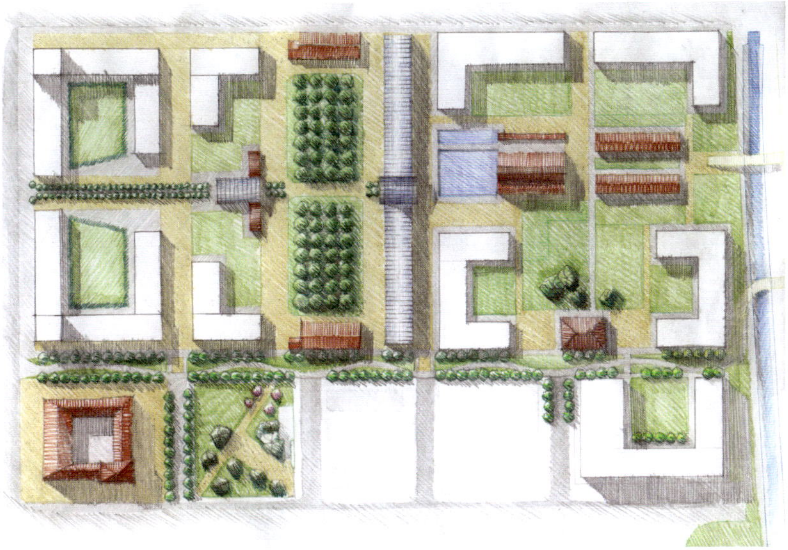

Plate #23 (also Figure 6.5) The master plan for the former abattoir of Monza.

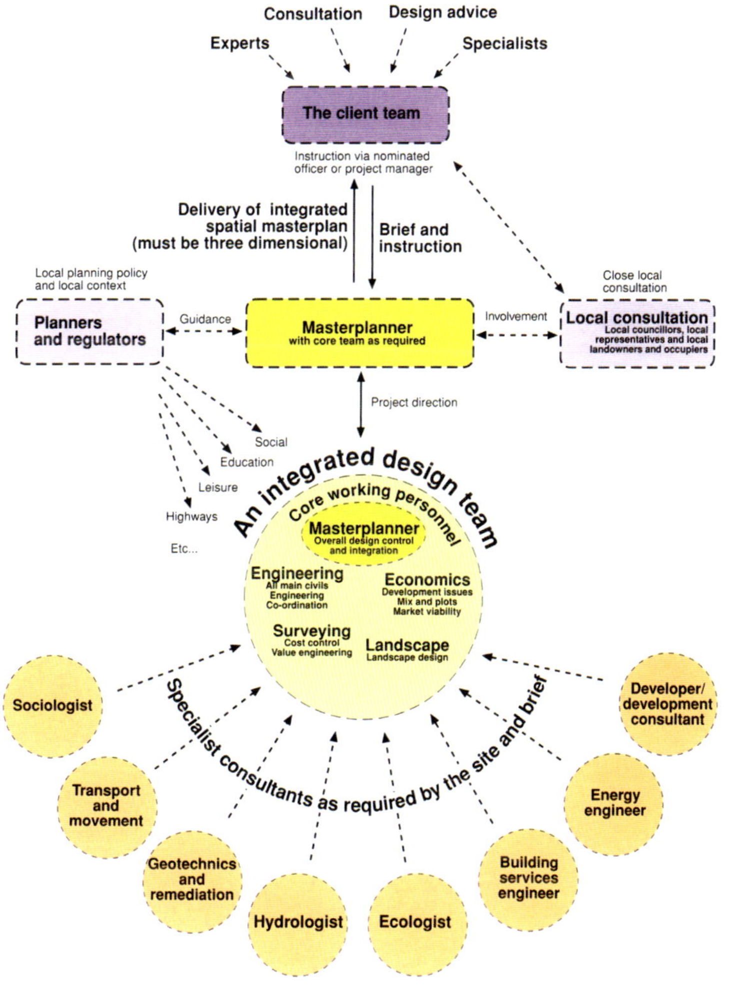

Plate #24 (also Figure 7.1) An integrated spatial master plan requires an integrated design team.

Plate #25 (also Figure 7.4) Paul Cret's plan of development for the University of Texas, 1933.

Plate #26 (also Figure 8.2) General plan of Riverside, Illinois, by Olmsted, Vaux & Co. Landscape Architects, 1869.

Plate #27 (also Figure 8.4) Madrid Rio existing conditions, 2004.

Plate #28 (also Figure 8.5) Madrid Rio proposed design, 2008. The project of Madrid Rio was designed by a team led by Ginés Garrido. The team consists of MRIO Arquitectos and West 8 Urban Design and Landscape Architecture. MRIO Arquitectos is a joint venture of three offices from Madrid: Burgos & Garrido Arquitectos, Porras + La Casta Arquitectos, and Rubio-Álvarez Sala Arquitectos.

Plate #29 (also Figure 8.8) Model in the Shanghai Urban Planning Exposition Hall.

Plate #30 (also Figure 8.9) A poster for the Vatnsmýri, Reykjavík, competition.

Plate #31 (also Figure 8.10) A poster for the Vatnsmýri, Reykjavík, competition.

Plate #32 (also Figure 9.1) Paul Cret's watercolor perspective of future development of the University of Texas campus, 1933.

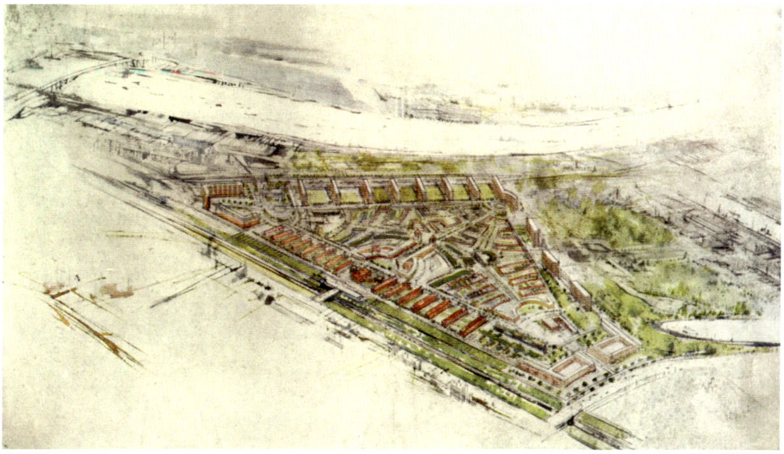

Plate #33 (also Figure 10.1) Greater London Plan by Sir Patrick Abercrombie. This layout indicates the application of the plan in Bermondsey for a density of 136 persons per acre (per 0.4 hectare).

Plate #34 (also Figure 10.3) Artistic representation of terrace houses for the plan in Bermondsey, London.

Plate #35 (also Figure 11.3) A new plaza creates vibrant open space within Thomas Jefferson University's health sciences campus in downtown Philadelphia, 2009.

Plate #36 (also Figure 11.4) Shanghai Houtan Park. The contaminated water has been cleansed and made touchable after a long journey through the vegetated terraces and human-made wetland. The steel structure is made of recycled materials from the site. Various productive crops are used in the park that are harvested by the park managers and that attract wildlife. The park covers about 10 hectares (24.7 acres). It is 1.6 kilometers (1 mile) in length and 10 to 30 meters (33 to 99 feet) in width. It can cleanse 2,400 cubic meters (3,139 cubic yards) of contaminated water daily (even one drip of water takes one week to run from the source to the sink), and it had attracted thirty-seven bird species just one year after it was built. It has become a unique park for local people as well as visitors from all over the world.

> Giancarlo De Carlo[2] was very aware of the fact that to listen to people does not mean obeying, or imply abdicating their own role; to participate is to educate. Which good medical doctor, having listened to the patient, would say exactly what he/she wants to hear? The listening attitude needs to be taught from a young age, and it grows with us. Being involved in participation does not mean convincing people, but acknowledging the requirements and translating them into good design. The art of discussing has to do with that noble thought of Norberto Bobbio[3]: "There is better in life than to persuade people about what you want to do, for instance, understanding what is the right thing to do." (Irace 2007, 14)

The designer must know how to manage—which does not mean to manipulate—participation and therefore to obtain as much as possible from the public (and the client) in order to direct the design (Carmona et al. 2003). The designer should not be overwhelmed by demands or succumb to shortcuts. In the foreword of Barbara Faga's (2006, vii–viii) book on public consensus, Alexander Garvin, former vice president for planning, design, and development for the Lower Manhattan Development Corporation (Goldberger 2004; Nobel 2005), told of an episode in his career that is enlightening about people's expectations in the public participation process:

> In 1968, I attended a meeting with about 100 residents of the Bushwick section of Brooklyn, New York, which at that time was a depressed, lower income neighborhood that had been largely neglected by public officials. A "professional planner" taped an enormous sheet of paper across one end of the room. Using a Magic Marker he listed numbers on one side of the page. Then he asked: "What do you want in Bushwick?" One by one he filled in desires listed by some of the people in the room. Suddenly a very angry welfare mother took the floor. "We don't need a wish list," she screamed. "We want things to happen, but we don't know what is realistic. You're the professional! You should tell us what the alternatives are, how they can be paid for, and what you recommend. *Then we'll decide*." From that moment I understood the difference between a serious public process and a charade.

---

2 Giancarlo De Carlo was the Italian architect editor of the journal *Spazio e Società*—Space & Society, Wolf Prize in Art Laureate in 1988, a member of Team 10, and designer of the urban plan of Urbino and of its University buildings. He was born December 12, 1919, and died June 4, 2005.

3 Norberto Bobbio was Italy's leading legal and political philosopher. He was born October 18, 1909, and died January 9, 2004.

Citizen participation is often a challenge and a difficult task because of resistance and suspicion from citizens. Michael Dobbins, in *Urban Design and People* (2009, 25), argues that

> citizen empowerment has been difficult and halting from the beginning. Important advances have been made, yet it's still, like democracy itself, a messy work in progress. The first line of resistance is predictable: People whose traditional powers were being impinged upon were unwilling to share. Then there are the internal challenges: How do traditionally marginalized people rise to trust the opportunity to participate? Too often their efforts have been ignored or rebuffed, resulting in oppositional activism at best or apathetic resignation at worst.

In her book on public participation experiences, Barbara Faga (2006, 21) of AECOM (formerly EDAW), and author of the foreword to this book, states that "the narrow channel between adapting the design and selling out can be excruciatingly hard to navigate—or not." In Boston, EDAW was involved in the design of Wharf District Park, a 5-acre (2-hectare) urban park reconnecting the harbor with downtown. Faga (2006, 21) writes: "[During the meetings with the population,] we were asked to include so many attractions and details in the design that the simplicity of the park would be lost. Gary Hack, [former] dean of the School of Design at the University of Pennsylvania . . . noted that if we had put everything the Boston public asked in the Wharf District Park, it would have ended up looking like an elaborate 18-hole miniature golf course."

There is no question that public involvement requires additional effort, time, and money, at least in the short run. However, if the public opposes a project, the costs of a delayed or failed project may even be higher. Public involvement is also difficult, complex, and, at times, emotionally draining, but it is necessary and worthwhile if, in the end, a project is accepted by those people affected by the change.

Public Participation and Public Involvement

Public participation and involvement in urban design processes, as in planning generally, is a way to address change that affects people's lives. Under some circumstances, public participation is a mandatory task for the designer. In other situations, public participation is a way to reduce possible conflicts or to find a way to minimize them. As Jonathan Barnett (1982, 35) pointed out about roles and opportunities for the exchange of ideas between designers and the public involved:

> If planners and designers ask the right questions, a few meetings with community groups can also tell them as much about the residents as a sociological survey, without insulting the residents and making them feel they are regarded as guinea pigs, which, unfortunately, is the effect of most surveys. Community meetings are also a good way to assess local priorities. . . . Planners and designers should not expect much in the way of specific positive suggestions from community meetings; it is necessary to make specific proposals to the community. These will get plenty of reaction. When people see the changes they suggested showing up on the drawings at the next meeting, they will begin to believe that they really are participating in drawing up the plan.

In general, public involvement "is not a single event, such as a public hearing, but a series of coordinated activities that provide different kinds of participation opportunities at different stages of a decision-making process" (Creighton 1981, 54). James Creighton, in a manual for public involvement (1981, 55–56), made four observations:

1. *Different publics will be involved at different stages of the decision-making process.* During the technical phases, participation is likely to be limited to leaders of groups, representatives of stakeholders, or staffs of agencies.
2. *There are appropriate levels of involvement at each step in the decision-making process.*
3. *Public participation will increase as the decision-making process progresses.* The overall pattern in public involvement is that more and more people will participate as the process comes nearer to a decision.
4. *The public involvement program must be integrated with the decision-making process.*

Public participation is effective throughout the entire design process. In the early phases, participation plays the role of supporting the designer in defining project goals. Public participation in the initial phase (see Chapter 2, Prerequisites) can help identify values that a community wants to take into consideration in the final design. There are some circumstances under which a community promotes a design development, indicating the goals that it would have to reach.

In the United States, the role of communities as promoters of planning and design initiatives is part of history and public policy. Alexis de Tocqueville, a French scholar of legal systems who visited North America in the first half of the nineteenth century, observed that Americans prefer to solve problems without waiting for their government to act. There is extensive literature on the role of citizens in planning and design, including *The Use of Land: A Citizens' Policy Guide to Urban Growth* (1973), edited by William Reilly, and the literature connected with the advocacy planning of the 1970s, as promoted by Paul Davidoff, Linda Davidoff, Robert Goodman, and others (Checkoway 1994). Jane Jacobs (1961) vividly described the deleterious consequences of not involving affected citizens in urban design decisions (Flint 2009).

The role of the public in planning and design commonly has to do with the defense and the protection of a way of life: "Faced with haphazard development and its accompanying costs, forward-thinking communities across the country [USA] are working to find strategies that will enable them to protect and enhance their distinctive and desirable qualities. Successful communities incorporate many elements—commercial vitality, jobs, good schools, a mix of housing types, adequate transportation systems, and a proper scale for human interaction" (Diamond and Noonan 1996, 34).

Michael Dobbins (2009, x) emphasized the role of the public in urban design as a public service no matter if his client ranged "from single patron to the city's 7.5 million citizens." According to Dobbins:

> *Urban design* came to describe the design and functionality of all urbanized places—how they look and how they performed. Furthermore, the emphasis in urban design is on *public places*—the streets, parks, plazas, the open spaces that everyone shares. . . . Urban design is the design of the public environment, the space owned by all, as it connects to, frames, and is framed by the private environment—that space owned by individuals or corporate entities. Urban design is the public face and public base of human settlements. People proud of their places are the mark of good urban design.
>
> In 40 years of practice as a public sector urban designer, in addition to the usual base of urban design theory and practice, I have identified at least three important themes that get short shrift or are ignored altogether. [The first is that] people are the core of successful urban places. If a place looks good, feels comfortable, and meets its functional expectations, it will attract people and

engender their embrace, ongoing interaction, and stewardship. Such a happy outcome is more likely to occur if representatives of the people who are or will be in the place play an active role in guiding the design and development decisions and priorities that make places happen. (2009, x)

Public participation, according to James Creighton (1992, quoted in Steiner 2008, 27), generates the following benefits:

- Improvement of the quality of a decision
- Minimization of costs
- Building of consensus
- Increasing ease of implementation
- Avoidance of worst-case confrontation
- Maintenance of credibility and legitimacy
- Anticipation of public concerns and attitudes
- Development of public expertise and creativity

Experiences in public participation in urban design suggest that motivations are connected with the desire to make proposals for change and to participate in that change.

Participation at Ground Zero

An important experience in public participation is connected with the atrocious terrorist attacks on the World Trade Center of New York City on September 11, 2001. A few weeks after the attacks, a myriad of civic groups asserted their role in the rebuilding process, which has been considered—for many reasons—the most important urban design project of recent years. According to Paul Goldberger (2004, 48–49), the strongest voice in the process

> seemed to belong to Robert Yaro, president of the Regional Plan Association, a . . . civic group whose interests spanned the tristate area [New York, New Jersey, and Connecticut]. . . . Yaro realized that rebuilding the trade-center site, whatever form it took, would have regional implications. . . . He thought that the Regional Plan Association . . . was ideally suited to coordinate an effort to combine the civic voices in the region. He convened a whole consortium of civic organizations [almost ninety] into something he called the Civic Alliance to Rebuild Downtown New York.

The group formulated a set of principles for the future of the site calling for an open planning process with significant public participation for the effort to encompass all of Lower Manhattan, not just the 16-acre (6.5-hectare) World Trade Center site. The Civic Alliance organized several initiatives, including workshops, general meetings, and focused discussions on specific topics, including transportation and cultural programs (Civic Alliance 2002a, 2002b).

The most significant initiative was Listening to the City (Civic Alliance 2002c), a program that began with a meeting of 4,300 participants, followed by a smaller meeting of 200 participants and an online dialogue of some 800 additional people.

Listening to the City was designed to emphasize both guided discussion and free expression of ideas. Participants "were asked to accept the program established by the Port Authority [the New York State and New Jersey agency, which owns the land and the buildings of the World Trade Center] and explain which features of the design schemes they liked and disliked. Participants then selected the single most important piece of advice they wished to give the planners from among the themes of that discussion" (Civic Alliance 2002c, 2).

This experience emphasizes the role of planning and urban design as a social act in which designers need to redefine their role: "Designers and planners can no longer presume to direct or instruct the public toward an easy consensus. Regardless of how design professionals view the creative process, the public now expects, and will take full advantage of, a more democratic method of creating public spaces. The people are demanding public process" (Faga 2006, 34).

The Role of Public Participation in the Urban Design Process

Public participation has several purposes, including to inform the public about progress, to verify outcomes of surveys, to check whether goals and issues are being met, to offer options, to introduce design possibilities, and to obtain a consensus, when necessary, to move the process forward.

The dialogue between designer and private client has the same purposes as public participation, but the education and involvement techniques may differ. In both cases, it is necessary to select the appropriate participation technique, to carefully organize meetings, and to choose what to present and how. A first draft concept plan, a list of goals, a vision to share, and a series of design schemes are often the most suitable intermediate dialogue opportunities (see Chapter 5, Options). The final design and a clear, detailed description of the process through which the designer reached the ultimate plan are the material for the concluding presentation. The organizing and managing of the dialogue sessions are important for achieving a successful design as well as its implementation. A dialogue that degenerates into different parties occupying opposing positions will usually produce negative consequences for the final design, for project implementation, and for how the design is regarded going forward.

A particular type of public involvement is continuing or permanent participation. Continuing or permanent citizen involvement is not restricted to the design of a specific project or to a goal; rather, it continues without time limits. It is a practice unlikely to influence specific details of an urban design. More often, it involves decision-making processes related to urban or regional policy and, thus, would affect an urban design project indirectly by creating rules for the effort. Although continuing involvement in urban design is rare, it cannot be completely excluded. Continuing involvement may be adopted, for example, where it may improve project implementation and management. Ongoing participation may inform implementation committees if a plan of great complexity takes many years to complete (Creighton 1981, 131).

Public Participation in Different Design Contexts

Three out of four contexts to which we refer throughout this book (workshops, competitions, and direct assignments) require different types of public participation or, sometimes, no participation at all (see chapter 2, Prerequisites).

In the context of workshops, public participation occurs in two ways: direct and consultative. Direct participation refers to the involvement of people (skilled or not in the fields of design or in topics considered in the project), representatives of associations, or groups of interested parties potentially affected by the design. In a workshop, public participation can also be consultative or informative (see Figures 6.1 and 6.2). This approach is accomplished by informative meetings, focus groups, design workshops, and presentations at the beginning, during, or at the end of the process.

In a competition, public participation is usually limited to individual participants because of time constraints (usually very short), distance (national or international open competitions involve groups often located very far from the study area), language, and organizational difficulties (e.g., how to organize a public meeting for all teams participating in the competition). However, public participation in a competition can be planned before the brief is prepared. In this way,

Figure 6.1 Brainstorming strengths, challenges, and ideas at an Imagine Austin Comprehensive Planning community forum workshop, organized by the City of Austin Planning and Development Review Department, held at the Baty Elementary School on November 9, 2009. (Courtesy City of Austin.)

information about public expectations is available to all participants and known to the jury.

In direct assignments, public participation can be organized by the client together with the urban designer. If the client is a private company whose essential interest is the commercial potential of the project, public participation is unusual unless required by public entities. Public consultancies may be initiated to avoid the risks of extending the time of the project or the prospect of reducing profit, or in the worst case, to open conflicts with parties, which could stop the project.

In general, public participation can have a significant role in urban design. In describing several North American cases (plus that of Fortaleza in Brazil), Barbara

Figure 6.2 A chip exercise workshop, where participants allocated future growth across the city of Austin and in different forms. This workshop was part of the Imagine Austin Comprehensive Plan process, organized by the City of Austin Planning and Development Review Department, held at the Eastview Campus of Austin Community College on April 27, 2010. (Courtesy City of Austin.)

Faga (2006, xxi) observes that in public participation processes there are "moments of brilliance and leadership, good intentions gone wrong, common pitfalls to be expected, and roadblocks that seemingly arise out of nowhere."

Public Participation in the Vatnsmýri, Reykjavík, Competition

An important aspect in the preparation of the Vatnsmýri competition was the early consultation with interested parties and the public. According to the City of Reykjavík organizers, it was important that the competitors received accurate information about the views of the public and interested parties about planning and possible utilization of the site: Vatnsmýri, a 371-acre (150-hectare) area near the center of Reykjavík. It was equally important that the competition judges had this information, so that they could consider and evaluate the proposals based on the same starting point. In this way, it was more likely that consensus could be achieved on making the winning proposal a reality.

> The opinion of the public was solicited by providing an open forum in the Reykjavík Museum of Arts on 29 September and 1 October, 2005. During the month of September there was an exhibition in the museum on planning [*What Kind of City Do You Want?*] and Reykjavík planning history and this exhibition formed the backdrop for the open forum. The emphasis was on gauging the public's preferences regarding the urban environment and how to allocate the land in Vatnsmýri. In addition, two walks were offered to inquire about attitudes toward natural and cultural heritage in the area. Participation was invited by conspicuous advertisements in newspapers and on the radio. (Reykjavíkurborg 2007, 28)

An estimated five hundred people visited the Reykjavík Museum of Art during the two consultation days. Some were active in their participation and gave suggestions and ideas, which were included in the documents attached to the brief (Reykjavíkurborg 2007, 28):

- Urban development in Vatnsmýri should be dense and mixed, akin to that in central Reykjavík or in European city centres. Generally, there was a preference among participants for modest building height while a few wanted very tall buildings.
- Vatnsmýri should offer culture and education in addition to residences. Diversity in culture, services, and architecture is preferable.
- It is important for the development to include sheltered and attractive public spaces with good connections to the nearby outdoor recreation areas.
- There should be increased emphasis on walking, biking, and public transportation.
- The cultural and natural heritage should be respected.

For the competitors, the document included useful information about settlement patterns, density, relevant landmarks, urban environment visions, open and entertainment areas, and other planning ideas. Prior to the competition, there was also a series of meetings with companies and institutions located adjacent to the Vatnsmýri area. The purpose of these meetings (the minutes of which were included in the document "Stakeholder Meetings") was to reveal local attitudes toward development and the opportunities that the project might offer, for the information of competition entrants. These suggestions were also included in the competition brief (Reykjavíkurborg 2007, 28–29):

- A dense development is preferable in Vatnsmýri as this would also accommodate services and an opportunity to live near the workplace or school.
- Businesses and institutions in Vatnsmýri should be focused on knowledge and innovation.
- It is important that internal links within the area are strong to encourage synergy between different parties and access to services. These links should at least be provided by public transportation, walking, and bicycling paths.
- A strong connection with the city centre is important due to the services and culture provided there. This could be shaped by extending the Lake, a green sector or a boulevard southwards.
- The development in Vatnsmýri should be the venue for vibrant city life, characterized by quality and diversity. It should be interesting, bold and noteworthy. It should refer to local traits and consider the local climate.

Types of Public Participation

Lawrence Susskind and Jeffrey Cruikshank (2001, 24) affirm that "a good process produces a good outcome; and a better process, a better outcome." According to Sherry Arnstein (1969, in Steiner and Butler 2007, 32), there were eight levels of public participation at the end of the 1960s, from greater to lesser involvement: (1) citizen control, (2) delegate power, and (3) partnerships are considered different grades of *citizen power*; (4) placation, (5) consultation, and (6) information are levels of *tokenism*; and (7) therapy and (8) manipulation are the two degrees of *nonparticipation*.

The International Association for Public Participation (IAP2, 2007) developed a hierarchy spectrum with five levels of public impact:

1. *Inform*. To provide the public with information and assistance in understanding the problems, alternatives, opportunities, and/or solutions. Techniques: fact sheets, websites, and open houses.

2. *Consult.* To obtain public feedback on analysis, alternatives, and/or decisions. Techniques: public comment, focus groups, surveys, and public meetings.
3. *Involve.* To work directly with the public to ensure that public concerns and aspirations are consistently understood and considered. Techniques: workshops and deliberate polling.
4. *Collaborate.* To partner with the public in each aspect of the decision, including the development of options and the identification of the preferred solution. Techniques: citizen advisory committees, consensus building, and participatory decision making.
5. *Empower.* To place the final decision making in the hands of the public. Techniques: citizen juries, ballots, and delegated decisions.

Techniques to Involve People in Design Processes

There are many forms of public consultation, ranging from obligatory meetings to well-orchestrated events. Many techniques for involving people have been created, put into practice, and refined over the years in England, the United States, and Canada as a result of the town meetings heritage (Platt 1991). Specific skills, defined rules, and applied practices have evolved over the years (Creighton 1981, 1992, 2005; Faga 2006; Steiner 2008; Dobbins 2009).

Some of the principal public participation techniques are the same as those presented earlier in this book (see Chapter 2, Prerequisites). *Task forces* and *citizens' advisory committees*, for example, can work alongside through the entire process with different roles. At the early stage of the process, a task force can act on a voluntary basis or be created by an agency planner or the designer in charge to establish the general goals of a project or to work on a specific task and charge relating usually to a single problem or subject (Gil and Lucchesi 1979). Citizens' advisory committees can provide recommendations to the urban designer or planner with respect to the plan throughout the process or at a single stage of the process.

Almost all of the techniques to involve the public at the beginning of the design process (as described in Chapter 2, Prerequisites) can be adapted to support the designer and create an uninterrupted dialogue throughout the process. Some of the most common techniques to build this continuous interchange are the following.

- *Focus groups.* Social scientists, planners, and designers ask focus groups to ascertain or assess public views and opinions about issues or to help set goals: "A focus group consists of between 7 and 10 people who are not acquainted with each other, but who share similar backgrounds. The focus group participants are brought together, typically for a two-hour session, in a quiet, private room. An experienced facilitator guides and focuses discussion by asking open-ended questions of each group member" (Leach 1992, quoted in Steiner 2008, 31–32).

- *Delphi* and *Policy Delphi*. The Delphi technique was developed in the 1950s by the Rand Corporation as a means of technological forecasting. It is a technique that relies strongly on experts. A panel of eight to twelve experts is asked to predict the future of a project or an issue. These predictions are compiled and distributed to the panel without identifying the authors. The panel reviews the other experts' documents, and all experts are given the opportunity to change their own. The process is continued until the panel members reach a consensus or remain firm in their forecasts (Steiner 2008). Policy Delphi derives from traditional Delphi, but whereas the latter is characterized by anonymity, in the Policy Delphi experts interact openly.

- *Town meetings*. Public meetings can be difficult to manage, especially if the designer sees this technique as a way to consult rather than as a means of informing. The *Working Guide for Planning and Designing Safer Urban Environments*, by the Safe City Committee of the City of Toronto (1992, 8–9), makes some specific and practical suggestions for managing public meetings:

> By remunerating parents for childcare, not going too late (i.e. a 7 to 9 or 9:30 p.m. meeting) and holding meetings in a wheelchair accessible location, you will lessen the chances of excluding women, the elderly, and people with disabilities. . . . The meeting might include a review of the plans, a safety audit of the existing neighbourhood [or on other issues related to the purpose of the design] and/or set questions on specific aspects of the project. It is better to go into the meeting with specific questions you want answered by the community representatives than engaging in a general discussion to resolve anything. . . . It is a good idea to think ahead about literacy issues related to handouts and visual materials. Quite often, site plans are too complex to be visualized by non professionals. . . . Colours can also be used to enhance key points. . . . It is also a good idea to expect people to suggest solutions to the problems they raise. This both cuts down on unfocussed complaints and tells people that the consultation is more than a meaningless exercise.

• *Workshops*. A workshop or charrette is the central event of a larger process [called] *Dynamic Planning*, a multiday, collaborative planning and design effort with the goal of arriving at a comprehensive, feasible plan. . . . A charrette involves a multidisciplinary team of professionals developing all elements of a plan. The team works closely with stakeholders. . . . Its capacity to bring all the decision makers together for a discrete amount of time to create a solution makes it one of the most powerful techniques in a planner's toolkit. (National Charrette Institute 2007, quoted in Steiner and Butler 2007, 41).

The basic elements of workshops are as follows:

- The information collected by the organizer needs to be prepared in advance and shared between the participants.
- All interested parties must be involved from the beginning.
- The workshop requires from two to seven days depending on the character of the problem and its difficulty.
- Workshops must produce a feasible plan.
- Design is used to achieve a shared vision.

A workshop is especially useful in achieving agreement among different individuals or groups within a short period of time. It provides an effective means for resolving impasses among public groups, government bodies, and private entities. This technique could be used to reduce the time required to make a decision and to marry ideas from experts and lay people.

• *Other techniques*. More recent techniques to involve people have become available with a wider diffusion of the Internet. Some of these techniques are briefly described at People and Participation Net (http://www.peopleandparticipation.net), a site funded by the United Kingdom Department for Communities and Local Government (Community Empowerment Division), the Ministry of Justice (Democratic Engagement Branch), and the Sustainable Development Commission. The website is based on a book with the same name (Involve 2005) and aims to be a central portal for information and inspirations about participation to practitioners around the world. The techniques include the following:

- *ePanel*. This is a way for councils or other organizations to carry out regular online consultations with a known group of citizens.

- *Webchat*. This is a discussion held online with a small group of preselected participants who are given a distinct login and password. Webchats are readable by anyone; registration is normally required to contribute and may be restricted to certain groups.
- *Online consultation*. This type of consultation utilizes the Internet to ask a group of people about their opinion on an issue (typically, a policy in the development stages). An unlimited number of participants can be sent information about the subject or given access to download it online and then be asked to respond via e-mail or to comment on the website.
- *Blog*. A blog provides a quick, informal way to disseminate information to the wider public or to specific groups. Most blogs allow readers to comment on the content, so the blog can become the focus for a continued discussion among site visitors. Blogs can play an important role in public engagement alongside more traditional involvement techniques, such as workshops.

Transforming the Places of Production: The Workshops

In 1999 and 2000, the Regional Plan Association and Milan Polytechnic organized a gathering to examine American and Italian experiences with the redevelopment of underutilized sites and obsolete infrastructure in the metropolitan regions of New York City and Milan (Fossa et al. 2002). Rather than facilitate an exchange of information and case histories between American and Italian experts, the structure of colloquia enabled participants to explore issues through three concurrent site workshops in both the New York (October 16–22, 1999) and Milan (April 9–16, 2000) metropolitan regions. For each of the six workshops, an interdisciplinary team of approximately fifteen Italian and American architects, urban designers, and planners worked with a local client to develop specific reuse plans for a site or an industrial district. The plans were the product of an intensive four days of tours, meetings with local interested parties, and teamwork. The results were presented at public meetings at each site and at final plenary sessions.

The three New York metropolitan workshop sites focused on Long Island City and Cohoes, New York, and on Raritan, New Jersey.

- *Long Island City, New York*. As with many urban manufacturers, the business of printing takes place in a complex environment where mutually dependent clients,

Figure 6.3 Long Island City, New York. (Photograph by Danilo Palazzo.)

graphic artists, brokers, press operators, and binders interact daily. Over time, this agglomeration economy has taken root in special districts in Lower Manhattan. Rising real estate prices are disrupting this social ecology. The workshop team investigated how a new center for printing could be created in Long Island City, an industrial neighborhood just across the East River in New York City (see Figure 6.3).

• *Cohoes, New York*. In 1837, the largest cotton mill in the United States was built at the confluence of the Hudson and Mohawk Rivers and the Erie Canal. The 828,821-square-foot (77,000-square-meter) Harmony Mill complex and thousands of units of company-owned housing helped make Cohoes a classic company town and a cornerstone of America's industrial revolution (see Figure 6.4). While this rich history is now celebrated by a state urban cultural park designation, the mills themselves are only 50 percent occupied and are in disrepair. The goal of this workshop was to find new manufacturing uses that match the mill's nineteenth-century architecture, the town's tourism potential, and the needs of the residents for the still-occupied worker housing.

• *Raritan, New Jersey*. Like many of the small towns in the New York metropolitan region, Raritan grew up around the railroad. At one time, the Raritan River

Figure 6.4 Cohoes, New York. (Photograph by Danilo Palazzo.)

and the woolen mills along it were the lifeblood of the town's economy. Later, the railroad supported not only commuters to New York City but also industry. Two of these industrial sites, adjacent but on opposite sides of the tracks, were the focus of this workshop. Both sites face increasing pressure for redevelopment. Together these sites represent a range of urban design and planning issues that affect the industrial properties along the rail lines.

The three Milan metropolitan region workshop sites were Porta Genova (Milan), Monza, and Valtellina (Sondrio).

- *Porta Genova, Milan.* Close to the historical and business center of Milan, this underutilized rail yard and station in a former industrial area is an important redevelopment opportunity for the entire city. The site is just outside Milan's historical center, close to the *Navigli* (canals) and a regional agricultural park. Old rail yards are common issues in many western European countries.

- *Monza.* Monza is a city of about 120,000 inhabitants located along the Lambro River, just northeast of Milan. Its rich history dates back to the sixth century BC when the Lombard queen Theodelinda established a residence and the still-standing cathedral. The workshop examined potential new uses for a former prison and a former abattoir. Both of these structures, located in a mixed-use area close to the historic city center, were largely abandoned, the only use being an animal fair that occupies part of the abattoir once a year.

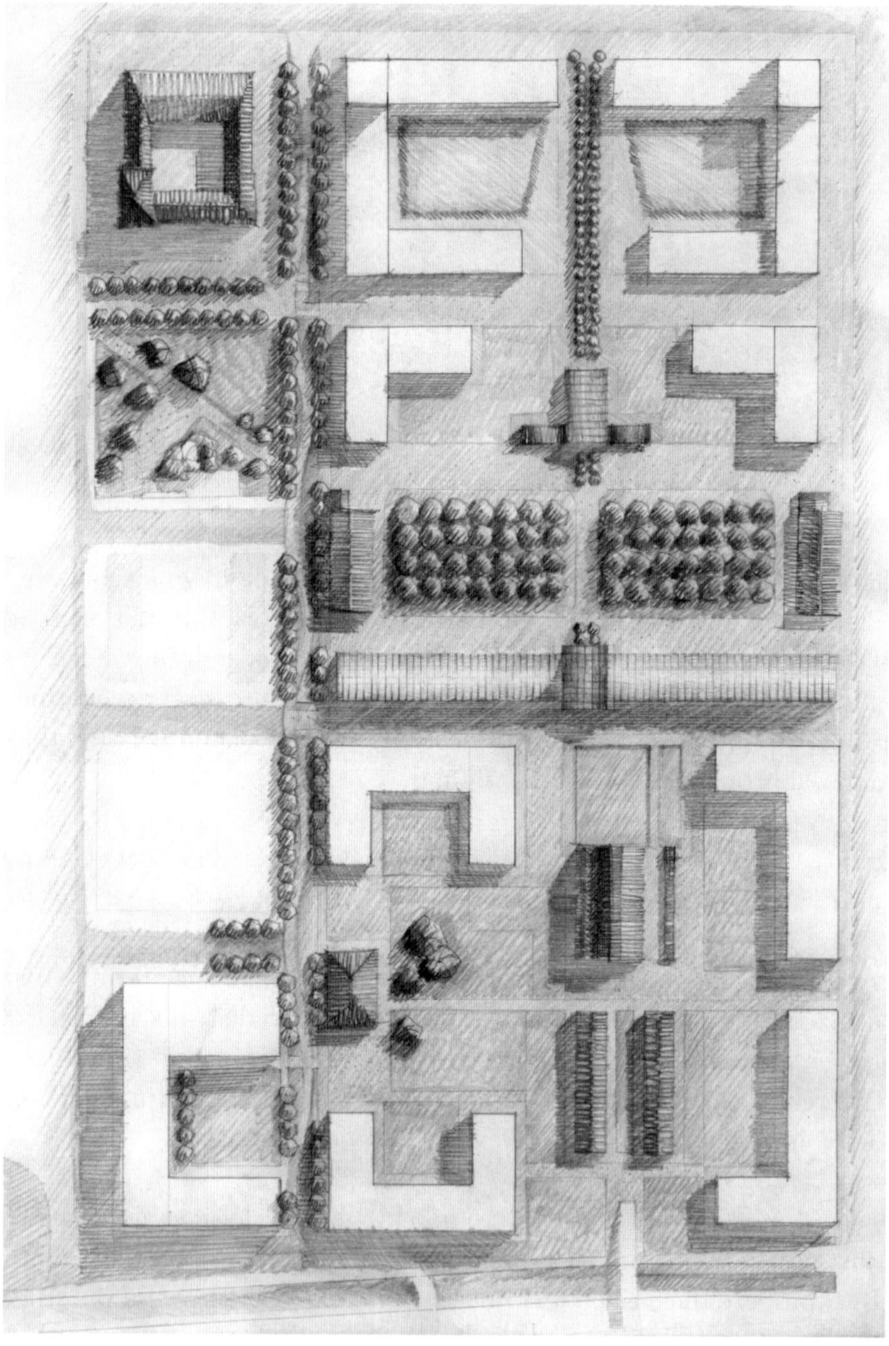

Figure 6.5 (also Plate #23) The master plan for the former abattoir of Monza. (Drawing by Elena Stevanato. From Palazzo 2002.)

- *Valtellina, Sondrio*. Located at the base of the Alps, Valtellina is an important river valley, well known for its hydroelectric plants and vineyards. It is a popular destination for tourists in winter and summer. Small and medium enterprises blossomed after the Second World War. Many of these businesses are located directly along a principal highway and the Adda River. However, this industrial and manufacturing system has suffered through recent economic transformations that led to the abandonment of industrial buildings. The design study examined how to integrate a new highway into the Valtellina landscape and economy.

The designs produced during the workshops have had concrete results and have also led to new exploratory plans. The workshop of Long Island City served, above all, to help the Borough of Queens develop urban design policies to encourage productive reuse. These policies reinforce the potential interrelations of public spaces on the waterfront with those reclaimed from the rundown part of the Sunnyside Yard and for the visual image of Queens in contrast to the urban landscape of Manhattan. At Raritan, the municipality adopted ideas emerging from the workshop for the renewal of the industrial area along the railroad. At Cohoes, the property owner of the area accepted the advice of the workshop for reusing the former cotton mill as a high-tech productive complex. He presented the project to the municipality, and it was accepted, thereby solving the problem concerning a building that had been abandoned for many years.

The Porta Genova workshop outcomes have become the base for the Milan city planning department to elaborate on specific criteria for evaluating new urban programs in the area. In Monza, the city government has given the Milan Polytechnic the task of carrying out the results of the workshop, passing from an instant plan to a master plan for the area of the former abattoir (see Figure 6.5/Plate #23). In Valtellina, the project of the Lombardia regional government for the new highway Ss36 in the two workshop areas (Bolgia and Sassella) was partially changed following the results of the workshop. This change respected the agricultural and environmental values and greenway potential for flood-prone areas along the river.

Summary

Two measures of success for an urban design are how well it is received, first, by the client and, ultimately, by all those affected by the design: the people who will live, work, or recreate in the new urban places. One way to ensure that people will react favorably to an urban design is to involve them in its creation. To do so, the designer must be willing to engage in dialogue, certainly with the client but often with a broader public as well. Dialogue informed by ecological understanding can do much to advance the sustainability of the planet by connecting local decisions to regional and global processes. Such dialogue can contribute significantly to a successful master plan.

7. Master Plan

The master plan is the definitive product of the urban design project. It pulls together all previous steps of the design process and presents them in an organized fashion. Although specific circumstances will dictate the scope and content of a master plan, most plans have common characteristics and features. The master plan describes and maps the overall development concept for the study area, including present and future visualization, land-use allocation, design guidelines, plantings and public spaces, built form, infrastructure, and service provision.

The level of detail in a master plan will vary according to the project's scale, the nature of the task, the specificity of the site and its values, and the complexity as determined by environmental, social, and cultural conditions (prerequisites). Master plans differ, depending on planning systems from country to country and, as in the United States, from state to state (see Chapter 10, Implementation). Master plans can provide a means to implement a comprehensive plan and even become a local plan. In other circumstances, the master plan can operate as a general plan ready for elaboration (see Chapter 9, Details) and implementation through design guidelines and other tools (see Chapter 8, Presentation).

The Origins of the Master Plan

The term *master plan* was coined in the United States in the 1920s to indicate a tool that "describes the vision of a coherent and unified city brought about through a single plan" (Abbott 1985, 2). According to Edward Bassett (1938, 67): "The term, 'master plan,' arose following the establishment of planning commissions.

Twenty-five years ago [around 1915] one did not hear of such commissions, but since then, increased attention to community planning has caused their establishment under provisions of law." Frederick Law Olmsted Jr. recognized at the beginning of the twentieth century that the practice of city planning was producing a radical change in urban form. Olmsted Jr., in parallel with Daniel Burnham, Benjamin Marsh, and John Nolen, produced planning tools that organized the whole city instead of just parts, such as the road network, city parks, or the water system. According to Mark Abbott (1985, 2–5):

> The master plan binding is not just an expedient way of holding together the extensive maps, the "before-and-after" drawings, and the bold declarations of the future that are contained inside. The plan's binding is the manifestation of the idea. It acts as an articulation of the belief that the city can be formed into a single, identifiable entity with a particular structure and character. . . . For Olmsted and his colleagues, the master plan was far more than a different approach to the problems of the city. The plan, for them, symbolized a whole new way of thinking about the world. . . . The problems which the plan was intended to address were the problems that all of the people faced. . . . The master plan implied that urban people lived not as individuals, but as citizens, as members of the city. The plan was a *res publica*—a public thing—that represented a conscious choice of the kind of world the citizens wanted to inhabit.

The master plan seeks to guide how a city will change physically and socially. The tool was adapted to various realities, dimensions, scales, and contexts over time. The master plan, "as a declaration of the possibility of control over the urban environment, . . . defined community . . . not as a passive geographic condition or a sharing of common beliefs and practices, but as [part of] an active process of shaping the city with one's fellow citizens. For the master planner, existing as a public document, the plan belonged to all of the citizens. . . . [The master plan] represented a set of goals which all the people shared" (Abbott 1985, 5).

Abbott (1985) describes the changes that have taken place with the master plan in the United States from its beginnings to the last quarter of the twentieth century. He highlights the progressive removal of the physical dimension from the master plans applied to cities and, beginning in the 1960s, the abandonment of the master plan as a comprehensive instrument to control cities and communities. Although the master plan has been replaced by other urban management and governance tools, it endures in the urban design project.

The master plan can guide rule choices to transform cities and metropolitan regions by describing the physical configurations in urban plans, other strategic planning documents, and architectural designs. It also offers a visualization of the urban design project and can be seen as a link between an urban plan and an architectural project.

In urban design, the master plan represents the final document within which the definitive proposal is described and represented. A simplified master plan can also be used within an urban plan as a tool for evaluating the choices for the physical form of the city that the plan suggests.

Planning: Delivering a Fundamental Change, better known as *Planning Green Paper*, issued by the UK Government, Department of Transport, Local Government and the Regions, in 2001, encourages "masterplanning to improve the quality of development" (point 5.5, p. 29). A few pages later, the document specifies that master plans can be properly used in large sites: "Large sites can take time to plan properly. They are also highly significant in relation to our objectives to involve local people in planning the future of their community and to improve the quality of development. Masterplanning developments can help speed up the planning process by indicating clearly the nature, type and design of development expected on a particular site or area" (point 5.39, p. 39).

Master Plan Characteristics and Goals

Key master plan characteristics continually evolve and can be summarized as follows:

- *Visualization* of how urban transformation choices affect the actual situation. This component of the master plan deals with the translation of main design ideas from words to images to facilitate their transmission to the public. This may also be seen as a way to return to the community the proposals formulated during the visioning process (see Chapter 5, Options).
- *Active involvement* of local residents at the beginning of the process (see Chapter 2, Prerequisites) and along the design development steps (see Chapter 6, Dialogues) to achieve and to assess a set of mutual values to be used throughout the design process. The master plan needs to describe how values and goals established will be totally or partially fulfilled.
- *Volumetric* and *urban setting prefiguration* of the spaces involved together with the constraints and opportunities (see Chapter 4, Synthesis) that come from considering the environmental and ecological characteristics of the site and

its surrounding area. The foreshadowing of the future site organization should describe how to address the challenges humans are facing, including climate change, reduction of the dependence on fossil fuels, urbanizations, food production, and so on.

- *Rules to implement the plan*, which must take into account public and administrative bodies and private individuals involved, as well as the potential role of the communities to be implicated in the years during and after the implementation of the plan.

In the United States, master plans matured in a more complex way than in other nations, as illustrated by projects of New Urbanist architects and planners (Calthorpe 1993; Duany and Plater-Zyberk 1997; Calthorpe and Fulton 2001) as well as other initiatives (Regional Plan Association 1998; Regional Center Partnership of Somerset County et al. 1999). In Europe, the use of a master plan is most common in the United Kingdom. However, it is widely diffused in other European countries.

The key purposes of a master plan can be summarized as follows:

- It *defines*, through meetings and dialogues with private and public parties, economic values—that is, benefits for individuals (e.g., in the form of enhanced real estate values) and for society as a whole, and which occur in social and environmental forms (e.g., a safe place, regenerative potential, and/or reduction of energy uses) (Carmona, Magalhães, and Edwards 2002).
- It *details* functions, dimensions, typological and functional characteristics, facilities to be provided, and potential synergies among public and private parties.
- It *recognizes* the potential functions that can be developed at the site by private developers, together with public entities or nongovernmental organizations, or independently through various arrangements and agreements.
- It *establishes* a framework to link the designer's hypotheses for the project and the urban area policies and infrastructure plans already adopted as well as existing community services and the transportation network.
- It *offers* a projection of an area in its urban context as it will be after the transformation has been completed (through images and narratives).
- It *illustrates* volumetric anticipations with graphic and cartographic representations to show the possible configurations of a given site. In these anticipations,

much attention is paid to public spaces, to the spaces "between" buildings, to specific functions, and to details about architectural and landscape materials.

- It *specifies* the "rules" for consequent architectural and landscape designs and for detailing the master plan. The more the client needs to control the transformation—or if the client, together with the designer, believes the meaning and the philosophy of the whole master plan can be altered by the design of single buildings and of specific open areas—the more exacting the rules will be. These rules can take the following topics into consideration:
    - buildings to be maintained, demolished, and transformed
    - height of buildings and distances between them
    - single and mixed functions, including complementariness
    - spatial roles and hierarchies
    - positioning and size of facilities
    - plant and material palettes for the outdoors
    - signage and street furniture standards
    - places and characteristics related to the larger city and broader regional contexts.

According to Urban Task Force (1999, 73):

The spatial masterplan is a synthesis of the design-led approach to urban development. . . . Unlike conventional two-dimensional zoning plans (which tend simply to define areas of use, density standards, and access arrangements), the "spatial" masterplan establishes a three-dimensional framework of buildings and public spaces. It is a more sophisticated visual "model" that:

- allows us to understand what the public spaces between the buildings will be like before they are built;
- shows how the streets, squares and open spaces of a neighbourhood are to be connected;
- defines the heights, massing and bulk of the buildings (but not the architectural style or detailed design);
- controls the relationship between buildings and public spaces . . . ;
- determines the distribution of uses, and whether these uses should be accessible at street level;
- controls the network of movement patterns for people moving on foot, cycle, car or public transport;

- identifies the location of street furniture, lighting and landscaping; and
- allows us to understand how well a new urban neighbourhood is integrated with the surrounding urban context and natural environment.

The conception of the master plan, as shown in the previous chapters, requires the involvement of a range of professionals, the client, commonly agency staff, and the public (as synthesized in Figure 7.1/Plate #24). The size and the competencies of the group of experts depends on the site's specificities, the resources available (money and time in the first place), and the capacity and sensibility of the urban designer to understand the place and the task given. The preparation of the master plan document might also need the expertise of graphic designers and other experts to better communicate its contents (see Chapter 8, Presentation).

In the United States, the term *master plan* is used in both general and comprehensive plans to define the tools to manage development and urban transformation with a strong emphasis on design. This is often referred to as *project planning*. City-scale master plan contents are usually clearly defined by state laws. For example, the first part of the General Laws of Massachusetts Administration of the Government, Title VII, Cities, Towns and Districts, Chapter 41, "Officers and Employees of Cities, Towns and Districts: Improved Method of Municipal Planning" (see http://www.mass.gov/legis/laws/mgl/41-81d.htm), describes the general contents of a master plan and how the plan applies to a "city or town or such part or parts thereof" (Part I, Title VII, Chapter 41, Section 81D). A master plan

> shall be a statement, through text, maps, illustrations or other forms of communication, that is designed to provide a basis for decision making regarding the long-term physical development of the municipality. The comprehensive plan shall be internally consistent in its policies, forecasts and standards, and shall include the following elements:
>
> 1. Goals and policies statement which identifies the goals and policies of the municipality for its future growth and development. Each community shall conduct an interactive public process, to determine community values, goals and to identify patterns of development that will be consistent with these goals.
> 2. Land use plan element which identifies present land use and designates the proposed distribution, location and inter-relationship of public and private land uses . . .
> 3. Housing element which identifies and analyzes existing and forecasted

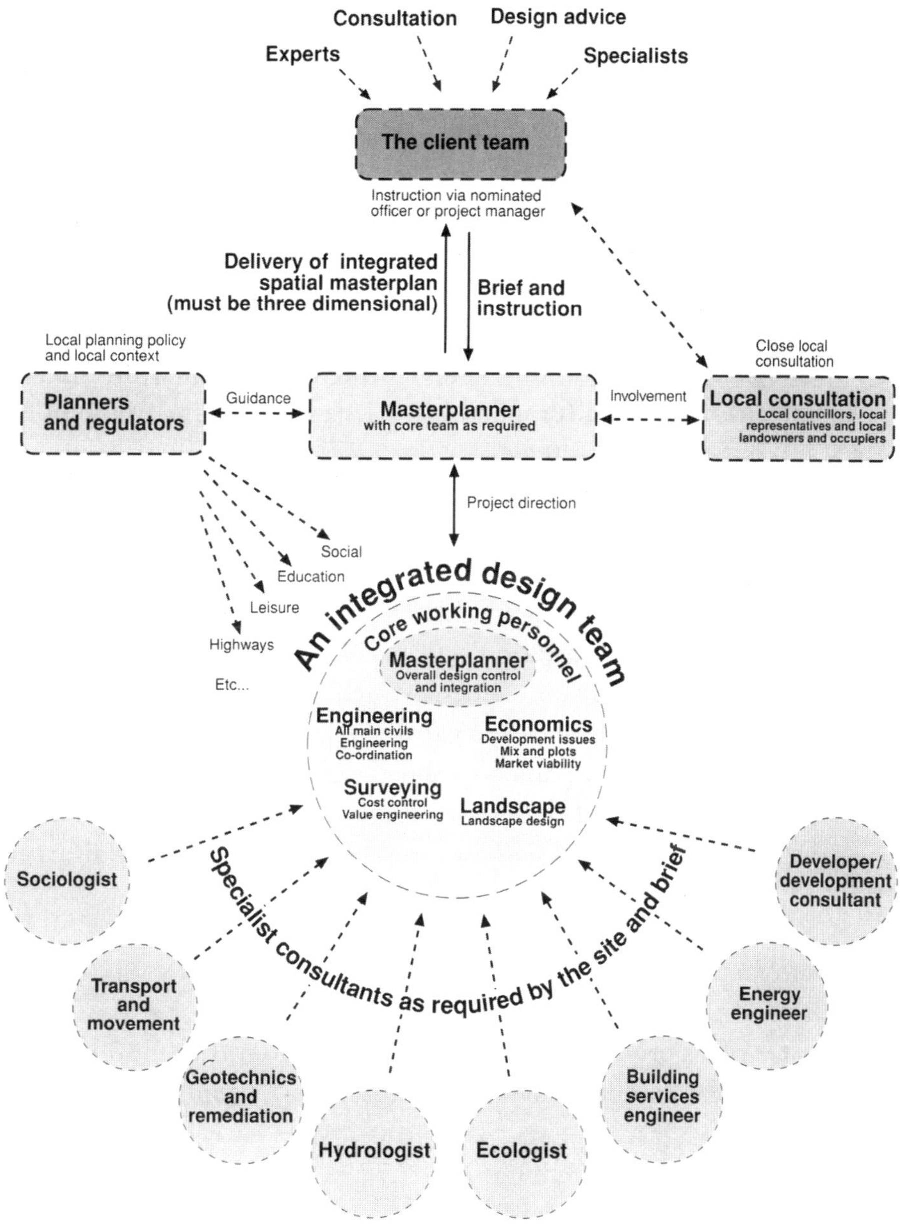

Figure 7.1 (also Plate #24) An integrated spatial master plan requires an integrated design team. (From Urban Task Force 1999, 76. Courtesy of Andrew Wright Associates.)

housing needs and objectives including programs for the preservation, improvement and development of housing.

4. Economic development element which identifies policies and strategies for the expansion or stabilization of the local economic base and the promotion of employment opportunities.
5. Natural and cultural resources element which provides an inventory of the significant natural, cultural and historic resource areas of the municipality and policies and strategies for the protection and management of such areas.
6. Open space and recreation element which provides an inventory of the significant natural, cultural and historic resource areas of the municipality and policies and strategies for the management and protection of such resources and areas.
7. Services and facilities which identifies and analyzes existing and forecasted needs for facilities and services used by the public.
8. Circulation element which provides an inventory of existing and proposed circulation and transportation systems.
9. Implementation program element which defines and schedules the specific municipal actions necessary to achieve the objectives of each element of the master or study plan. Scheduled expansion or replacement of public facilities or circulation system components and the anticipated costs and revenues associated with accomplishment of such activities shall be detailed in this element.

Through an analysis of master plan contents from the United States to Europe and Australia, some common elements emerge despite the disparities. Per a study of eleven master plans produced since 1995 in several countries for different development types, similar contents and common graphic vocabularies are employed.[4]

The Master Plan Contents

A final master plan generally consists of a report, generously enriched by images, maps, artist and computer simulations, diagrams, and other visual communica-

4 To review the eleven cases, see Bristol Airport 2006; City of Nottingham, 2001; HafenCity, Hamburg 1999; Ballymun Regeneration Limited 2004; Dublin Docklands Development Authority 2008; Palazzo 2002; Centre for Addiction and Mental Health 2001–2002; University of Cincinnati 1995/1999; Cesar Pelli & Associates and Balmori Associates 1999; University of South Florida Polytechnic 2009; Sydney Airport 2009.

tion tools (see Chapter 8, Presentation). In most cases, the master plan consists of a single document that combines text with images. A standard scale is usually chosen to simplify prints and reproductions. Other formats can be adopted, especially when the design team uses maps that are hard to read at a small size.

The master plan should be concise without forfeiting completeness. A wastefully laborious document, consisting mostly of written parts, may not be read by the intended audience. Prose and graphic presentations of a master plan must be accessible and easy to understand but should not gloss over complex or even controversial issues. The following elements are common to most master plans.

Executive Summary

An executive summary describes the highlights of the master plan in plain language.

Introduction

The introduction includes the reasons why the master plan was prepared, an overview of the process the designer employed in developing the urban design, deliberations of private and/or public entities that promoted the project, as well as the laws and regulations that led to its preparation. The introduction may also contain short descriptions of the plan's methodological aspects and the composition of the responsible team. The introduction sometimes provides a preview of the vision and the challenges that the urban design project is meant to address.

In some cases, the master plan begins with a short preface written by administrators or agency managers, who guarantee the contents and recognize their responsibilities in the document development and those of the organization they represent.

Purposes and Vision

The master plan can respond to various economic, cultural, and environmental goals. This section of the master plan should clearly describe the goals, the motivations, and the expectations and should include any demands coming from the client or any interested parties who have been directly involved during the design process, as well as recommendations included in official plans or obtained during meetings. The vision—a concise and strongly evocative account of the intentions of the plan—can be recorded here if the designer thinks it beneficial to mention analytical findings at this point.

General Background

In the background section, the site is first situated in its city and regional context. Then its dimensions, morphology, existing buildings, and environmental characteristics are described. The physical description can contain specialized data, such as information about climate, geology, terrain, water, soils, plants, and animals. To these data, characteristics of the property are added, which include historical and current uses; population and economic forecasts; the transportation network and parking; accessibility for cars, bikes, and walking; and green spaces. Urban planning information is frequently included, such as descriptions of policies, plans, and projects under discussion or realization by local governments or private developers that could interfere with or complement the master plan. The description need not be limited to the site area. Characteristics of the wider city and the regional context are also fundamental.

Surveys and Analyses

The master plan describes the survey and analysis outcomes for the project. Analytical results are explained and, if necessary, a synthesis of the outcomes is presented through one or more of the techniques available and appropriate (see Chapter 4, Synthesis). The plan authors specify which analyses have been executed directly and which have been drawn from other sources. For unusual surveys, it is necessary to explain outcomes in the same tone as the rest of the report and to attach the full analysis report in the appendices. Examples may include more thorough analyses of material and structural degradation of the buildings that compose the site; historical analysis that has used specialized archives; or technical, scientific surveys on, for example, acoustic pollution, road network performance, or quality of ground waters.

In general, surveys and analyses should aim to enrich the knowledge about a place relevant to the design and, in some cases, to evaluate possible consequences of the design proposals. A standardized system brings out those elements that are most useful for the master plan.

The Preferred Design

This section presents a detailed description of the project itself and the process that led to the final design, in particular the various steps from the synthesis of the analyses to goals and options chosen, their translation into a concept plan, results from dialogues with various parties, and the production of the final design (see Figures 7.2 and 7.3). Solutions or options considered at one time but discarded later can be mentioned here. The final design is structured into themes that can

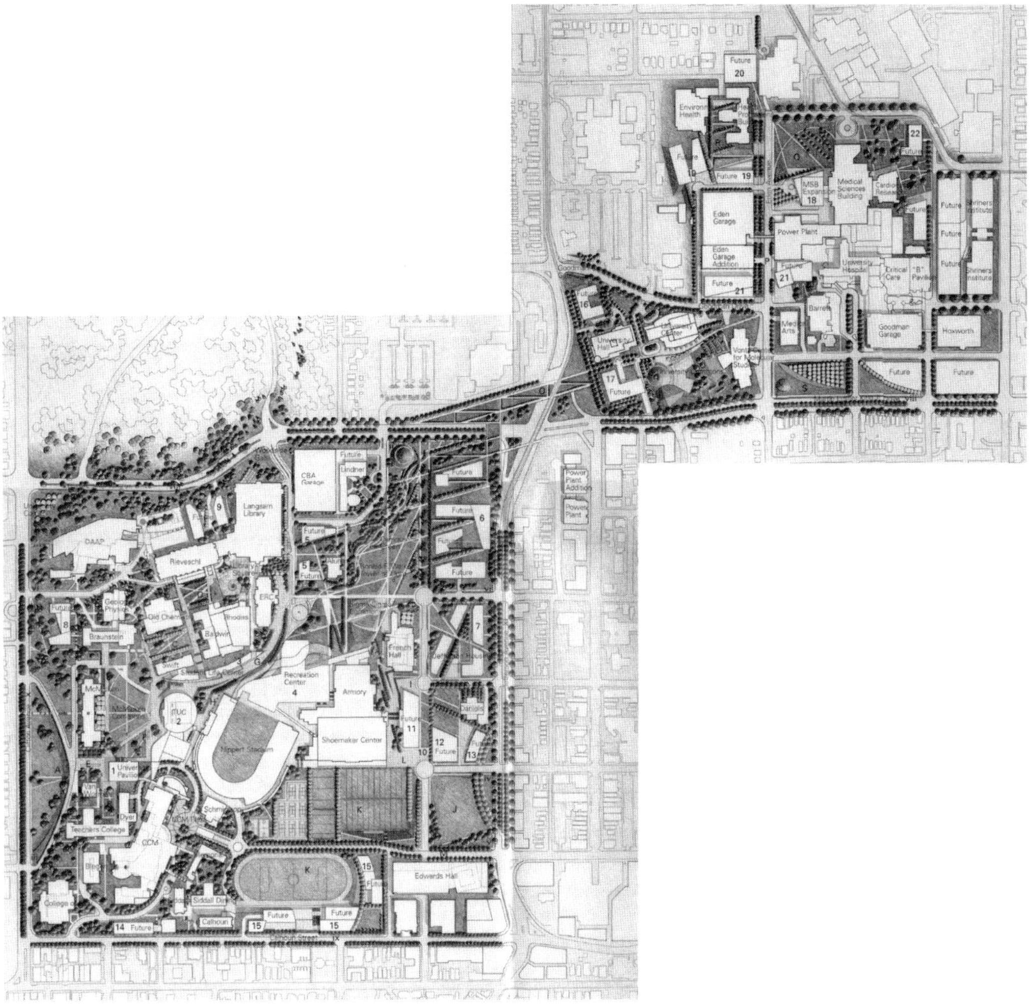

Figure 7.2 University of Cincinnati master plan by Hargreaves Associates, Landscape Architects, Planners, 2000. (Courtesy Hargreaves Associates, New York.)

vary according to the character of the project (transportation, green areas, public spaces, protection areas, buildings, and density) or in portions of the whole site. If the master plan is a long-term undertaking, the project may be split into phases and specific actions.

Cost and Implementation

A master plan can necessitate estimates of costs and revenues generated by the design. An estimate incorporates the values of areas, development costs, and potential gains. The master plan provides a budget summary with diagrams and tables.

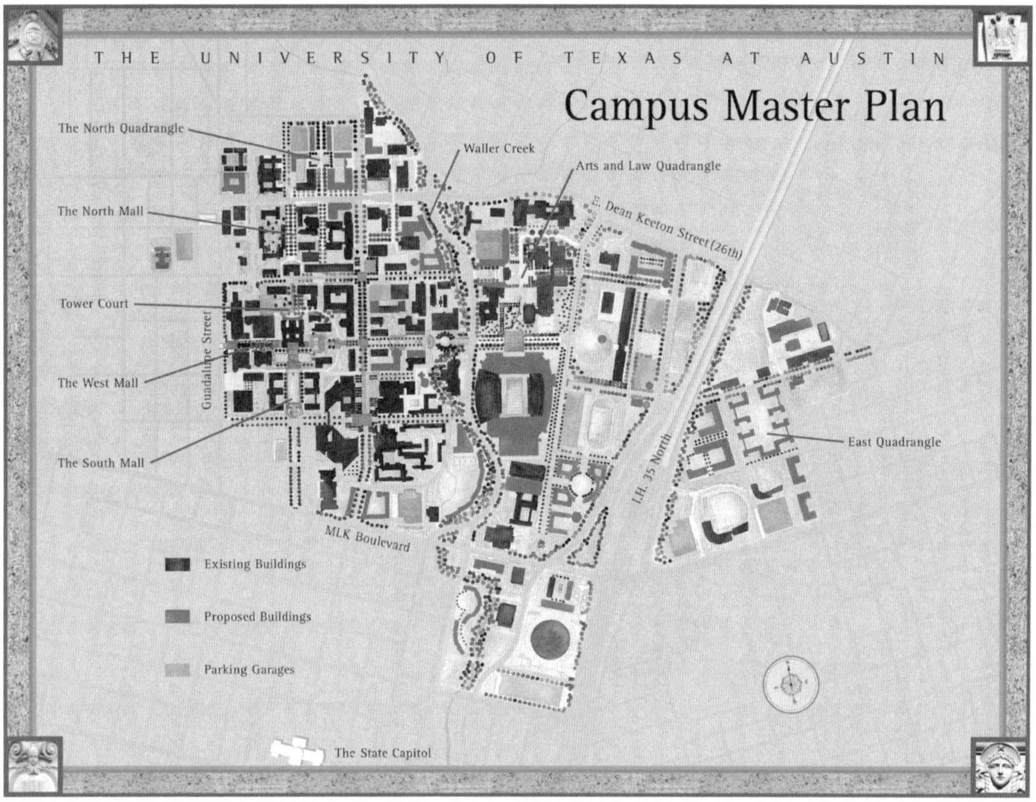

Figure 7.3 The University of Texas at Austin campus master plan by Cesar Pelli and Balmori Associates, 1999. (Courtesy Pelli Clarke Pelli Architects, New Haven, Connecticut.)

If the designer or the client deems it useful, an entire financial report can be attached. Potential sources of financing may be documented. Implementation steps include official agreements, approvals, certifications, and reviews essential for the master plan.

Other Sections

Some of the following specific sections can be added to complete the master plan, depending on the designer, the client, or the character of the commission.

Design Guidelines

These contain details related to green areas (plant specifics), street furniture for public spaces (benches and lighting systems), paving, and buildings (heights, widths, and distances). The purpose of design guidelines is to provide rules for detailed studies as well as for architecture and landscape architecture projects.

Master Plan Visualizations

These can be narrations, images, or physical models, using communication tools that stimulate both emotions and thought, with the aim to increase attention to the project (see Figures 7.4/Plate #25 and 7.5). A good narrative description of what the site will become, still or animated visual descriptions, or a scale model can accomplish more than a cold technical description (see Chapter 8, Presentation).

Building Typology Investigation

A building typology investigation may become necessary to demonstrate that buildings in the master plan can fulfill client requests. The master plan establishes the "rules" for design development, but it must also demonstrate how such rules can be applied.

Case Studies

Case studies provide precedents that can be exceptionally persuasive instruments. Comparable examples can aid not only the designer but also the client and the public. Case studies in a master plan should include location, realization period, area, functions and their percentages, methods of implementation, and project costs (see Box 4.2 in Chapter 4).

Appendices

Appendices typically include any of the following documents that were not included in the master plan:

- A list of design team members with their affiliations and qualifications
- Extended versions of documents prepared by the designer (or by other experts) during the process
- A complete account of all analyses
- A diary and/or minutes of all meetings
- Administrative documentation, such as deliberations, bills, budgets, or agreements
- Correspondence between the subjects relevant to the master plan (which can be published only with the approval of their senders and recipients)
- Rough drafts of any agreements between the involved parties

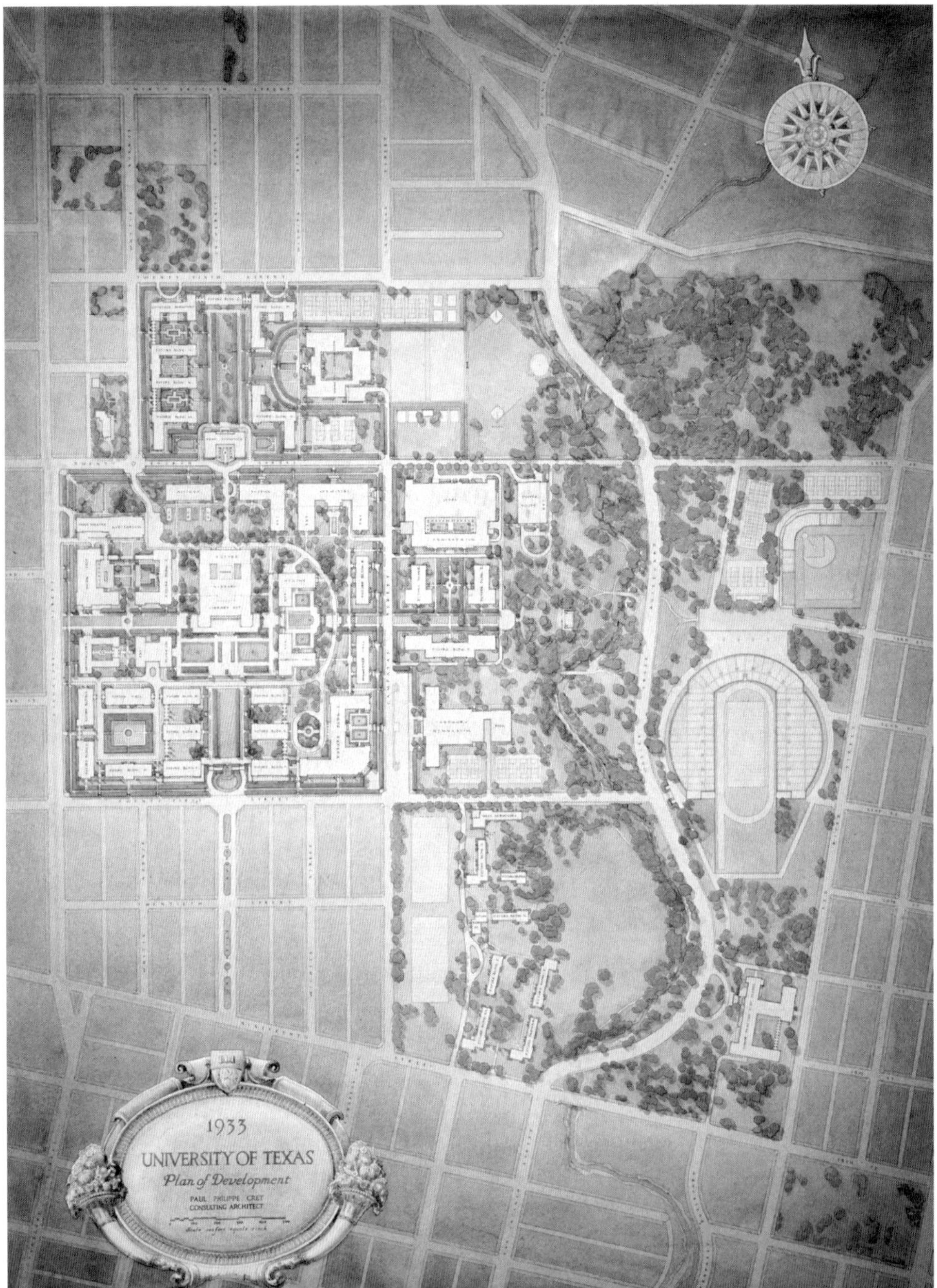

Figure 7.4 (also Plate #25) Paul Cret's plan of development for the University of Texas, 1933. (Courtesy Alexander Architectural Archive, University of Texas Libraries, the University of Texas at Austin.)

Figure 7.5 A visualization of the park area of the former abattoir of Monza. (Drawing by Elena Stevanato. From Palazzo 2002.)

- Full version of relevant laws and policies
- Reference citations

The entire document, appendices, and maps can be saved on CD-ROM or DVD and can be included with the report or be released separately. After the master plan is released, the designer can upload a copy of all the documents to a website for downloading.

Summary

In addition to recording the process and presenting the design, the master plan is a communication tool that indicates how the design will be realized. A master plan motivates everyone involved in the project to support its realization.

8 ■ Presentation

Designers communicate the final version of the urban design project to interested parties through presentations.

When asked about traditional urban design ideas at a conference on town center management, Sir Peter Hall, an English planning scholar, said that "the concept of urban design should not be taken in its old-fashioned sense—producing nice drawings to pin on the wall" (Madanipour 1996, 97). Urban design involves more than nice drawings; rather, it addresses significant urban challenges. However, how a design is presented can be as important as the project itself because, especially when it comes to graphic communication, the medium often, indeed, is the message. A good but poorly presented design may find itself losing ground to one that is mediocre but better presented. On the other hand, good presentation cannot offset a bad concept. Effective communication draws on the best material generated for the project through specific steps in the process.

When communicating an urban design project through a master plan, the designer must understand the differences that exist among verbal communication, PowerPoint or other computer-generated presentations, written reports, and posters. It is important to know which materials will be most effective and how to employ physical or virtual models and/or design simulations.

Such effectiveness is determined, in large part, by a clear idea of the audience for whom the message is intended. An understanding of the audience helps shape the language, the form, and the contents of the presentation. A project can be communicated to the public, to a private client, to a competition board, or to a committee composed of public officials. The designer needs to select appropriate methods of presentation tailored to the needs of each audience. Messages need to be adapted to the competencies of the audience and their expectations. It is useless, for example, to describe all the particulars of analysis and survey in a public meeting or, on the contrary, to avoid details and information during a presentation in front of a planning council. At this stage, it is also important to consider previous meetings that have occurred during the design process in order to be in harmony with these dialogues.

The three most frequently used media in urban design presentations are (1) summary reports; (2) verbal, PowerPoint, and video presentations; and (3) posters. Each has its own possibilities and limitations—for example, a report cannot replace a verbal presentation linked to a series of PowerPoint slides; a poster should take full advantage of the potential of its dimensions. A summary report is the design description presented through written text and images. The Internet can distribute a report to virtually anyone in the world, and anybody anywhere can print it and read it in its entirety or look at selected parts. Whatever the media, the design should be described in a precise, unambiguous, clear, and inclusive manner.

A PowerPoint presentation usually requires someone to describe the images. Without a narrator, the slides might be confusing. Instead of a live narrator, a PowerPoint presentation might include music or recorded comments.

Posters communicate without commentators, similar to reports in their static nature and unlike the dynamic quality of a slide presentation. Posters have the advantage of strong communication through large-format images. They can be commented on and explained during a presentation, but their nature is essentially to summarize a project using images and small amounts of text. Posters are common in urban design competitions with a specific number of posters to be included—for example, a plan view of the project on-site; images of the entire project (renderings, photomontages, photographs of models, perspectives, or drawings); concept description; and any drawings and diagrams that explain the project further.

Summary Report

Master plans, as noted in Chapter 7, consist of common elements. A summary report may be adapted from the larger master plan report for presentation purposes. The summary may have many or some of the same sections of the master plan, including the following (adapted from Carter 2007, 11) :

- *Executive Summary*. The summary should present the design's "strong ideas," methods, and outcomes in a few pages.
- *Strategy, Process, and Method*. The designer needs to describe the starting point, the process, and the method used during the process.
- *Existing Conditions*. This part of the report documents the relevant ecological, social, and economic characteristics.
- *Analysis*. The outcomes of original surveys and the results of analyses, reviews, and related syntheses of existing conditions are displayed through diagrams, maps, drawings, and other media.
- *Goals and Objectives*. Project goals depend on the method adopted during the design process (for instance, participatory, up-down, or exploratory). If the process is limited to interactions between the client and the designer, goals focus on specific demands. If the process is more open, the original client demands could be broadened by issues that emerged from formal or informal meetings.
- *Preferred Design*. The design presents two-dimensional drawings and three-dimensional visions of the final project and is accompanied by a project description and, depending on the situation, by a development program that clarifies phasing, forms of implementation, participants involved, and timetables.
- *Design Guidelines*. Urban design projects can include suggestions about design details, alternative proposals, architectural styles, open space treatments, and energy-saving measures.

In general, a summary report should be written clearly and concisely. A report can contain or be written as a narration of daily life at the site after project implementation. Describing the future can also help the public to imagine the project through words that can support visual representation.

Sometimes, it is essential to produce such a report. In competitions, the report has a defined dimension, often quite short. For example, in the competition for the Vatnsmýri area, Reykjavík, Iceland (see Chapter 6, Dialogues), the rules required three tables in the A1 format (23.4 by 33.1 inches, or 594 by 841 millimeters), accompanied by a report of no more than one thousand words. Under less rigid circumstances, a report, especially if addressed to a wide audience, can allow more images and, consequently, reduce written parts without forgoing certain basic principles:

- The person writing it must know the target audience.
- The ideas need to be clearly organized.

- The report should be subdivided into chapters, paragraphs, and subparts.
- An index should be included with corresponding page numbers and an abstract.
- Parts adapted from secondary sources need to be distinguished from original work.
- Information should be synthesized in diagrams with clear interpretations.
- Extensive literature exists about how to write for various audiences (e.g., Alley 1996; Sides 1999; Strunk and White 1999; Gustavii 2003; Davis 2005; and Day and Gastel 2006).

Riverside, Illinois

In 1868, Frederick Law Olmsted Sr. and Calvert Vaux presented a preliminary report to the Riverside Improvement Company (see Figure 8.1) on what was to become Riverside, Illinois, an early example of a suburb where natural features became an integral and essential part of everyday life (see Figure 8.2/Plate #26). To this day, Riverside remains a good example of how a suburban new community can be designed.

The preliminary report by Olmsted and Vaux is an excellent example of data synthesis. The report clearly displays how environmental knowledge becomes the means for designing an extraordinary place. Following are excerpts from the original report (Olmsted and Vaux 1868):

> Gentlemen: You have requested a report from us, upon an enterprise which you desire to bring before the public, and which appears to rest on the following grounds:
>
> First. Owing partly to the low, flat, miry, and forlorn character of the greater part of the country immediately about Chicago, . . . the city, as yet, has no true suburbs or quarters in which urban and rural advantages are agreeably combined with any prospect of long continuance. . . .
>
> Second . . . under these circumstances, sites offering any very decided and permanent advantages for suburban residences . . .
>
> Third. You have secured a large body of land, which, much beyond any other, has natural advantages for this purpose.
>
> Fourth. . . . By a large outlay, these advantages could be developed to the utmost, and could be supplemented by abundant artificial conveniences. . . .
>
> We propose to review these grounds so far as they are not matters of fact easily put to the test of observation by those interested. . . .

Figure 8.1 The Riverside Improvement Company. (Courtesy Frederick Law Olmsted Society of Riverside, http://www.olmstedsociety.org/resources/maps-of-riverside.)

We proceed to consider the intrinsic value of your property for the purpose in view. The question of access first demands attention. . . . There is a double-track railroad from Chicago of remarkably good construction, with its first out-of-town station, at which every train is required to stop in the midst of your property. . . . Turning next to your present property, we find that it extends for a distance of two miles [3.22 kilometers] upon the banks of the Aux Plaines River. Upon the river side, the land has a somewhat higher elevation than at any point nearer Chicago. . . . We were informed that there were deep beds of clay upon the property; but wherever we happened to test the subsoil, as we did at several points, we found a porous stratum at no very great distance from the surface. . . .

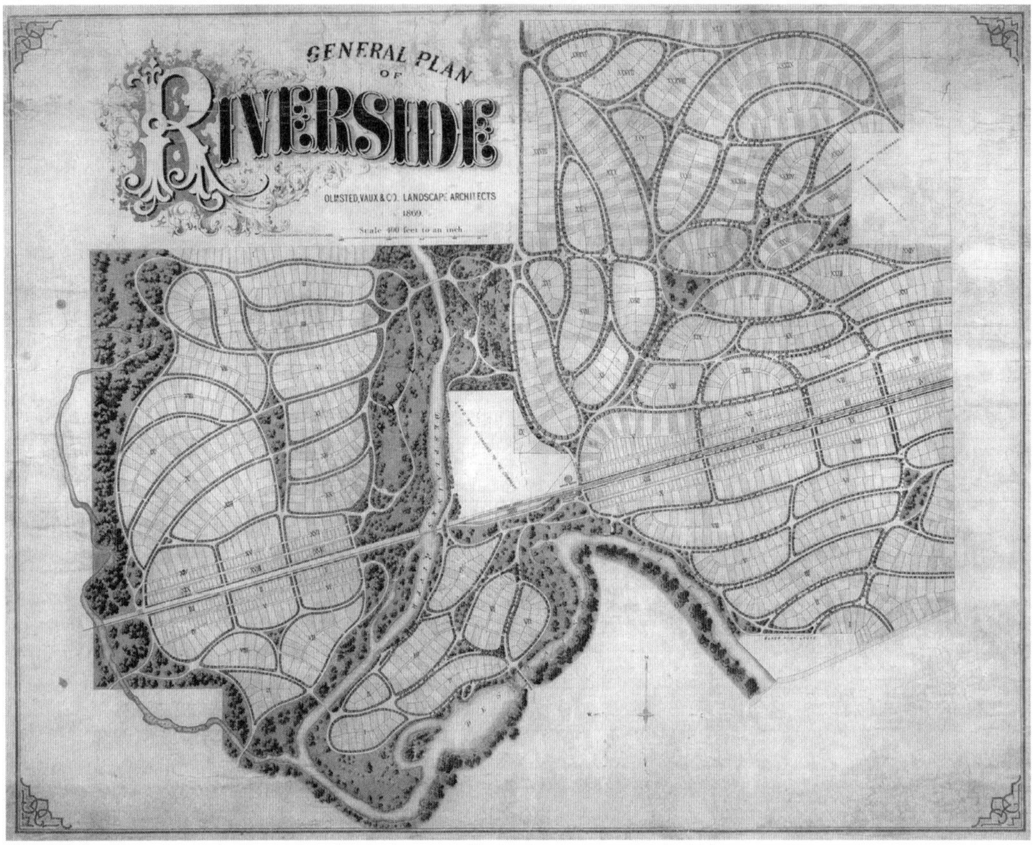

Figure 8.2 (also Plate #26) General plan of Riverside, Illinois, by Olmsted, Vaux & Co. Landscape Architects, 1869. (Courtesy Frederick Law Olmsted Society of Riverside, http://www.olmstedsociety.org/resources/riverside-history.)

> The more elevated parts of the ground, and the banks of the river everywhere, are occupied by groves of trees. . . .
>
> The water of the river is said to be ordinarily very clear. . . . It abounds with fish and wild fowl, is adapted to pleasure boating, and can be improved in this respect. . . .

Olmsted and Vaux provided a site description with brief, but essential, information about natural features, such as water, subsoil, trees, and physical geography, as well as Riverside's accessibility to nearby Chicago. They then defined some draft design ideas about building masses, distances from roads, tree plantations, landscape improvements, and public provisions.

> We cannot judiciously attempt to control the form of the houses which men shall build, we can only, at most, take care that if they build very ugly and inappropriate houses, they shall not be allowed to force them disagreeably upon our attention when we desire to pass along the road upon which they stand. We can require that no house shall be built within a certain number of feet of the highway, and we can insist that each house-holder shall maintain one or two living trees between his house and his highway-line.
>
> A few simple precautions of this kind, added to a tasteful and convenient disposition of shade trees, and other planting along the road-sides and public places, will, in a few years, cause the whole locality, no matter how far the plan may be extended. . . . If the general plan of such a suburb is properly designed on the principles which have been suggested, its character will inevitably also, notwithstanding its tidiness, be not only informal, but, in a moderate way, positively picturesque. (Olmsted and Vaux 1868, selected from 4 to 29)

The positive results of the Olmsted and Vaux vision continue to the present (see Figure 8.3). Riverside is a pleasant, leafy community with a diversity of housing types and a short commute by train to downtown Chicago.

Verbal, PowerPoint, and Video Presentations

During the dialogue and presentation steps, PowerPoint slide shows are the most widely used tools in urban, landscape, and building design. A presentation is a succession of images containing text, diagrams, animations, videos, and multimedia elements, put together for projection on a wide screen. The use of slide presentations grew rapidly, when ordinary software packages began replacing film-based transparency slides. Microsoft's PowerPoint and Apple's Keynote have become standards. According to *BBC News Magazine* (August 19, 2009), after the first twenty-five years of PowerPoint, there are 500 million users worldwide and 30 million presentations each day.

Some of the main reasons slide presentations are so widespread follow:

- They are easily produced by almost anyone with simple design training.
- The interface potential is strong, with media available in digital format (movies, digital photography, sounds, texts, tables, and renderings).
- Raster and scanned images can be imported easily.
- Images and slides can be modified in real time.
- They can be transmitted quickly through e-mail or uploaded to a website.

Figure 8.3 Riverside, Illinois, 2004. (Photograph by Danilo Palazzo.)

Unfortunately, the wide diffusion of the tool does not correspond to an equally wide familiarity with the communication mechanisms relating to this medium. The leading authority on visual communication, Edward Tufte (2003, 5), is an especially strong critic of PowerPoint, arguing, for instance, that "bullet outlines dilute thought." He observes further that "presentations largely stand or fall depending on the quality, relevance, and integrity of the content. The way to make big improvements in a presentation is to get better content . . . [and that the design formats provided in PowerPoint] will not salvage weak content" (22). It is not rare to see presentations with obvious shortcomings, such as the following:

- Excessive use of text animations and transition effects between slides ("Audiences rarely complain about too little embellishment, but are easily distracted and offended by too much. When in doubt, increase the quality and density of the content and reduce the level of decoration. The emphasis should be more matter with less art" [Gaskins 2007, 17])

- Inappropriate colors, especially regarding contrast between the background and text (pale gray on dark gray, or yellow characters on red background, or worse, the reverse)
- Too small or too large text (the first challenges the reader's eyes; the second can limit the information conveyed)
- Too many type styles and sizes (this can pose readability problems)
- Too much text on the slide (a presentation is not a report, and readers cannot absorb long text, listen to the presenter, and take notes at the same time)
- Messages overwhelmed by graphics (especially if they are the ready-to-use good-for-anytime vignettes)
- Poor and/or standardized graphic design (such as gray sandy backgrounds with black Times New Roman type)
- Presenters reading slide text (this can be boring)
- Long sequences of slides without verbal comments (the audience can lose interest)
- The use of a slide presentation hard copy to substitute as the report (again, a presentation is not a report; if it is delivered before the presentation, the audience will be less interested by the "live performance")

Craig and Amernic (2006) distinguish different types of literature about PowerPoint, arguably the most powerful and ubiquitous communications technology for presentations. The first type provides technical advice on how to prepare presentations (Jones 2003; Shwom and Keller 2003). The second type outlines the advantages and disadvantages of the tool. Much PowerPoint research information is accessible through keyword search using Google, although some work appears in scholarly journals, such as Jones (2003).

Some of the advice can be summarized as follows:

- Declare the contents of the presentation in the first slides.
- Use graphic and written elements that work as navigators (e.g., a clear title that summarizes the page content; a histogram or a marker to point out, on each slide, which point of the presentation the audience is watching; and an index constantly visible in a portion of the slide with the title of the part under presentation highlighted and the number of the current slide followed by the total number of slides).
- Devote each slide to a single topic.
- Do not use a report page as a slide.

- Keep the presentation within the required time length (if there is one).
- Use diagrams to translate concepts through images.
- Present a project history. Different narrative strategies can be adapted depending on the audience and the purpose of the presentation (e.g., a linear presentation that starts with the contract and progresses through the specific steps until a master plan is prepared and implemented). Or, the presentation can be organized starting with the final project and going back and forth to explain the basis for design choices and the process adopted to reach the result.
- Treat the slide presentation as a speech outline and a tool for the audience to understand what is being said.
- Summarize figures and facts.
- Do not fill up the slide with text: conventional wisdom is to use no more than six lines.
- Do not use more than two different fonts, one for titles and one for text.
- Do not use too many type sizes. Select them carefully—every word must be legible even from the back of a crowded room.
- Before the presentation, test the projection to check font sizes, readability from a distance, and visual effects, as well as how the projector works and whether it is, indeed, working.

Good speaking abilities also enhance a presentation. Craig and Amernic (2006, 151) explain that "whether a PowerPoint presenter is the centre of attention or more of a stagehand will be a function of the communication ability of the presenter. Good presenters will most likely still be the centre of attention, using PowerPoint appropriately as a valuable communication aid to buttress their rhetoric. Poor presenters, such as nervous freshman students making their first assessable class presentation, will most likely be stagehands, with PowerPoint used as a dominating prop and their visual presence barely discernible."

In slide presentations and in verbal communications references to others, completed projects are often considered. Such projects, which also can be included in posters and reports, should have common elements with the design being presented. The purpose of including these images is to stimulate emotions in the audience or in readers to help people imagine themselves and their relatives and friends in the future in a setting similar to the finished project. When selecting images, it is necessary to adopt principles of respect, balance, and caution. An excessive or unbalanced use of reference images should be avoided. It is always important to credit the author of the project and the source of the image used.

Use evocative images of built architecture and public spaces, such as children playing, people biking or engaging in sports, and retired academics resting in the shade of a tree on a park bench. Our personal preference is to avoid images of children flying kites, which have been so overused that they fail to be evocative.

A typical representation tends to answer questions—for example, What will this area be like after the development? What will be the differences compared to now? One of the more popular representation techniques that can be employed in a slide presentation to a large public, especially in urban regeneration projects and when the design is applied to already utilized sites, is the *before and after* representation. Examples are presented by Peter Calthorpe and William Fulton in *The Next Metropolis* (2001).

The Dutch design firm West 8 used aerial photographs to illustrate changes for the Puente del Rey in Madrid. A 2004 photograph was used to illustrate the existing conditions of the river corridor (see Figure 8.4/Plate #27). A vision of how the corridor would look in 2008 after the design had been implemented was then used to illustrate the changes (see Figure 8.5/Plate #28). Likewise, the American firm STOSS LU used similar before (see Figure 8.6) and after (see Figure 8.7) aerials to illustrate their design for the Fox Riverfront in Green Bay, Wisconsin. These representations can use several techniques: digitally constructed photos, real photos with overlapped images, sketches, and digitally constructed aerial maps.

During the presentation session, it can help to display physical models. In contrast to rapid models used in other steps of the process, physical models for the communication phase are more defined and precise. Models can be costly, depending on the materials used. However, the effects are valuable and commonly result in immediate interest from the public. For example, Chinese designers use large-scale models of their cities most effectively to show how future urban spaces will look, as, for example, at the Beijing Planning Exhibition Hall and the Shanghai Urban Planning Exhibition Hall (see Figure 8.8/Plate #29).

Videos are becoming increasingly popular in urban design, for several reasons:

- The ease of producing a video by a design team at a moderate price
- The diffusion of digital video cameras to collect interviews on the design matters for users, stakeholders, clients, and public officials; to describe through images the actual state of the site, or to document similar projects
- The opportunity to post a video on Internet sites that everyone can access

Figure 8.4 (also Plate #27) Madrid Rio existing conditions, 2004. (Courtesy Area de Gobierno de Urbanismo y Vivienda del Ayuntamiento de Madrid.)

Narrated video presentations might be used instead of, or in parallel with, verbal communication. During its recent bid for the 2016 Olympic Games, Chicago presented a video (http://www.chicago2016.org/videos.html) with a dynamic view of the city and the master plan for proposed new venues. Madrid has produced a similar video for its proposal for the 2020 Olympic Games (http://www.youtube.com/watch?v=BhBTec7IrUU&feature=related).

Presentations of Ground Zero Proposals

The Lower Manhattan Development Corporation (LMDC) was established in autumn 2001 by the governor of New York to oversee reconstruction of the former World Trade Center area (see also Chapter 5, Options). A fiasco ensued in July 2002 after a set of preliminary suggestions emerged for the site that were considered dull and unexciting by the public. As a result, the LMDC issued, in mid-August 2002, a call open to architects from around the world. A total of 406 teams responded (involving approximately 900 architects).

Figure 8.5 (also Plate #28) Madrid Rio proposed design, 2008. The project of Madrid Rio was designed by a team led by Ginés Garrido. The team consists of MRIO Arquitectos and West 8 Urban Design and Landscape Architecture. MRIO Arquitectos is a joint venture of three offices from Madrid: Burgos & Garrido Arquitectos, Porras + La Casta Arquitectos, and Rubio-Álvarez Sala Arquitectos. (Courtesy Area de Gobierno de Urbanismo y Vivienda del Ayuntamiento de Madrid.)

LMDC spent several weeks reviewing the submissions and finally reached a short list of seven. These seven groups, consisting of many significant architects and urban designers, were invited to present their proposals for Ground Zero in December 2002 at the Winter Garden in New York City. Each team had twenty minutes to present its project. Paul Goldberger (2004) described the different presentation styles.

According to Goldberger (2004), Daniel Libeskind "did not talk about square footage or economics, and he barely used an architectural term in his presentation. He talked about commemoration, memory, mourning, and renewal, and he did it with the zeal of a preacher. 'Life victorious,' were his final words, to sustained applause" (9). Norman Foster followed with a different style: "Instead of earnest appeal to the emotions, Foster delivered crisp, self-assured professionalism . . . , unlike Libeskind, he spoke without notes" (9). Richard Meier presented his group's project starting with a joke: "We're the New York team—some say we're the dream team" (11), but he seemed unsure of himself compared to Foster and Libeskind.

Figure 8.6 Existing conditions, Fox Riverfront, Green Bay, Wisconsin. On the east (downtown) side of the river, adjacent parcels were empty, abandoned, or in use as parking lots. Nearby buildings turned their back on the riverfront. Unsurprisingly, there was little social or civic life here, and no reason to visit; the elevated walk along existing bulkhead walls prevented any direct access down to the river—as well as up to the city from boats. Access from the west side, also ecologically degraded, was no better. (Photograph by Mike Roemer, RoemerPhoto.com. Courtesy StossLU.)

Rafael Viñoly was permitted to present three different schemes, and "he was so concerned that his three designs not be confused with one another that he spent most of his time trying to present them separately instead of pointing out that all three expressed a similar underlying idea. . . . Viñoly's presentation seemed somewhat rushed and almost disheveled" (12–13). Greg Lynn presented the design of United Architects. His presentation turned out "to be clear, straightforward, and organized, and he managed, more than any of the others, to strike a balance between talking about general emotional issues surrounding Ground Zero and describing the specifics of his group's project in a way that made sense to an audience of nonarchitects" (14). Steven Peterson gave a plain presentation, but "the

Figure 8.7 Fox Riverfront, Green Bay, Wisconsin. The project reimagines the riverfront as the new center of civic life—Green Bay's new front porch on the river. On the city side, the linear corridor is rendered as a series of discrete activity spaces oriented to the river and designed to encourage connections from the city to the river and vice versa. On the opposite side, the focus is on softening the edge between water and land; new wetlands, stormwater processing terraces, and river access points improve the ecological health and social function of the site. (Courtesy StossLU.)

architecture . . . seemed tame by comparison to everything else. Peterson and Littenberg seemed to be offering Brooks Brothers when all the other architects came selling Prada" (16). Last was the SOM presentation made by Roger Duffy, whose "presentation ended the day on a relatively quiet note" (17).

Posters

The poster has become an increasingly popular form of communication of the urban design project. Academic and professional conferences and seminars often include poster sessions where researchers can display the outcomes of their studies. Urban design, landscape architecture, and architecture competitions commonly

Figure 8.8 (also Plate #29) Model in the Shanghai Urban Planning Exposition Hall. (Photograph by Kathryn Chang.)

require that projects are presented on one or more posters with specific dimensions. Design and planning students' intermediate and final assessable presentations are often in poster format.

The character and style of a poster will vary. The same topic can be organized and displayed differently depending on the audience. A few principles should be considered:

- Make a scale drawing of the poster layout, and solicit comments on its overall design.
- Develop a hierarchy of information for the poster, and give the most important information the most visibility.
- Display information clearly (Where does the design story start? What is its focus and its center of interest? What is the main message?).
- Do not fill the poster with too much information. Components should support the design idea, and open spaces between informational items help highlight the proposal (all extraneous material should be eliminated).
- Make the poster legible from ten to thirteen feet (three to four meters) away.

- Make all lettering legible from six to seven feet (two meters) away.
- Highlight specific information and elements with formatting and size variations.
- Consider contrasts between background and text colors.
- Use a scale for the design that best fits on the poster, the ideal one for making pertinent details clearly evident, unless the scale is predetermined.
- Be brief and succinct. "Studies show that you have only 11 seconds to grab and retain your audience's attention so make the punch line prominent and brief. Most of your audience is going to absorb only the punch line" (Mandoli 2007).
- Use posters created by others for inspiration (see Figures 8.9/Plate #30 and 8.10/Plate #31).

Choosing What to Present

At the conclusion of an urban design process, prior to preparing a summary report, a PowerPoint presentation, and/or a poster, the designer needs to identify the appropriate materials and media. The products prepared for the project will depend on different factors, such as the time spent on the process, the number of people involved, and the complexity of the task. The material prepared can frequently reach seemingly unmanageable proportions, even at the end of a workshop. Materials can be in different formats: text or spreadsheet files, notes, hand-drawn sketches, images, computer- or hand-drawn maps, physical models, notes, intermediate slide shows, paper documents, documents downloaded from the Internet, and website links.

A recursive process, which may involve all the team members, can be used to select what to include in a presentation. Materials selection can use a modified *triage* technique. Originally used in battlefield situations, triage is a medical strategy applied at the scene of a mass casualty incident to rank order patients who need immediate transport to a hospital to save their lives, those who can wait longer for help, and those who are beyond hope for recovery. Patients are divided according to injury severity using color codes:

- Green: minor (minor injuries)
- Yellow: delayed (non-life-threatening injuries)
- Red: immediate (life-threatening injuries)
- Black: deceased (no care needed)

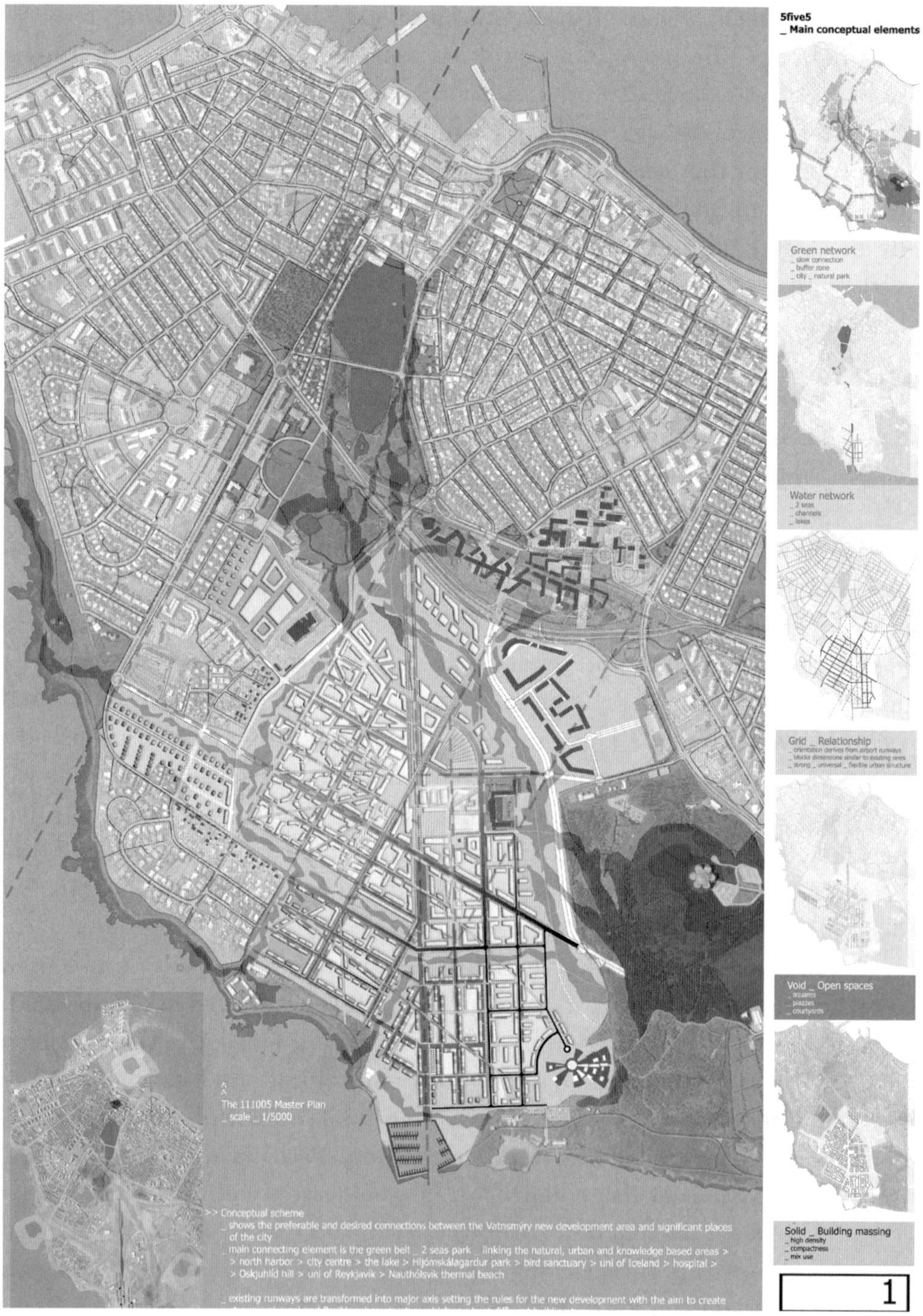

Figure 8.9 (also Plate #30) A poster for the Vatnsmýri, Reykjavík, competition. (By Team 111005: Massimo Tadi, Danilo Palazzo, Petr Janoš, Andrew Winkler, and Emre Kishali.)

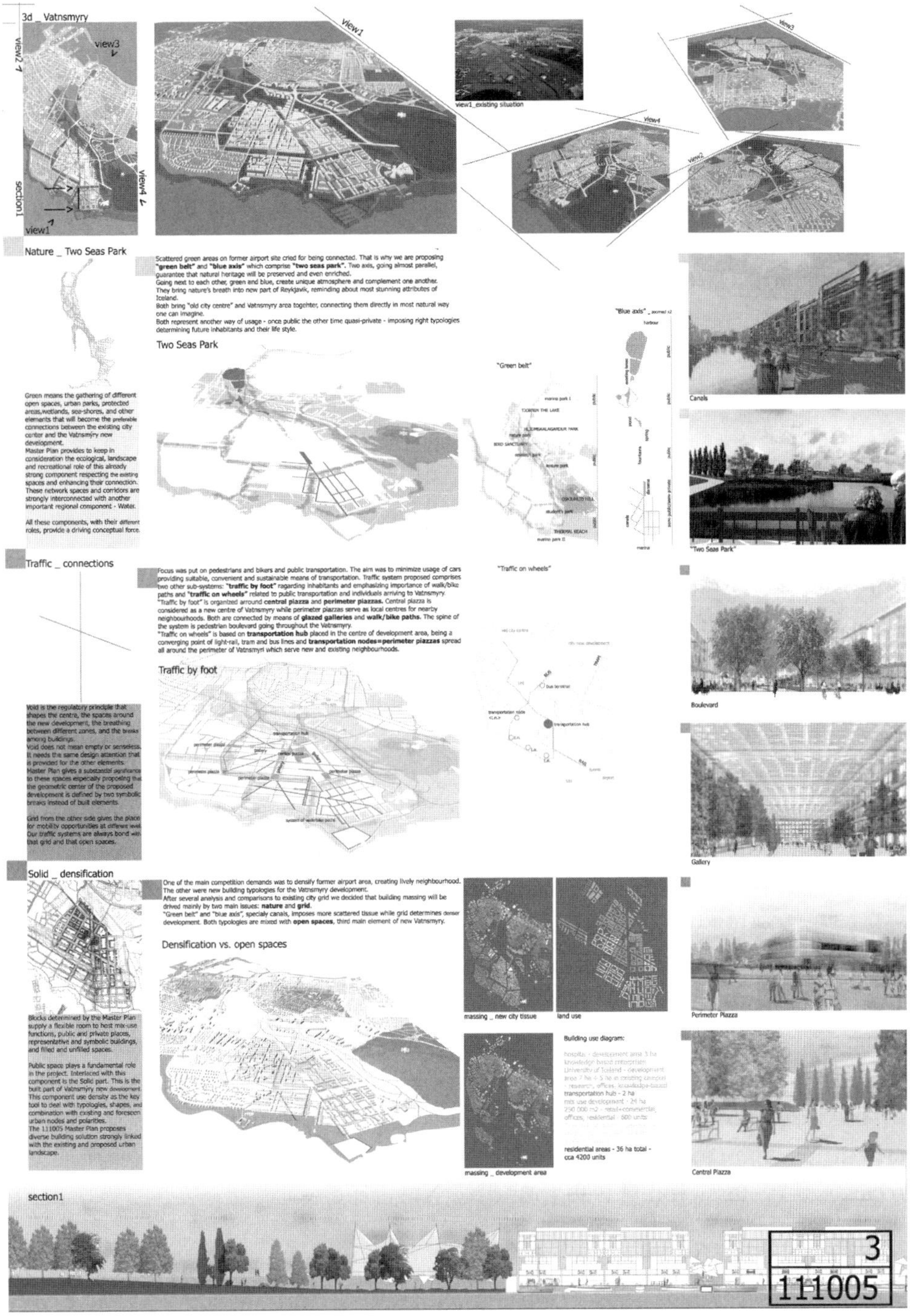

Figure 8.10 (also Plate #31) A poster for the Vatnsmýri, Reykjavík, competition. (By Team 111005: Massimo Tadi, Danilo Palazzo, Petr Janoš, Andrew Winkler, and Emre Kishali.)

In the design process, triage can help in selecting materials for presentation. Colored tags can be applied to hand- or computer-generated drawings or printed matter. For instance, the following subdivisions can be used to differentiate the material:

- Black (B) could represent material that will definitely not be included in the final presentation.
- Red (R) could represent material that will definitely be included in the final presentation.
- Yellow (Y) and green (G) could define two intermediate levels of importance for what materials to include.

If a material is still included after selections are made by all team members, it becomes part of the final presentation.

Choosing a Method of Presentation

Posters, for their dimensions, are the most appropriate support for images that can be produced with particular computer software or by artists. Both types of simulation can be used in different media, such as slide presentation or reports.

Three-dimensional computer-graphic programs are popular among urban designers, architects, and landscape architects. Computer simulations are especially useful in revealing ecological relationships. Until relatively recently, only specialized laboratories, a few research centers, and a limited number of private design firms could afford the specialized hardware and software that is now accessible on a much wider scale. Applications of common CAD and virtual imaging programs are often freeware—that is, downloadable legally from the Internet and free of charge. Most desktop and laptop computers can produce short animation videos.

Widespread use of such programs has some negative effects, however. First, in some cases, computer simulation is considered the real project and not, as it should be, its simulacrum. Second, excessive use of short videos can produce, in a skilled audience, a suspicion that the simulations hide design inconsistencies. In some cases, this suspicion is well founded. Nevertheless,

> the graphical language of urban design has an important role to play in promoting urban quality; creating visions which inspire and motivate; engaging communities and others involved in planning and development; and presenting information objectively and honestly for assessment purposes.

> The technology now available provides designers and producers of graphic images with enormous choice. The graphic vocabulary continues to evolve. This brings exciting opportunities and challenges in choosing the right mix of techniques combining computer-generated images, hand drawn plans and sketches and photography in new ways. (Meeda, Parkyn, and Walton 2006, 2–3).

Artistic simulations are used less frequently because of the ability required, not because they are less effective than computer simulations. Professional illustrators are often commissioned to produce, under the guidance of designers, persuasive images to include. A remarkable historical example is that of Mariemont, a residential new town outside of Cincinnati, Ohio, designed by John Nolen in the 1920s (Rogers 2001). Considered one of the fathers of American city planning and landscape architecture, Nolen, with Charles Livingwood and with illustrations by Andrew Avinoff, produced an advertising brochure entitled "A Descriptive and Pictured Story of Mariemont—A New Town" in 1925 (see Figures 8.11 and 8.12).

> The brochure, filled with black-and-white illustrations, was to be distributed free of charge to interested parties. . . . When published eventually in 1925, the sixty-four-page brochure was a guidebook rich in illustrations, both photographic and rendered by architects, as well as an account of the village's prehistory, twelve reasons for living in Mariemont, Nolen's philosophy of town planning, Livingwood's detailed overview of the new town's advantages, and charts and statistical lists. (Rogers 2001, 115)

In urban design communications, some elements are commonly used to confirm the design hypothesis and as "persuasive supports." The latter are used during dialogue sessions and to present with other professionals and the involved public.

Summary

The success or failure of an urban design project often rests on how it is presented. The art of communication involves transferring information, thoughts, and opinions from one party to another. Urban designers commonly use techniques to convey information about their plans through verbal, written, and visual communication. As the master plan is clarified through this presentation, the urban designer also must go into greater detail to elaborate and help realize specific aspects of the plan.

Figure 8.11 The primary promotional brochure for Mariemont, Ohio, was published in 1925 by Charles Livingood and John Nolen, with the cover illustration by Andrew Avinoff. (From Rogers 2001, 116. Courtesy Millard F. Rogers, Jr.)

Figure 8.12 This drawing was made in 1922 by John Nolen to illustrate Charles Livingood's ideas for buildings to be erected in Mariemont, Ohio. (From Rogers 2001, 36. Courtesy John Nolen Papers, Carl A. Kroch Library, Cornell University.)

9 Details

A detailed design study is often needed to elaborate on and define the master plan. Reasons for detailed studies include if a client requests further exploration; a regulatory agency wants to assess the plan in more detail; a feasibility analysis is necessary; more specificity is needed to carefully guide the design of elements within a plan, such as buildings and open spaces; or the economic viability of the plan must be determined. Although a detailed design might follow quickly after the master plan, at other times the request to detail the project can occur months—or sometimes years—after the presentation and delivery of the master plan.

One common situation relates to buildings. The master plan presents the volumetric prefiguration of city spaces, with which the urban designer guides other architects and landscape architects to detail the components of future architecture, mobility infrastructure, and public spaces. Buildings in a master plan are often designed as simple volumes, without architectural details aside from height requirements, number of floors, or building orientation. A detailed study can be requested to assess feasibility, to investigate possible typologies, and to estimate the quantitative performance of buildings.

Master plan details may require contributions from experts in fields beyond those involved in earlier stages of the urban design process. Issues regarding mobility infrastructure, community services, landscape architecture, public or green spaces, natural areas protection or recovery, energy, economic feasibility, funding development partnerships, and plan management may require that specialists be consulted.

Economic Assessments

If the design is produced for a private developer, the client will certainly want to know what costs and profits are projected. The urban designer will work with a real estate specialist to prepare a *pro forma,* a financial assessment that models the anticipated results of the urban design project. A government client may also require a pro forma to determine project costs and projected new tax revenues.

These economic analyses do the following:

- Bring about a better allocation of resources, leading to enhanced returns from the investment
- Ascertain the feasibility of investment projects
- Assess the viability of a project beforehand

Economic feasibility depends on the sustainability of the project's effects, which are assessed to ensure the following:

- The project provides sufficient incentives for the investors.
- Sufficient funds are available to complete the project operations.
- The distribution of project benefits and costs is consistent with project objectives.
- Environmental impacts are included in the analysis.
- Costs, contributions, and roles of the public are defined.

Economic feasibility compares anticipated costs for implementing urban design projects with the expected revenues of the project. Urban renewal programs, for example, outline measures (typically, infrastructures and facilities) to be implemented by public entities (municipalities, regional agencies, or state governments) to facilitate private investment in the project and to eliminate influences that would make the project less inviting. In urban renewal or regeneration projects, public bodies often act in partnership with other public entities and sometimes with nongovernmental organizations.

Project costs are compared with potential financing sources. The objective of the economic assessment study is to identify the potential gains for real estate companies who may be interested in providing financial support for amenities (e.g., cultural venues and infrastructure) that do not generate profits but are requested by public entities. A feasibility study analyzes the possibility of positioning—a series of activities and the ability of a project to generate revenues with support from private real estate developers—to cover the cost of the requested amenities.

A simple method for appraising the viability of an urban design development proposal is the *residual method of evaluation* (Marsh 2001, 110). The residual method has three functions:

1. To determine the value of the land and therefore how much the developer can afford to bid in attempting to acquire the land from the landowner
2. To calculate the overall value of the completed scheme and the level of profit the proposal will produce for the developer
3. To assess the likely level of costs that will be incurred by the developer during construction in order to identify a cost ceiling that must not be exceeded if the development is to remain profitable.

The value of land—the "residue"—is determined by what can be developed on the site, the demand for that site, and the availability of alternative spaces elsewhere. Writes Marsh (2001, 110): "Obviously, great care must be taken in using residual valuations and while similar market transactions on other comparable developments in the area will provide some checks and balances, it is important to be aware that development projects almost always have characteristics that are unique to them and this will affect value."

Design Guidelines

A master plan can define details through design guidelines (or design statements) that establish standards and related performance criteria for an area or type of development. Design guidelines can be organized in different ways depending on the circumstances and purposes of the project. One method is related to specific elements, such as facades, windows, entrances, lamps, fences, benches, material, and pavements. Another method is to divide the scope of the master plan into smaller parts and describe how to implement the design proposal in those areas. Many American university campus master plans provide good examples of design guidelines.

The Design Guidelines in the Campus Master Plan of the University of Texas at Austin

Cesar Pelli & Associates (now Pelli Clarke Pelli Architects), Balmori Associates, and Danze & Blood were the designers of the 1999 University of Texas at Austin campus master plan. The purpose of the plan was to "support and embody a sense of community for students, faculty, and staff and to create a sense of place that will remain strong and clear in the memories of the graduates. Another objective is to reverse the current tendency toward decentralization of planning in response to growth. The new master plan . . . addresses the planned growth of an already mature campus" (Cesar Pelli & Associates and Balmori Associates 1999, 33).

The location of the original 40 acres (16 hectares) of the University of Texas at Austin campus was chosen in 1881. Plans by Cass Gilbert in 1909, by James M. White in 1923, and by Green, La Roche and Dahl in 1928 contributed to the campus core, but it was the 1933 master plan by Paul Cret that "most significantly established the future design direction for the 40 acres [16 hectares] and served as the model for the overall character of the University" (Cesar Pelli & Associates and Balmori Associates 1999, 11). Cret was a French-American architect, born in Lyon, educated at the École des Beaux-Arts in Paris, who arrived in the United States in 1903 to teach at the University of Pennsylvania. He served as campus architect for the University of Texas from 1930 until 1945. In addition to his 1933 plan, Cret helped design nineteen buildings on campus (see Figure 9.1/Plate #32).

The Pelli team designed the campus with the mind-set that "responsibility for the future development of the University should be assumed only after understanding, respect and love of its past have been acknowledged, because it is in these earlier buildings and open spaces that we find the essence of our community. These buildings are flexible and enduring, and these open spaces encourage interaction and pedestrian comfort. They should be the model and inspiration for future development" (Cesar Pelli & Associates and Balmori Associates 1999, 28).

The campus master plan defined seven objectives and organizing principles (Cesar Pelli & Associates and Balmori Associates 1999, 33):

1. To return the core campus to pedestrians and keep vehicular traffic to the edge of the campus
2. To use the architectural language of Paul Cret's original works as the point of departure for the design of new structures
3. To establish a community of landscaped open spaces, working in concert with buildings to extend and reknit the campus
4. To add substantially to on-campus housing, thus creating a more complete academic community
5. To establish new centers of student activity, reinforcing housing and academic uses to enhance a full on-campus life
6. To concentrate future construction in the core campus rather than on the fringes

Figure 9.1 (also Plate #32) Paul Cret's watercolor perspective of future development of the University of Texas campus, 1933. (Courtesy Alexander Architectural Archive, University of Texas Libraries, the University of Texas at Austin.)

7. To enhance public perceptions of and access to the campus through strengthened identity and wayfinding programs

Based on the second principle, any new buildings on the University of Texas at Austin campus "must correspond in massing, scale, proportion, materials and building character to its most revered structures. . . . Architects who add new buildings to a campus had an obligation to understand and respect the character of its most exceptional parts" (Cesar Pelli & Associates and Balmori Associates 1999, 35, 43). To help future designers, the master plan provides a series of images and descriptions of existing buildings and significant building elements, such as the facade composition, entrances, iron works, lamps, materials, textures, colors, soffits, and ceiling patterns (see Figure 9.2).

The characteristics of open spaces are described building on the typologies of existing courtyards, green and park space types, walking streets, plants, lawns, pedestrian site lighting, and paving patterns and textures. Additional detailed elements include benches, trash and recycling containers, kiosks, and food carts. In the master plan, components—from facade to benches to paving patterns—are organized into palettes so that future designers can use them to achieve cohesion between new open spaces and buildings and existing ones.

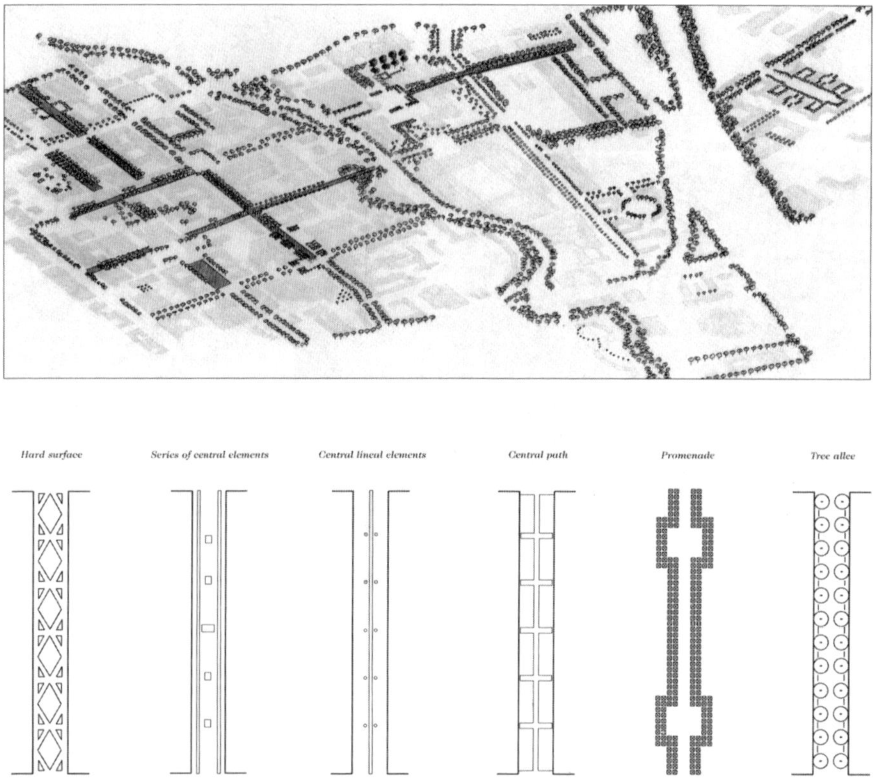

Figure 9.2 The University of Texas at Austin: diagrams of various conceptual treatments for new malls using planting, paving, and sculptural elements. Master plan by Cesar Pelli & Associates and Balmori Associates. (Courtesy Pelli Clarke Pelli Architects.)

The "Rule Book" of the University of Cincinnati Master Plan

The University of Cincinnati master plan was prepared by Hargreaves Associates of San Francisco in 1991, updated in 1995 (Update 1), and updated again in 2000 (Update 2). The plan defines guidelines as "the 'rule book' of the master plan intended to direct campus development toward achieving goals and objectives set forth by the Mission. These guiding fundamentals should persevere through future evolution of the University and subsequent updates to the master plan" (Hargreaves Associates 1995, 17). The guidelines are so strong and well defined that amending them requires a vote of the University of Cincinnati Board of Trustees. The campus master plan had to incorporate the need for approximately 1 million square feet (about 93,000 square meters) of new academic and research space.

Between the master plan goals, reaffirmed in the second update of the master plan (Hargreaves Associates 2000, 1), was "the creation of a physical environment reflecting the idea that learning takes place at all times in a range of places in and beyond the classroom." The master plan policies and guidelines are divided into seven parts:

- A *Connective Strategy* addresses the relationship between the east and west campuses, the links between individual buildings, and between the buildings and other parts of the campuses (see Figure 9.3).
- *Open Space Policies* contain the planning framework that could be used "as the basis for new path connections and for design articulation of the connective open spaces [to unify] the character of the entire campus" (Hargreaves Associates 1995, 22) (see Figure 9.4).
- *Policies for Specific Open Spaces* include rules for certain campus "regions." These rules are intended as guidelines for future development without presenting "the solution"; rather, they point out some elements to be considered by future designers.
- *Building Policies* specify rules defined by Hargreaves Associates starting from the recognition of force fields: "those three-dimensional spatial characteristics generated by buildings, landforms, and vegetation, projected into space along particular alignments or axes. . . . Force Fields set the planning framework for the addition of new buildings. Adding buildings within this framework becomes a process of infill" (Hargreaves Associates 1995, 19, 36) (see Figure 9.5).
- *Campus Elements* present proposals for the gateway system, lighting types, site furnishings, and a representation of standard furniture.
- *Infrastructure Policies* relate to parking, disability access, circulation for cars and bicycles, and utilities.
- *Enforcement* sets out the rules for implementing the master plan, defining the composition of the *Design Review Committee,* in charge of the enforcement of the master plan, and of the *Art Advisory Committee* and *Art Review Committee*, responsible for selecting artists and reviewing any art work on campus. This part also defines the master plan update process (Hargreaves Associates 1995).

In 2003, the Signage Committee of the University of Cincinnati, led by environmental graphic design expert Kelly Kolar, produced *Signage Policy and Standards* (University of Cincinnati 2003), a directive "created to provide a consistent and uniform signage wayfinding system applicable to all the University of Cincinnati

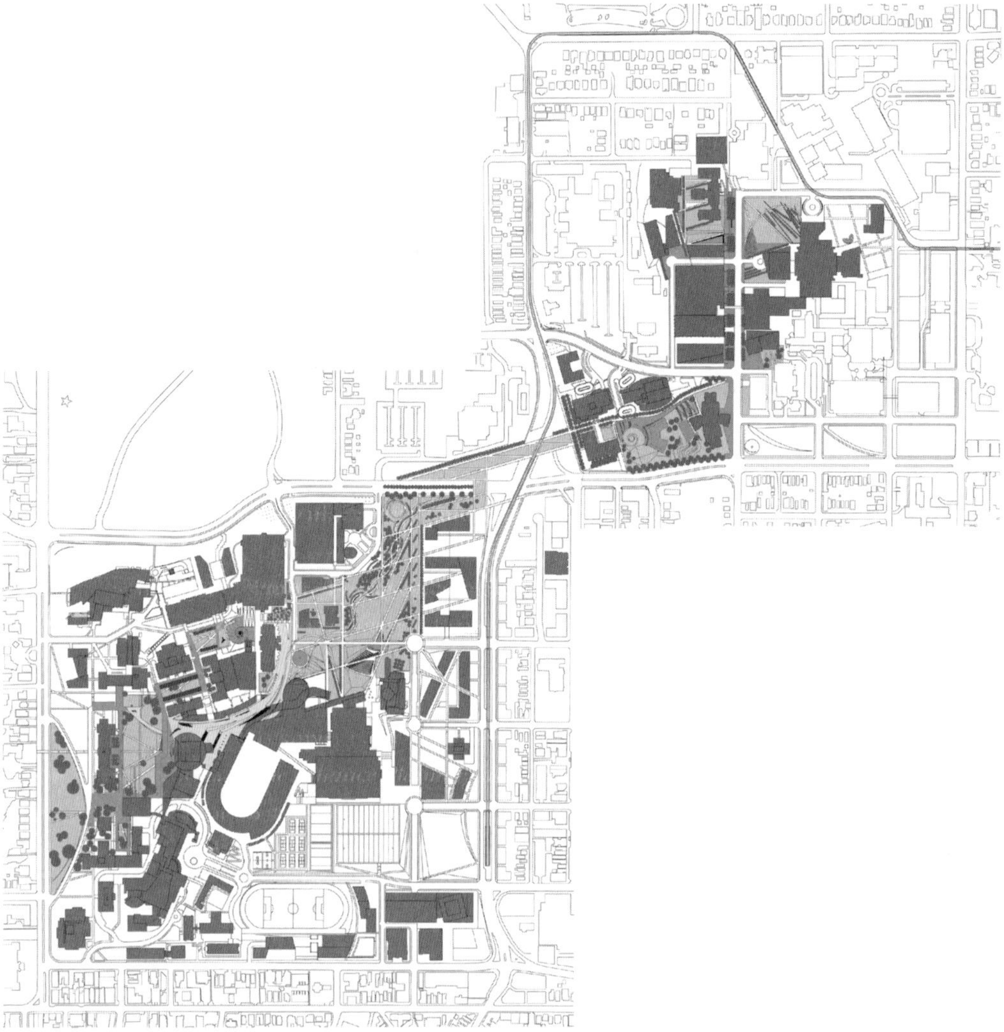

Figure 9.3 University of Cincinnati: the connective quadrangle. The diagram establishes a direct open space connection between West Campus and East Campus. Master plan by Hargreaves Associates of San Francisco, California, 2000. (Courtesy Hargreaves Associates, New York.)

campuses" (ii). The document detailed and specified the guidelines about *Campus Elements*, and specifically "Campus Gateway System" and "Wayfinding" as described in the Master Plan Update 1 (Hargreaves Associates 1995, 48–50) and Update 2 (Hargreaves Associates 2000, 46–47), which stated: "A primary goal of the wayfinding system is to give students, faculty, staff and visitors a sense of

Figure 9.4 University of Cincinnati: connective open spaces. Master plan by Hargreaves Associates of San Francisco, California, 2000. (Courtesy Hargreaves Associates, New York.)

safety through the implementation of a signage system that provides clear circulation routes. . . . The wayfinding system will improve connectivity by: creating a sense of place for the University as a whole through a single signage system unified across both campuses" (Hargreaves Associates 2000, 47).

The Cincinnati plan is an outstanding example of renewal for an aging campus. In addition to giving the university a facelift through new buildings by starchitects

Figure 9.5 University of Cincinnati: force fields. The force fields are "those three-dimensional spatial characteristics generated by buildings, landforms, and vegetation, projected into space along particular alignments or axes." Master plan by Hargreaves Associates of San Francisco, California, 2000. (Courtesy Hargreaves Associates, New York.)

like Michael Graves, Peter Eisenman, Frank Gehry, and Morphosis, it also identified areas for preservation and conservation. While historic buildings were restored, large parking areas were transformed (by Hargreaves) into parks. Eventually, sustainability concerns were also incorporated into new building designs. In 2008, the CARE/Crawley Building opened as part of Cincinnati's College of Medicine with a LEED Silver Rating from USGBC.

Battery Park City Green Building Guidelines

Increasingly, design guidelines also include standards for green building. New York City's Battery Park City Green Building Guidelines require developers to incorporate energy and environmental considerations into the design and construction process for new buildings on the 92-acre (37-hectare) section of land adjacent to the World Trade Center site. The guidelines were written by a team of architects, engineers, energy specialists, and construction managers in 2000 and have resulted in one of the "greenest" neighborhoods in the United States.

The guidelines are included in a "how to" booklet that explains the required green strategies, the rationale behind each strategy, potential sources of funding, and what kind of documentation developers are required to submit to be in compliance (Hammer and Hinge 2009). The guidelines have been updated several times since 2000 to reflect changing knowledge, such as the ever-evolving LEED standards, and they cover residential, commercial, and institutional buildings. Some key requirements for residential buildings follow (Hammer and Hinge 2009):

- Buildings must achieve 30 percent greater energy efficiency than would be achieved under the current state building code.
- Buildings must install a photovoltaic system capable of supplying 5 percent of the building's anticipated peak electricity demand.
- Each new building's electrical distribution system must be designed to allow maximum use of demand-response technologies and strategies.
- Apartments must receive 30 percent more natural light than the level called for under current New York City building code requirements.
- Developers must employ a waste management program capable of recycling 80 percent (by weight) of all waste materials generated during the construction process.
- Developers must maximize use of building materials manufactured within 500 miles (804.7 kilometers) of Battery Park City to reduce transportation-related energy use.
- Buildings must provide enclosed storage space for bicycles.
- Dedicated parking spaces for hybrid electric and other high-efficiency automobiles must be provided.
- Developers must commission all mechanical systems in the building post-occupancy to ensure they are working as intended.

While construction costs in Battery Park City are 5 to 15 percent higher than in nearby neighborhoods without green building standards, developers recoup costs quickly because they can charge rent and sales prices 4 to 5 percent higher due to the popularity of the buildings. Often, the buildings with green features sell out before they are completed, despite their higher cost (Hammer and Hinge 2009).

Even with higher construction, sales, and rent costs, the longer-term costs for energy are lower. The buildings are also designed to enhance the health of the residents. In addition, new Battery Park City buildings have been designed by important young architects, such as Rafael Pelli (of Pelli Clarke Pelli) (see Figure 9.6).

The Mobility Feasibility

The master plan may need to go deeper into circulation and infrastructural issues. The definition of a walking path or a road within the site can require more information about road sizes, compliance with technical rules, and feasibility. Some options may seem possible but need to be assessed and verified at a local level. Other issues can include pedestrian mobility for people with disabilities.

If these issues are not fully considered during the master plan design, then the client may require the designer to modify or update the master plan proposals during the implementation phase. This, in turn, might require reconsideration of other important parts of the design or, at the very least, cause delays and add to costs.

Pedestrian Mobility along the Gonzaga Axis in Mantua

During the preliminary study of the Gonzaga Axis in Mantua (see Chapter 5, Options), pedestrian mobility for all users, including those with disabilities, was examined. The main design goal was to renew interest in the Gonzaga Axis for tourists visiting the many buildings and places that compose the city's historic center. The guiding design principle was to define new ways to recognize the walkway. In general, a route's identity can be established using (1) signs to guide the tourist, (2) maps to orient the occasional visitor toward where to go and what to find, and (3) systems of horizontal (floor) signs or special paving.

Signs, together with maps, are the most widespread means for directing tourists in a historical urban center. To be effective, signs must be visible, contain information in a concise manner, and be primarily in a graphic format. The risk is that these signs rapidly become part of that background "noise" quickly invisible in historical centers and cities in general.

Maps pose a different set of issues, including language. The growing tourist market means visitors coming from different countries and cultures. English, while considered an Esperanto, is not the mother tongue for many tourists who

Figure 9.6 The Visionaire, a LEED Platinum thirty-three-story residential condominium building in Battery Park City, Lower Manhattan, featuring a high-efficiency fresh-air supply and exhaust system; centrally filtered water; an in-building wastewater treatment system that resupplies toilets and central air-conditioning makeup water; and rainwater harvested on the pesticide-free roof gardens. Design by Rafael Pelli. (©Pelli Clarke Pelli Architects. Photograph by Pelli Clarke Pelli.)

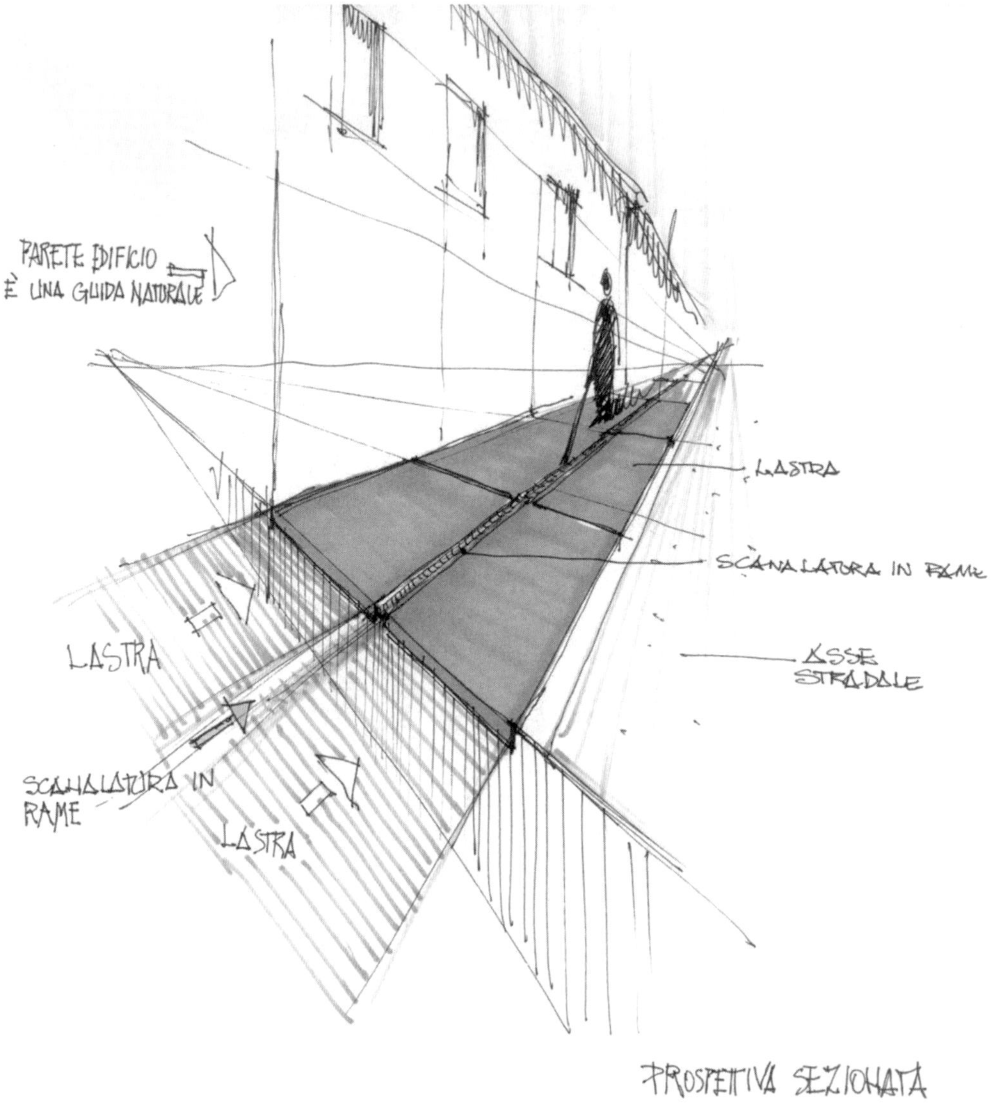

Figure 9.7 The first paving solution for the Gonzaga Axis, Mantua, Italy. (Drawing by Elena Stevanato. From Treu 2001.)

visit the historic cities from Italy to China to Brazil. Horizontal signs offer a compromise solution. Unlike vertical signs, they are less invasive and do not require knowledge of the local language.

Various solutions have been applied in European and North American cities. For instance, a simple colored line can run along sidewalks. In Mantua, because of

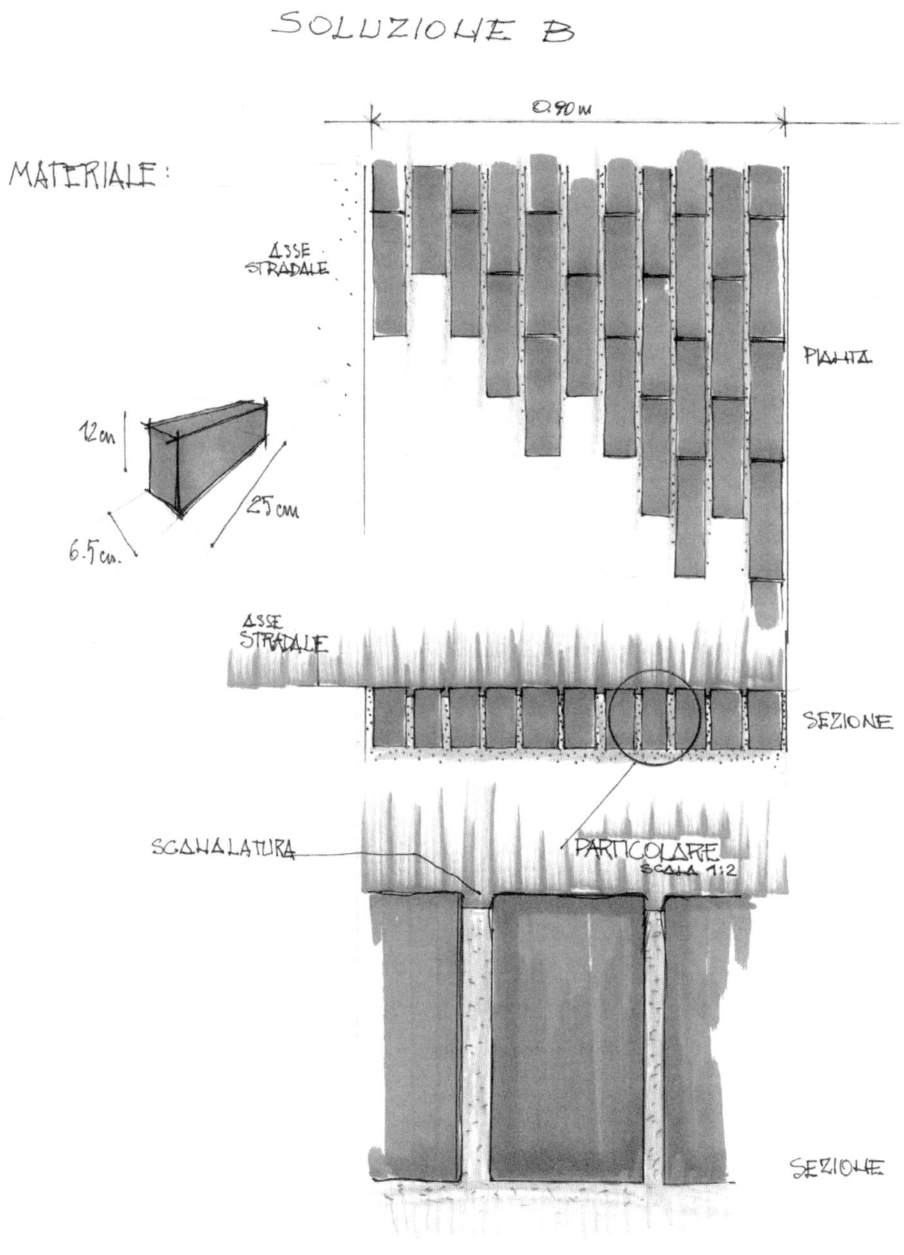

Figure 9.8 The second paving solution for the Gonzaga Axis, Mantua, Italy. (Drawing by Elena Stevanato. From Treu 2001.)

the historical texture, this was not an option. Other solutions were proposed that better respected the city's history.

The hypothesis was that special paving could be used along the Gonzaga Axis to be a symbol of the routes connecting two of Mantua's main monuments, which could benefit both the inhabitants of Mantua and tourists, plus people with several degrees of physical disability as well as blindness and near-blindness. Two proposed alternatives were assessed by Hbgroup of Milan, a team of experts in plans and research and development for the disabled and a broader range of users.

The two solutions tried to find a compromise between the following needs:

- To mark the route in unambiguous ways for all users
- To choose the solution among already existing paving solutions in the historical texture
- To guarantee accessibility for people with motor disabilities and for blind and near-blind users

The first solution entails rectangular natural stone slabs (18 by 36 inches, or 45 by 90 centimeters) placed side by side, in the middle of which a metal track is laid (see Figure 9.7). The track can act as an artificial guide for the visually impaired, and the relatively smooth surface of the slabs provides a good surface for wheelchairs. The paving can be placed as close as possible to buildings so that walls can serve as a natural guide for the visually impaired. The track can also serve as an artificial guide for blind users with white canes. The second solution suggests clay bricks set along the longer side (see Figure 9.8). Exposed bricks, like the slabs in the first solution, can be seen in much of the historical paving in Mantua. This solution has the advantage of being easily recognized, although it is more difficult and expensive than the other approach.

The consultants assessed the two solutions based on three factors: tactile, acoustic, and visual. Based on these three aspects, the first solution was favored because of the smooth surfaces and the uniformity of proposed materials, which would help those in wheelchairs particularly affected by irregular paving.

Summary

Detailed studies help illustrate the potential consequences of the master plan. Such studies can expose economic, social, and physical details of the plan. Design guidelines help ensure that ideas in the master plan are pursued. Thus, detailed studies form a bridge between the master plan and its implementation.

10 ■ Implementation

An urban design project is implemented in different ways depending on institutional and cultural contexts. Most official planning systems require a "comprehensive" plan document, with general and strategic contents. Some comprehensive plans are implemented by regulation and policy; others, through the availability of funding; and still others, through some combination. Project implementation usually requires consistency with planning policies and rules or an official amendment of those policies and rules. Sometimes, comprehensive plans result in public funds—through taxes, fees, or bonds—that can be used to realize urban design projects. Urban designers need to understand the planning context to get their projects implemented.

In the United States, planning systems vary from state to state (Delafons 1962; Bosselmann and Callies 1971; Clawson and Hall 1973; DeGrove and Stroud 1987; Platt 1991). In *The Political Culture of Planning*, Barry Cullingworth (1993, 194) noted that in the United States "much of land use planning operates through the agency of local government. . . . American local planning is characterized by a great variety: it ranges from local governments with no zoning, to those with highly active (or reactive) land use controls." Cullingworth and Roger Caves in *Planning in the USA* (2003, 17) observe that "land use planning in the US is largely a local matter. . . . This means that there is a great variety in the ways in which planning is carried out."

Cullingworth (1993) distinguishes between comprehensive plans (or general plans as they are called in some states) and more local site plans or zoning plans. In the more specific plans, private and public sectors must collaborate and negotiations have a relevant part in the process. In an usual development process, "the private sector is responsible for development proposals, while the public sector is responsible for regulating them. . . . The success of the private developer is measured simply: does the development return a profit? The public process is very different. . . . It is concerned to ensure that development accords with the standards set out in legislative instruments. . . . Its chronic shortage of resources, and its perpetual concern about future costs of maintaining the public estate, leads to try to secure the maximum amount of public benefit from developers" (18–19). Sometimes, the tools to implement comprehensive plans are called "action plans" in the United States.

Research conducted by the European Union Commission, Directorate General for Policy and Cohesion for the *EU Compendium of Spatial Planning Systems and Policies* (Hawkes et al. 1996) demonstrates that wide diversity also exists in planning systems among different European countries. The research reported that

> it should be understood that [the term] spatial planning when used in "EU sense" does not mean precisely *aménagement du territoire, town and country planning, Raumordnung, ruimtelijke ordening,* or any of a number of other terms used by Member State and regions to describe the particular arrangements for managing spatial development which apply in their territories. . . . Spatial planning refers to the methods used largely by the public sector to influence the future distribution of activities in space. It is undertaken with the aims of creating a more rational territorial organization of land uses and the linkages between them, to balance demands for the development with the need to protect the environment, and to achieve a more even distribution of economic development. (3, 4)

While the research acknowledged the variations among the member states of the European Union, the compendium also identified some common elements, including, at the municipal level, the relationship between general and detailed plans. Local authorities produce "spatial framework documents which set out general criteria for the regulation of land use change [and prepare] land use instruments which define the type of physical development which will be permitted at particular locations" (Hawkes et al. 1996, 7).

In Europe, therefore, a broad distinction can be made between general plans and detailed or implementation plans. Implementation plans in some European countries are binding. Implementation plans, both in the European sense of "detailed plans" and in American "action plans," are in many cases an appropriate tool for urban design projects.

The Roles of Urban Design in Planning

Regardless of the similarities or differences among American states and European countries, we contend that urban design, and design in general, can assist in the transition between general plan strategies and their spatial implications. Design "is a way of making a complex decision where a series of potential actions are interrelated and choices of one issue affect choices about others" (Barnett 1995, 179). This observation by Jonathan Barnett, a professor of practice at the University of Pennsylvania, acknowledges at least three roles of urban design in the context of its relationships with urban planning. The first role, less traditional, takes place within the production processes of general plans. The second one, more obvious in practice, happens in detailed plans. The third, which is gradually becoming more frequent, occurs while defining the design regulations and guidelines.

The first role of urban design within the general planning process is to assess and pre-appraise the spatial consequences of forecasted land-use transformations.

> Zoning regulations inevitably shape buildings and these design consequences should be anticipated and intended. Subdivision of land into lots and streets is not just a way of offering parcels for sale, but shapes a new neighborhood. Building public housing is not just a way of eradicating slums or moving people out of substandard quarters, but creates new communities. Urban renewal in city centers is not just the removal of blighted buildings and unproductive ownership patterns, but a strategy to reorganize the downtown. (Barnett 1995, 180)

Where the general plan is typically a matter of rules and policies, planning decisions are frequently a major part of the design, and "skilled [urban] designers are needed to help make these decisions and carry them out" (Barnett 1995, 180) (see Figures 10.1/Plate #33, 10.2, and 10.3/Plate #34).

The second role of urban design takes place while preparing implementation plans, where urban designers work with clients, analyzing the site, sketching out alternative hypotheses, evaluating them, and synthesizing new possibilities from dialogues with clients and other interested parties.

The third role urban design can play is in defining and detailing regulations, rules, and guidelines to direct future developments. This role is perhaps the least

Figure 10.1 (also Plate #33) Greater London Plan by Sir Patrick Abercrombie. This layout indicates the application of the plan in Bermondsey for a density of 136 persons per acre (per 0.4 hectare). (From Abercrombie 1945, facing p. 82.)

developed, particularly for mature urban environments. However, historical and more recent examples do exist.

> The designer has to discover how to rewrite development regulations to ensure that appropriate design relationships are achieved. . . . [Urban designers] learned that Paris has been imposing design guidelines for more than two centuries. From 1784 onward, Parisian legislation related building height to street widths and imposed a setback angle for attics. In addition, façade controls could be adopted for important streets. The Parisian street-wall and attic control . . . became the prototype for the bulk control in New York City's 1916 zoning ordinance. Buildings could rise to a height that was a function of the width of the street, as in Paris, and then had to set back beneath an angled "sky exposure plane," which is the Parisian attic translated to the larger scale of the elevator building. Understanding the power of this one simple idea to affect the design of cities as disparate as Paris and New York encouraged designers to return to the elements of city design that were pushed aside by the doctrine of modernism but that turned out to be necessary for a coherent city. (Barnett 1995, 188)

Figure 10.2 Artistic representation of multistory flats for the plan in Bermondsey, London. (From Abercrombie 1945, facing p. 83.)

The Translation of the Master Plan: The Orsenigo Integrated Intervention Program

In the Italian planning system, the relationship between general plans and implementation plans, although defined by a national law of 1942 and by different regional laws, usually depends on the rules adopted by each specific single general plan. Some general plans precisely define rules that the implementation plan will develop in detail. Others are less precise and give only broad indications about how to implement the plan. When the space between the general plan and the implementation plan is too wide, the implementation plan can produce conflicts and negative reactions among citizens, officials, and other interested parties.

In Orsenigo, a hamlet located 6.2 miles (10 kilometers) from Como and its homonymous lake, a master plan was designed during a workshop organized by the Milan Polytechnic. A few months after the public presentation of the master plan, the municipality, together with the owner of the area, asked the team to convert it

Figure 10.3 (also Plate #34) Artistic representation of terrace houses for the plan in Bermondsey, London. (From Abercrombie 1945, facing p. 83.)

to a detailed plan to be implemented. The master plan provided an overall design, which had been communicated and shared with the public. It now needed to be transformed into a formal planning tool: the Integrated Intervention Program. In Italy, the Integrated Intervention Program is a binding agreement governed by a partnership between public and private entities for a site.

The Orsenigo municipality requested that the implementation plan reassert the guiding principles that emerged from the master plan, specifically to achieve the following:

- Regeneration of an area very close to the historical center, perceived by the population as "abandoned" and "neglected," with the creation of a multifunctional place that, while giving preference to housing (as required by the general plan), would host other uses and public spaces
- Enhancement of the surrounding landscape views and the relation with the historical center and the current urban pattern, respecting the existing character
- New construction needs to preserve alignments, volumetric relationships, building heights, and visual perspectives
- Presence of public spaces, green areas, as well as pedestrian and bicycle paths, integrated into the existing network, thus representing an alternative to automobile use

- Consistency with the master plan, acknowledging that the implementation plan, as an operating tool to transform the area, would have to specify some details and relationship elements that were underestimated during the workshop

The design of the implementation plan began by taking account of the surrounding landscape. Landscape features acted as an important element for organizing urban design choices. The distant view of the mountain ranges of Lecco and Bergamo, the open view on Brianza's small lakes, the terraced cultivation in closer view, and the church that emerges on the top of the hill on which rests the historical center of Orsenigo are all morphological characteristics that emerged.

Another aspect considered was the site's location in the city context. The derelict industrial area acts as a hinge between the historical center and the more recent settlement and is adjacent to the core of existing services. The final design of the Integrated Intervention Program (see Figure 10.4) respected the general plan forecasts about the volumetric concentration along the longest side of the area and the request for public facilities (a new city hall and public library, parking, and public spaces). In addition, access to the area and to the historical center was studied. As a result, an existing road was eliminated and replaced with a new one.

The implementation program divided the site into four distinct districts. The design rules for buildings and public spaces were described in a "Map of the Alignments and of the Regulating Lines," which is legally binding. The map specifies the following:

- Building fronts
- Alignments between distinct buildings
- Building footprints
- Building orientations
- Maximum dimensions of the building bulk admitted, the maximum number of floors, and the types of building roofs
- Limits of private areas that establish the borders with public spaces

The "Map of the Alignments and of the Regulating Lines" becomes the translation tool of the master plan that leaves appropriate flexibility for specific building and landscape designs. The "Map of the Alignments" respects the general plan and prescribes some "fixed points," which allow future designers to make original interventions. Charles Eames observed that "design depends largely on constraints," which is certainly true in urban design (Neuhart, Neuhart, and Eames 1989, 15).

Figure 10.4 The master plan of Orsenigo, Como, Italy, 2007. (Courtesy Integrated Intervention Program. Team leaders: Danilo Palazzo and Massimo Tadi.)

Design Guidelines and Spatial Rules: Envision Central Texas

The definition of design guidelines and rules for the plan implementation is another role for urban design. As described in Chapter 5 (Options), Envision Central Texas (ECT), a nongovernmental organization, provided concept plans for community test-site planning areas in five counties. The concept plans served as pilot projects to assess different planning tools to be used and to allow possible solutions to be explored at a local level. The concept plans developed for the five counties were also included in the design guidelines (ECT 2003a, 2003c, 2003e, 2003k). In essence, Peter Calthorpe and his colleagues adapted basic New Urbanist design principles to Central Texas conditions and the ECT vision.

In the Bastrop test site, the urban design standards (ECT 2003a) deal with principles such as placement and massing, a list of building types, recommendations for materials and other building-specific characteristics, axonometric and plan drawings of the basic building types, and street sections. The design guidelines will help to implement the concept plan, which "envisions a village center and neighborhood center located strategically along primary connector streets. The plan is intended to provide a vision for the evolution of the site into a mixed-use, walkable district by creating a mixture of housing options, retail and office uses, enhanced civic uses and recreation spaces which will facilitate community gathering places" (2003a, 3).

The rules provided by the Bastrop design guidelines relate to the following features:

- *Building placement and massing* defines how to build along streets, how to orient buildings, and minimum building heights.
- *Permitted uses* provides a list of permitted land uses, such as commercial/mixed-use/civic areas, open space, and town center residential areas.
- *Employment and mixed-use building design* describes building characteristics in terms of street orientation and appearance, transparency of the ground floor, specific design elements to deal correctly with the region's cool winters and hot summers, and the choice of materials.

The guidelines illustrate design principles through plans and axonometric images of specific building types, such as anchor retail, in-line shops, offices, offices over a commercial ground floor, office/research, and residential over commercial.

A specific section of the guidelines is dedicated to residential buildings. The guidelines emphasize the importance of mixed-use and housing variety in terms of floorplans and varied exterior treatments and materials. Variations in building mass, entry and porch designs, window patterns, roof forms, and other architectural features are encouraged. Housing types are also differentiated and regulated in terms of lot size, density, and distinguishing features.

Residential building guidelines are provided to drive design in terms of orientation, rapport with streets and roads, characteristics of entrances, garages, front setbacks, materials, facades, roof forms, and visual characters. For different types of housing (e.g., garden apartments and townhouses), the guidelines present principles and examples of plans and axonometric visualization. The final two sections of the guidelines present parking requirements and examples of street sections. The ECT urban design guidelines, prepared by Calthorpe Associates, offer an example of how to implement a vision and have indeed been adapted through several projects in the Austin metropolitan area (see Figures 10.5, 10.6, and 10.7).

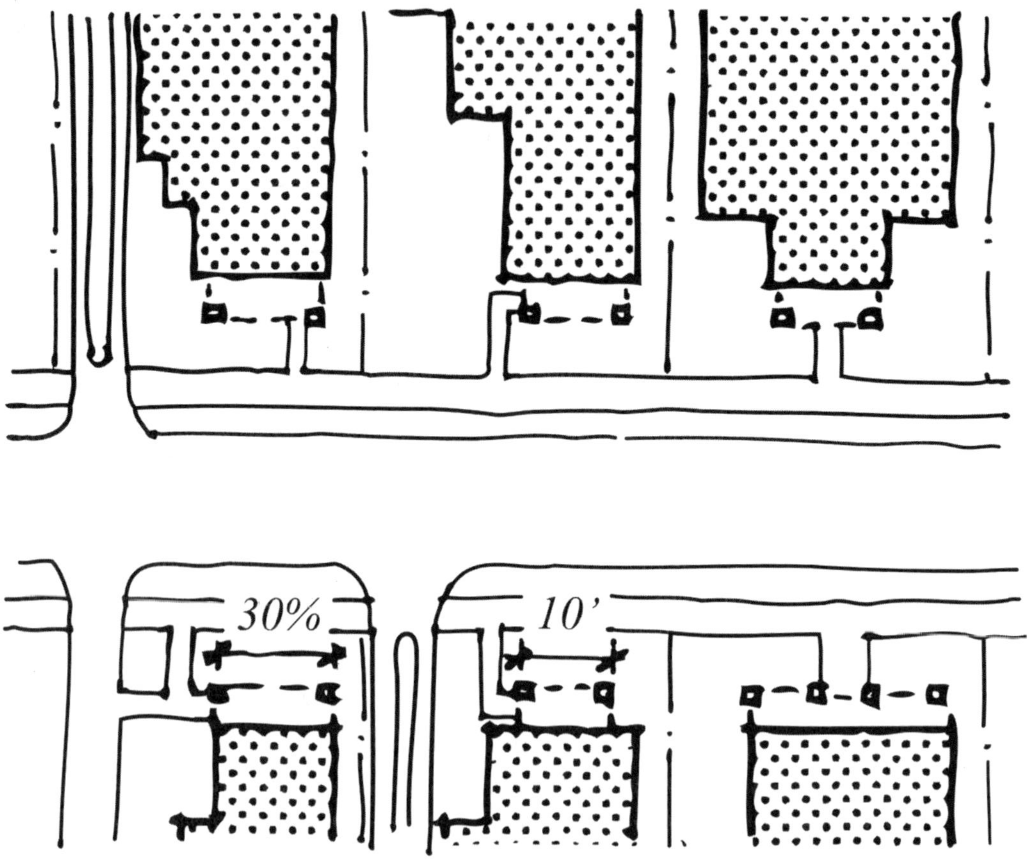

Figure 10.5 Envision Central Texas's Bastrop proposed urban design guidelines for the relation of buildings to streets. (Courtesy Envision Central Texas.)

Point Fraser Precinct Development

For another example, look at the Point Fraser Precinct Development in Western Australia. The development is on a 15.2-acre (6.13-hectare) brownfield site, located in Perth's central business district along the tidal river flat of Swan River. The Point Fraser Reserve is constructed on a reclaimed river foreshore with the aim of improving the health of the Swan River and connecting the city to the water's edge (City of Perth n.d.; Syrinx n.d.; and http://www.sustainablesites.org). The previous use of the site was predominantly as a parking lot and helicopter pad, with the foreshore area being hard-walled. The former site was underutilized and,

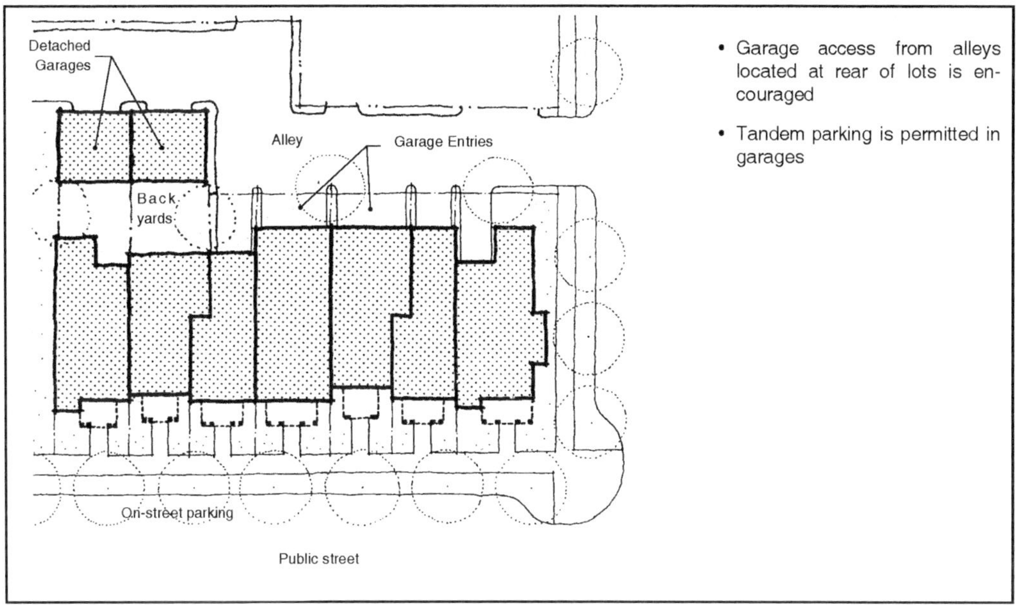

Plan

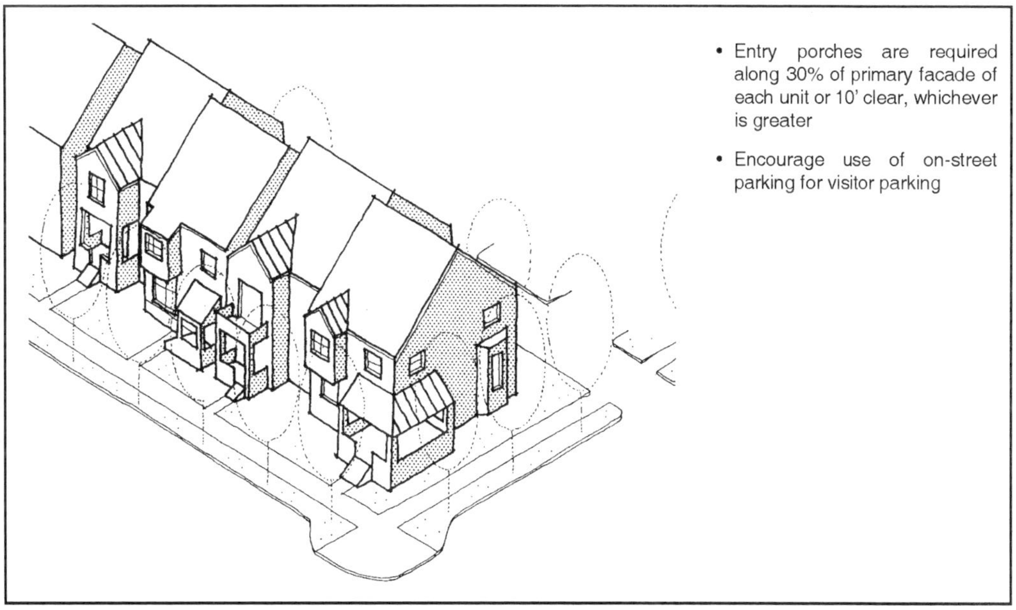

Axonometric

Figure 10.6 Plan and axonometric views of Envision Central Texas's Bastrop proposed urban design guidelines for residential front setback and garage access from alleys. (Courtesy Envision Central Texas.)

Landscaped Frontages. *Where parking lots abut streets, landscaped frontages are required.*

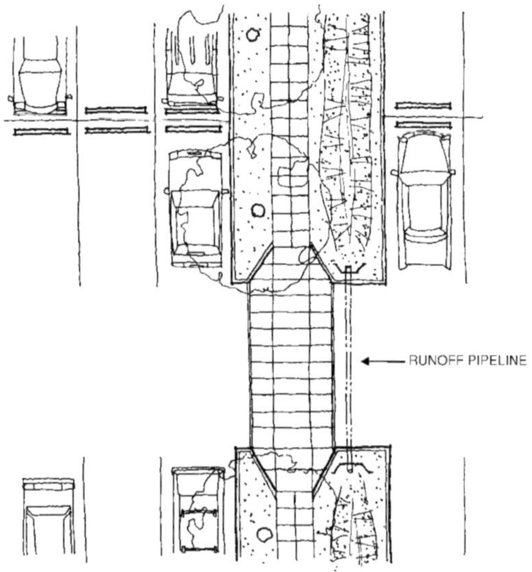

Plan View.

Section View

Figure 10.7 Envision Central Texas's Bastrop proposed urban design guidelines for plan and section of the relation between walkways and parking. (Courtesy Envision Central Texas.)

although prime foreshore land, offered little or no potential interaction with the public domain. Ecologically, the site contained acid sulfate soils and was geotechnically unstable and unpredictable. Culturally, Point Fraser's highly visible profile along the Swan River intertidal zone required the project design to be subtle while also encouraging maximum experiential engagement with the site (Steiner et al. 2010). The contemporary park now treats the urban stormwater discharge while providing dynamic spatial experiences that offer opportunities for human interaction with the natural environment (Figure 10.8).

Financing Urban Design Projects

The most direct way to implement an urban design is to pay for its realization. An urban design plan can be implemented through private or public funding as

Figure 10.8 The redevelopment of the park at Point Fraser in Western Australia included riparian restoration and the reestablishment of resilient and diverse native habitats, 2006. (Photograph by Syrinx Environmental PL. Courtesy Syrinx Environmental PL.)

well as through some combination of both. A developer client may have sufficient resources to pay for the project outright. The same may be the case for a city commissioning an urban design. In the latter case, the city may use its taxing or bonding authority to fund the project. Tax funds can be allocated through a capital improvement program. A developer may work with a city to pay for parts of the project, while the municipality uses its capital improvement program to underwrite the costs of streets, sidewalks, infrastructure, and parks. Even if a private developer or public agency is paying for the project, public approvals are usually necessary. This is why dialogue and communication with the public and elected officials are important through the design process. Public opposition can be an important barrier to implementation. In addition, the use of public funds requires political support.

Tax increment financing (TIF) is a popular tool in much of the United States. With this approach, the city pays for public improvements for the project upfront; then the taxes generated by new developments are used to pay back those costs over time. TIF districts may be established to undertake the improvements and collect the taxes over time. To form a TIF, the case for public benefits must be compelling to the city or county.

Some local governments have used their condemnation powers to realize projects in the United States. The Constitution protects private property in the Fifth Amendment. However, private property can be taken for a public purpose with "just compensation." Known as *condemnation*, this practice is controversial and has resulted in such negative reactions that many states have limited the authority of local governments to use this power. Its use may create more barriers to implementation than its value. As a result, the private developer or public agency may be better off simply purchasing the property outright. Still, in some cases, condemnation may be needed as a last resort to realize a project.

A nonprofit organization may also become engaged in funding project implementation. For instance, former University of Pennsylvania president Judith Rodin (2007) recounts how the university became involved in transforming much of West Philadelphia, an endeavor that continues to the present. For example, Sasaki prepared a vision plan for a site formerly owned by the United States Postal Service, converting a brownfield into new spaces for the University of Pennsylvania (see Figure 10.9/Plate #2).

Nonprofit organizations have the benefit of being neither private businesses nor governmental agencies and, thus, have greater political credibility in certain circumstances, especially in the United States. As a result, nonprofit organizations

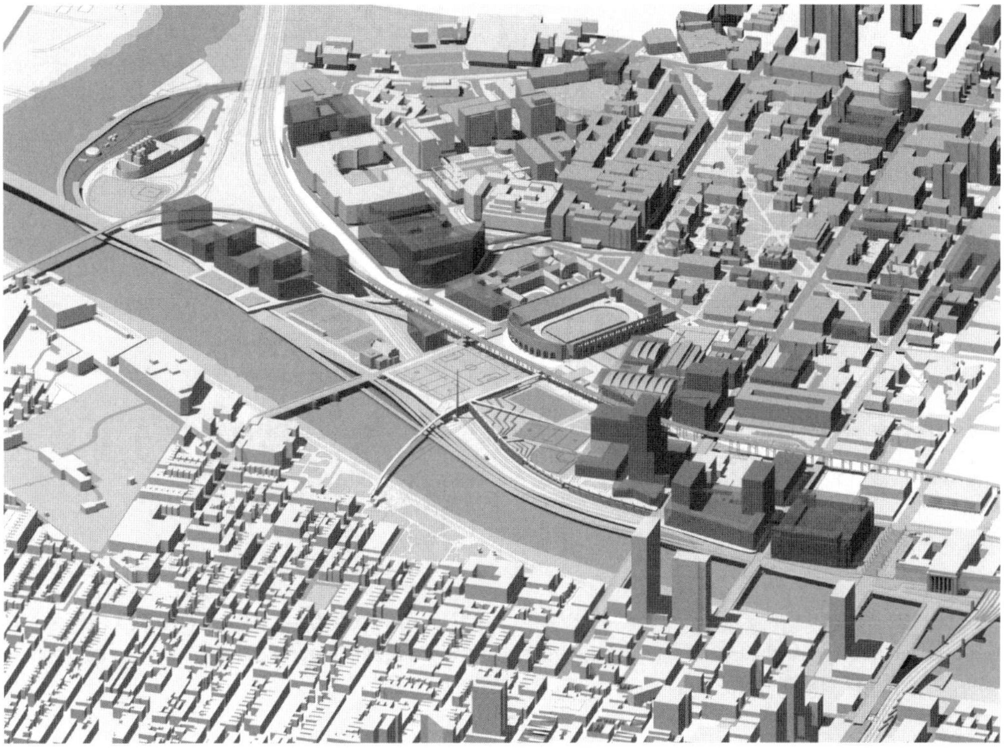

Figure 10.9 (also Plate #2) Penn Connects, a vision plan for the University of Pennsylvania: a regeneration of brownfield sites within the campus district. (Courtesy Sasaki Associates.)

may stay involved in a project through implementation and beyond to project management. An urban designer may engage an existing nonprofit in the project or may help create a new organization specifically for the project.

Summary

To be implemented, an urban design usually must fit within the existing structure of city plans and regulations. Official plans can be enhanced through urban design. Design guidelines are one important implementation tool. Public or private sponsors of the urban design can support its implementation by providing funds for realizing the plan. The role of nongovernment, nonprofit organizations and institutions may also be important.

In the end, the success of an urban design project rests on how it is implemented. A streetscape design by Wallace Roberts & Todd (WRT) for Washington Avenue on the edge of downtown St. Louis provides an example. The existing street was

Figure 10.10 For decades, Washington Avenue in St. Louis was the virtually empty spine of the city's once-thriving Loft District, a grossly underutilized historic urban resource. (Courtesy Wallace Roberts & Todd.)

Figure 10.11 Today, Washington Avenue is the "happening" place in downtown St. Louis. Hundreds of lofts have become condos, and the street is active with restaurants, al fresco dining, shops and galleries, and nightclubs. (Courtesy Wallace Roberts & Todd.)

cluttered, unfriendly, and ugly (Figure 10.10). The WRT design envisioned a lively street to provide a central spine for the historic Loft District (Figure 10.11). The realized WRT design provided the catalyst that helped repurpose the historic loft buildings into apartments and new ground-level retail. The streetscape promotes cycling, reuses granite curbs, includes trees and other plants, and helps infiltrate storm runoff.

11. Conclusion

In parts of Europe, all urban design possibilities can be fulfilled by an architect, an engineer, or a town planner. Especially in Northern Europe, Australia, and North America, and increasingly in Asia, these urban design opportunities may also be undertaken by a landscape architect or a landscape urbanist. These professionals may carry out an urban project without calling themselves urban designers, and they need not have been trained as urban designers.

Urban design probably does not need to obtain recognition as a technical or disciplinary field independent of architecture, urban planning, or landscape architecture. At least this recognition is not the purpose of this book. Instead, we aim to establish a process for ecological urban design and to present some techniques for anyone working in the urban design field. The proposed process can be adapted to different circumstances and possibly enhanced or simplified by those who want to use it in academic or professional environments.

The Role of the Urban Designer

One point we wish to emphasize here is that anyone working as an urban designer should consider two key issues. The first issue concerns the role of the urban designer compared to other fields of expertise. Even if denying any disciplinary independence in urban design, it is important to establish the limits of the urban designer's activity. We define the urban designer as "author and director of rules." The urban designer does not duplicate the role of the architect—whose task remains that of designing the project, an individual building, or clusters of buildings—or the landscape architect—who designs parks and other open spaces. The urban designer helps establish rules that the architect and the landscape architect need to follow. In a master plan, rules form guiding spatial policies for future development without compromising the role of other designers. Olmsted and Vaux in 1868, Nolen in 1927, and Hargreaves in 1995 and 2000 helped define the role of urban designers (even if they called themselves landscape architects, city planner, and landscape architect, respectively) as the ones who establish priority guiding principles and a site-oriented structural basis, which architects and other designers should follow.

The second issue concerns the resulting competences and the responsibilities. The urban designer develops skills in accord with demands from society and deals with the public during the design process. In some cases, it is indeed the designer who becomes the "broker and promoter of processes," consciously assuming the responsibilities arising from possessing a "design authority." In this sense, the urban designer's role is not neutral, not restricted to design and to delivering the project to the client. The urban designer cooperates actively with the client and the public to bring the project to its end. Several participatory processes, taking place in small or larger communities as a reaction to standardized design or to promote an alternative placemaking, highlight the active role of urban designers who do not merely make their skill available for that specific vision or project but, instead, organize the listening process, prepare participation in design initiatives, and become active agents of social creativity.

Urban Design Process and Responsibility

According to Kevin Lynch and Gary Hack (1984, 127): "Design is the search for forms that satisfy a program. It deals with particular solutions, while the program is concerned with general characteristics and desired outcomes. Design begins in the programming, and programs are modified as design progresses."

More broadly, Herbert Simon (1969, 55–56) observed: "Everyone designs who devises courses of action aimed at changing existing conditions into preferred ones. The intellectual activity that produces material artifacts is no different fundamentally from the one that prescribes remedies for a sick patient or the one that devises a new sales plan for a company or a welfare policy for the state. Design, so construed, is the core of all professional training: it is the principal mark that distinguishes the professions from the sciences."

Prerequisites, rules, and projects are part of a process aimed "at changing existing conditions into preferred ones" that is theoretically linear. The urban designer is firmly positioned in the middle and cannot intervene with prerequisites—they come from a collective subject, be it a general plan, the local government, inhabitants, a community, nature, or all of them together—or the architectural or landscape design. The process is only theoretically linear but is actually subject to multiple feedbacks. For example, the redefinition of prerequisites by the client can introduce, during the design process, an afterthought or even a radical change in the direction up to that point.

The process may also be subject to recurrence. At the partial conclusion of a phase, certain choices and, consequently, certain rules may be reviewed and revised.

The urban designer as author and director of rules does the following:

- *Explores* various design and operational solutions to reconcile general strategies, prerequisites, and expectations of the client and the public
- *Cooperates* with other experts involved in the process
- *Establishes* some fixed points, which will be transferred to architects responsible for building design or planners responsible for implementation
- *Evaluates* and *estimates*, in conjunction with experts, the consequences of the project and its options, including those of economic and financial nature and relating to the cost of the various solutions
- *Takes into account* issues of a procedural nature to select the "translations" of the choices into tools that can most effectively lead to implementation
- *Promotes* the process from a technical point of view to advance the master plan both as a final outcome and as a container for the "rules"

The urban designer must be able to use skill and at the same time be conscious of the responsibilities that arise. The activities of urban designers cannot be free of responsibilities—more precisely, of three specific responsibilities: the species responsibility, the generational responsibility, and the competence responsibility.

The *species responsibility* compels us, as human beings, to face the dominant role we have over the earth. We have to be conscious that our actions, throughout history, have led plant and animal species to extinction. Human activities have resulted in the destruction of entire environments, as well as the death of other human beings in catastrophes that we have unconsciously produced. We are, on the other hand, the same species that helps to heal damaged natural environments and that creates places of breathtaking beauty. The species responsibility compels us to face our seemingly contradictory behavior. We destroy, we construct, and we recover. We need to be conscious that every action will be judged—in the future—as part of the wide range of human behavior. We should be able to reject both hubris and cowardice. We are at the top of the food chain. We are responsible both for the past and for the future. We choose a profession that demands action, not rejection.

The *generational responsibility* obliges us to keep in touch with our legacy and to think about what we will leave behind. A good definition of sustainable development—"meeting the needs of the present without compromising the ability of future generations to meet their own needs"—can be interpreted as an "alliance between generations." In every single land transformation, we have to consider the contributions by past generations. At the same time, we have to safeguard the role of the current generation to define the shapes of development without compromising the role of future generations. Sustainable development means to act intentionally (which means that our actions should be driven by design) to increase the value of actual resources.

The *competence responsibility* (or the *design responsibility*) especially concerns those who act on the land and on the landscape with "design authority." Urban designers, architects, landscape architects, and urban and regional planners—more than other professionals and more than public administrators, private managers, landowners, and private citizens—must be able to use their skills and aptitudes to give expression to creative purpose, matching it with scientific knowledge and the capacity to manage processes.

Competence responsibility and design authority are not the same as authoritarianism or arrogance toward nature and people. To meet the aspirations of the people affected by a project (as noted by the European Landscape Convention and by an inherited aptitude of reflective practitioners all over the world) means to adopt the best possible techniques to reach an accurate interpretation of these aspirations and of the natural environment. Having design authority also means being expected to adapt the design process to the social and ecological context. The project is at least as important as the process involved to make it happen. The project may be the result of participatory design processes, an expression of active citizenship, rather than merely being advisory and fueled by the needs expressed by various interested parties. A project can be judged on paper, but its full appreciation is determined by its ability to become part of the urban and social texture. A project is evaluated based not only on the built environment it produces but also on the fulfillment of investments in expectations that the various participants have conceived during the entire process.

Urban Design Process and Stewardship

Over half a century ago, Kevin Lynch (1958, quoted in Banerjee and Southworth 1990, 383) wrote about approaching urban design through "additive structure," in which the "basic unit is rigidly standardized, inflexible [like a brick]. The flexibility lies in the myriad ways in which the constellation of units may be patterned, and in the interchangeability of parts. The total pattern is not highly organized, but is rather additive in nature: growth of units at the periphery does not change the structure at the center." Lynch introduced this concept in a 1958 article on "environmental adaptability," which he explained as the capacity that enables the organization of urban space to adapt to the changes in function, concentration, and communication. More recently, fractal theory suggests that the world is composed of self-similar systems. A fractal is a geometric shape that forms building blocks in nature. Another theory that fits Lynch's environmental adaptability is resilience and, specifically, urban resilience, defined by Marina Alberti and John Marzluff (2004) as a function of the patterns of human activities and natural habitats that control and are controlled by socioeconomic and biophysical processes operating at various scales. Peter Newman, Tim Beatley, and Heather Boyer (2009, 7) point to the need for cities to use resilience thinking "to cope with reductions in the resources that are used to make the city work."

In natural ecosystems, each species adapts its habitat for survival and reproduction. The city is a human ecosystem, and urban design is one of our tools for adaptation. We are learning more and more how to consider our impact on other species and future generations. We are also becoming more and more aware of how to design to maximize the ecosystem services provided by nature.

As we plot the future of our cities, it is apparent that there is not a single solution to how we adapt our cities. While there are many options, clearly some paths result in more benefits with fewer costs. The art of urban design is to find those ideal routes and then to communicate them to all involved.

The world continues to grow more urban every day, with more than half of the planet's population now living in metropolitan regions. As a result, the design of urban places has profound social and environmental consequences. People are attracted to cities for the opportunities they provide: jobs, entertainment, education, culture, and health services. Although urban life has many benefits, issues also abound: crime, poverty, pollution, homelessness, and health hazards. Exhaust from automobiles and from burning fossil fuels to heat and cool homes and for business and industry all result in respiratory infections and other health problems. Urban design should help to reinforce the benefits of living in cities, while minimizing the problems.

Throughout the twentieth century, cities served as the sinks for much of the planet's resources. Water, food, materials, and energy flowed into urban regions. Resources fueled industry and made our homes comfortable. Many governments, including the U.S. federal government, subsidized this flow. In the twenty-first century, we must reverse this trend and design urban places as sources for future resources. With its intention to affect the arrangement, appearance, and functionality of public space, urban design can do much to convert sinks into sources by replacing waste with opportunity.

In doing so, the concept of ecosystem services should prove useful. These are the natural services on which we depend on for life. Ecosystem services, for example, provide clean air and water, pollinate crops and disperse seeds, and help mitigate the extremes of climate. Twenty-first-century urban design will not diminish ecosystem services but, rather, will contribute to natural processes positively.

A growing number of urban design projects illustrate this potential. Brooklyn Bridge Park was designed to create new bird and marine habitat as well as to manage stormwater while providing new recreational opportunities for local residents (see Figures 11.1/Plate #15 and 11.2/Plate #16). In downtown Philadelphia, Andropogon Associates designed a plaza for Thomas Jefferson University over an underground parking garage. The plaza collects, stores, and uses stormwater and condensate from air conditioners of surrounding buildings (see Figure 11.3/Plate #35).

Turenscape created a waterfront park on a former industrial brownfield for the 2010 Shanghai Expo. The landscape of Shanghai Houtan Park was designed as a living system to include wetlands, flood controls, and reclaimed industrial structures and materials. The park includes new habitat for wildlife as well as water-cleansing features. During the 2010 Expo, the park helped accommodate massive pedestrian flows. After the Expo, it became a permanent public urban waterfront park for Shanghai (Figure 11.4/Plate #36).

And so we conclude with the promise of urban design. As we noted in the beginning, it is a field claimed by several professions but that rests more accurately at the ecotones between them. As an ecotone, urban design is built on each community at its intersections. Architecture contributes the knowledge of building design; landscape architecture, the design of open areas; and planning, an understanding of public policy. Law, engineering, business, the social and environmental sciences, history, and geography contribute as well. Ecology provides the connecting tissues that bring the disparate parts together in a new whole.

Most urban design books begin with a definition. We are unaware of one that ends with a definition. We would like to be an exception. For us, urban design

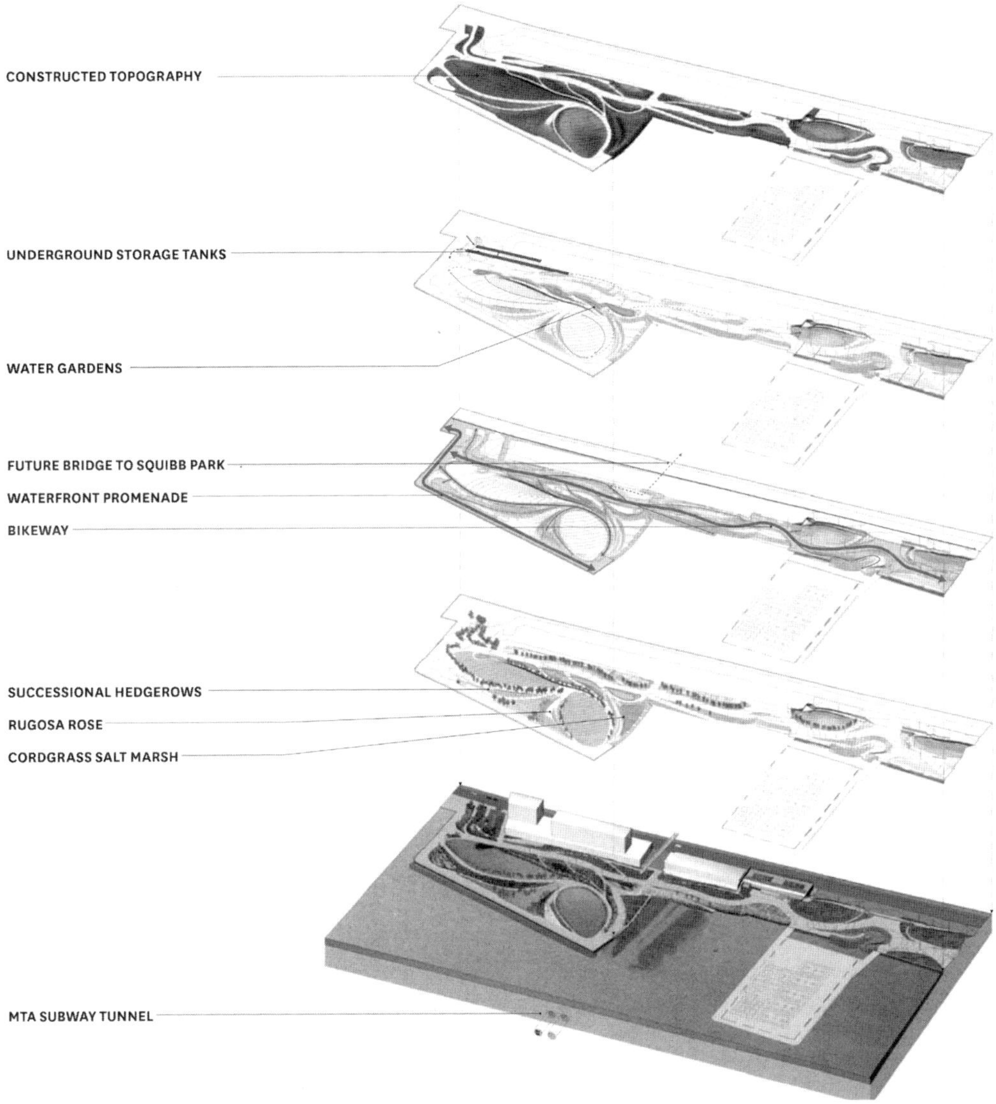

Figure 11.1 (also Plate #15) Axonometric drawing of Brooklyn Bridge Park systems at Pier 1, Pier 2, salt marsh, spiral pool, and upland areas, 2008. (Courtesy Michael Van Valkenburgh Associates.)

involves the artful and democratic arrangement of public spaces. This involves areas outside of private places we occupy for good portions of our lives, the areas where we are not private. As such, the design of such places requires great flexibility. Still, our road map may prove useful for that journey.

New ideas about city design and planning are necessary because urbanization

Figure 11.2 (also Plate #16) Spring in Brooklyn Bridge Park. (Photograph by Elizabeth Felicella. Courtesy Michael Van Valkenburgh Associates.)

poses significant social and environmental challenges. We live in the first urban century with more than half of the world's population living in urban regions for the first time. As the number of people in the world increases, the percentage of those dwelling in large city-regions is also expected to increase. The consequences of continuing to develop as we have in the past are clear: energy use and greenhouse gas production for buildings and transportation systems increase; water and air pollution spreads; valuable habitat and prime farmland are lost; and social issues, such as crime and poverty, are exacerbated.

Urban ecological design recognizes what should be obvious: people interact with other humans and with other species, as well as with their built and natural environments. The city is a human ecosystem. Through such design, urban ecosystem services can be enhanced. Ecosystem services can be defined as the benefits we receive from nature, such as food, water, and energy; regulating services, such as purification of water, carbon sequestration, climate regulation, waste decomposition and detoxification, crop pollination, and pest and disease control; supporting

Figure 11.3 (also Plate #35) A new plaza creates vibrant open space within Thomas Jefferson University's health sciences campus in downtown Philadelphia, 2009. (Courtesy Andropogon Associates.)

Figure 11.4 (also Plate #36) Shanghai Houtan Park. The contaminated water has been cleansed and made touchable after a long journey through the vegetated terraces and human-made wetland. The steel structure is made of recycled materials from the site. Various productive crops are used in the park that are harvested by the park managers and that attract wildlife. The park covers about 10 hectares (24.7 acres). It is 1.6 kilometers (1 mile) in length and 10 to 30 meters (33 to 99 feet) in width. It can cleanse 2,400 cubic meters (3,139 cubic yards) of contaminated water daily (even one drip of water takes one week to run from the source to the sink), and it had attracted thirty-seven bird species just one year after it was built. It has become a unique park for local people as well as visitors from all over the world. (Photograph by Kongjian Yu. Courtesy Turenscape.)

services, such as nutrient dispersal and cycling, and seed dispersal; and cultural services, including cultural, intellectual, and spiritual inspiration, recreational experiences, ecotourism, and scientific discovery. The pursuit of urban ecological design is critical as we address the need for cities to increase ecosystem services and to become resilient to future environmental challenges.

Bibliography

Abbott, Mark K. 1985. *The Master Plan: The Life and Death of an Idea*. PhD diss., Purdue University, West Lafayette, Indiana.

Abercrombie, Patrick. 1945. *Greater London Plan 1944*. London: Her Majesty's Stationery Office.

Ahern, Jack, Elizabeth Leduc, and Mary Lee York. 2007. *Biodiversity Planning and Design: Sustainable Practices*. Washington, DC: Island Press.

Alberti, Marina. 2008. *Advances in Urban Ecology: Integrating Humans with Ecological Processes in Urban Ecosystems*. New York: Springer.

Alberti, Marina, and John Marzluff. 2004. "Ecological Resilience in Urban Ecosystems: Linking Urban Patterns to Human and Ecological Functions." *Urban Ecosystems* 7: 241–65.

Al-Kodmany, Kheir. 2000. "GIS in the Urban Landscape: Reconfiguring Neighbourhood Planning and Design Processes." *Landscape Research* 25 (1): 5–28.

Alley, Michael. 1996. *The Craft of Scientific Writing*. 3rd ed. New York: Springer Science + Business Media.

Almy, Dean, ed. 2007. *Center 14: On Landscape Urbanism*. Austin: Center for American Architecture and Design, School of Architecture, the University of Texas at Austin.

American Institute of Architects. 2007. *Architecture Graphic Standards*. 11th ed. Hoboken, NJ: John Wiley & Sons.

American Planning Association. 2006. *Planning and Urban Design Standards*. Hoboken, NJ: John Wiley & Sons.

Arnstein, Sherry R. 1969. "A Ladder of Citizen Participation." *Journal of the American Institute of Planners* 35 (4): 216–24.

Anderson, Larz. 1995. *Guidelines for Preparing Urban Plans*. Washington, DC: American Planning Association Press.

Anderson, Larz T., William R. Klein, and Stuart Meck. 2007. "Plan Making." In *Planning and Urban Design Standards*, edited by Frederick Steiner and Kent Butler, 3–5. Hoboken, NJ: John Wiley & Sons.

Appleyard, Donald, Kevin Lynch, and John R. Myer. 1964. *The View from the Road*. Cambridge, MA: MIT Press.

Arizona State University. 2007. "Geographer's Computer Model Helps Predict Crowd Behavior." *ASU Insight* (May 25). http://asunews.asu.edu/files/20070525.pdf (accessed July 21, 2011).

Association of Collegiate Schools of Planning (ACSP). 2007. *Guide to Undergraduate and Graduate Education in Urban and Regional Planning*. 13th ed. http://www.acsp.org/sites/default/files/ACSP_13th_Edition_Guide_FullWeb_Printable.pdf (accessed July 28, 2011).

Bacon, Edmund N. 1974. *Design of Cities*. Rev. ed. New York: Penguin Books.

Baker, L. A., A. J. Brazel, N. Selover, C. Martin, N. McIntyre, F. R. Steiner, A. Nelson, and L. Musacchio. 2002. "Urbanization and Warming of Phoenix (Arizona, USA): Impacts, Feedback, and Mitigation." *Urban Ecosystems* 6 (3): 188–203.

Ballymun Regeneration Limited. 2004. *Ballymun Masterplan*. http://www.brl.ie (accessed June 16, 2010).

Banerjee, Tridib, and Michael Southworth. 1990. "Kevin Lynch: His Life and Work." In *City Sense and City Design: Writings and Projects of Kevin Lynch*. Edited by Tridib Banerjee and Michael Southworth, 1–34. Cambridge, MA: MIT Press.

Baradaran, Siamak. 2001. *The Influence of Deterrence Function in Large Scale Accessibility Models: Baltic Sea Region as a Part of Europe, GIS-Analysis of the Transport Infrastructure and Accessibility*. Stockholm, Sweden: Royal Institute of Technology.

Baradaran, Siamak, and Farideh Ramjerdi. 2001. "Performance of Accessibility Measures in Europe." *Journal of Transportation and Statistics* (September/December): 31–48.

Barnett, Jonathan. 1982. *An Introduction to Urban Design*. New York: Harper & Row.

———. 1995. *The Fractured Metropolis: Improving the New City, Restoring the Old City, Reshaping the Region*. New York: Icon Editions.

———. 2011. *City Design: Modernist, Traditional, Green and Systems Perspectives*. Oxford, United Kingdom: Routledge.

Bassett, Edward M. 1938. *The Master Plan: With a Discussion of the Theory of Community Land Planning Legislation*. New York: Russell Sage Foundation.

Batty, Michael, Martin Dodge, Bin Jiang, and Andy Smith. 1998. "GIS and Urban Design." London: Centre for Advanced Spatial Analysis, University College. http://www.casa.ucl.ac.uk/working_papers/paper3.pdf (accessed June 9, 2010).

BBC News. 2009. "The Problem with PowerPoint." *BBC News Magazine* (August 19). http://news.bbc.co.uk/go/pr/fr/-/2/hi/uk_news/magazine/8207849.stm (accessed July 13, 2010).

Beatley, Timothy. 2011. *Biophilic Cities: Integrating Nature into Urban Design and Planning*. Washington, DC: Island Press.

Beatley, Timothy, with Peter Newman. 2008. *Green Urbanism Down Under: Learning from Australia's Sustainable Communities*. Washington, DC: Island Press.

Benyus, Janine. 2002. *Biomimicry: Innovation Inspired by Nature*. New York: Harper Perennial.

Berrizbeitia, Anita, ed. 2009. *Reconstructing Urban Landscape: Michael Van Valkenburgh Associates*. New Haven, CT: Yale University Press.

Bevilacqua, Mario, ed. 2005. *Nolli, Vasi, Piranesi, Immagine di Roma Antica e Moderna* [Nolli, Vasi, Piranesi, Ancient and Modern Image of Rome]. Rome: Artemide.

Blyth, Alaistair, and John Worthington. 2001. *Managing the Brief for Better Design*. London: SPON Press.

Bosselman, Fred, and David Callies. 1971. *The Quiet Revolution in Land Use Control* (prepared for the Council on Environmental Quality). Washington, DC: U.S. Government Printing Office.

Brawne, Michael. 2003. *Architectural Thoughts: The Design Process and the Expected Eye*. Amsterdam: Elsevier.

Bristol Airport. 2006. *Master Plan 2006–2030*. Bristol Airport, Bristol, England (November). http://www.bristolairport.co.uk/about-us/our-future/master-plan.aspx (accessed February 14, 2011).

Buechner, Robert D., ed. 1971. *National Park, Recreation and Open Space Standards*. Washington, DC: National Recreation and Park Association.

The Builder. 1908. "The Systematic Study of Town Planning." *The Builder* 95 (December 12). http://www.library.cornell.edu/Reps/DOCS/liverpool.htm (accessed March 15, 2009).

Bürklin, Thorsten, and Michael Peterek. 2008. *Urban Building Blocks*. Basel, Switzerland: Birkhäuser.

Calatrava, Santiago. 2009. *University of South Florida Polytechnic, 2010–2020 Master Plan Update*. http://www.poly.usf.edu/Documents/CampusFacilities/I-4/Master-Plan/2010_MASTER_PLAN_UPDATE_091106.pdf (accessed June 17, 2010).

Calthorpe, Peter. 1993. *The Next American Metropolis: Ecology, Community, and the American Dream*. New York: Princeton Architectural Press.

———. 2011. *Urbanism in the Age of Climate Change*. Washington, DC: Island Press.

Calthorpe, Peter, Michael Corbett, Andrés Duany, Elizabeth Plater-Zyberk, Stefanos Polyzoides, and Elizabeth Moule with Judy Corbett, Peter Katz, and Steve Weissman. 1998. "The Ahwahnee Principles." In *Creating Sustainable Places Symposium*, edited by A. B. Morris, 3–6. Tempe: Herberger Center for Design Excellence, Arizona State University.

Calthorpe, Peter, and William Fulton. 2001. *The Regional City: Planning for the End of Sprawl*. Washington, DC: Island Press.

Cantrell, Bradley, and Wes Michaels. 2010. *Digital Drawing for Landscape Architecture*. Hoboken, NJ: John Wiley & Sons.

Carmona, Matthew. 2010. "Contemporary Public Space, Part Two: Classification." *Journal of Urban Design* 15 (2): 157–73.

Carmona, Matthew, Tim Heath, Taner Oc, and Steve Tiesdell. 2003. *Public Places–Urban Spaces. The Dimensions of Urban Design*. Oxford, United Kingdom: Architectural Press.

Carmona, Matthew, Claudio de Magalhães, and Michael Edwards. 2002. "What Value Urban Design?" *Urban Design International* 7 (2): 63–81.

Carmona, Matthew, and Steve Tiesdell, eds. 2007. *Urban Design Reader*. Oxford, United Kingdom: Architectural Press.

Carter, Don. 2007. "Urban Design Plans." In *Planning and Urban Design Standards*, edited by Frederick Steiner and Kent Butler, 10–13. Hoboken, NJ: John Wiley & Sons.

Centre for Addiction and Mental Health, Toronto, Ontario, Canada. 2001–2002. *Master Plan for the Centre for Addiction and Mental Health*. http://www.camh.net/News_events/Redeveloping_the_Queen_Street_site (accessed February 14, 2011).

Cesar Pelli & Associates and Balmori Associates, Inc. 1999. *The Campus Master Plan: The University of Texas at Austin*. Austin: University of Texas at Austin.

Checkoway, Barry. 1994. "Paul Davidoff and Advocacy Planning in Retrospect." *Journal of the American Planning Association* 60 (2): 139–43.

City of Nottingham, England. 2001. *Waterside Regeneration Interim Planning Guidance*. http://www.nottinghamcity.gov.uk/CHttpHandler.ashx?id=718&p=0 (accessed February 14, 2011).

City of Perth. N.d. "Point Fraser Redevelopment." http://www.perth.wa.gov.au/web/Council/Plans-and-Projects/Current-Projects/Point-Fraser-Redevelopment (accessed July 17, 2011).

City of Reykjavík, Department of Planning and Building. 2007. *Planning Vatnsmýri: Consultation Days*. http://www.vatnsmyri.is (accessed March 2, 2007).

Civic Alliance. 2002a. *Civic Alliance Planning and Design Workshop*. http://www.civic-alliance.org (accessed June 16, 2010).

———. 2002b. *Civic Alliance Planning and Design Workshop for Lower Manhattan: Executive Summary*. http://www.civic-alliance.org (accessed June 16, 2010).

———. 2002c. *Listening to the City: Report of Proceedings*. http://www.civic-alliance.org (accessed June 16, 2010).

Civic Alliance and Regional Plan Association. 2002. *A Planning Framework to Rebuild Downtown New York*. http://www.rpa.org/civicalliance/pdf/Framework0827.pdf (accessed July 28, 2011).

Clawson, Marion, and Peter Hall. 1973. *Planning and Urban Growth: An Anglo-American Comparison*. Baltimore, MD: Resources for the Future, Johns Hopkins University Press.

Congress for the New Urbanism. 1996. *Charter of the New Urbanism*. http://www.cnu.org/charter (accessed February 7, 2011).

———. 2009. *Canons of Sustainable Architecture and Urbanism: A Companion to the Charter of the New Urbanism*. http://www.cnu.org/canons (accessed February 7, 2011).

Corner, James. 2002. "Origins of Theory." In *Theory in Landscape Architecture: A Reader*, edited by Simon Swaffield, 19–20. Philadelphia: University of Pennsylvania Press.

Craig, Russell J., and Joel H. Amernic. 2006. "PowerPoint Presentation Technology and the Dynamics of Teaching." *Innovative Higher Education* 31: 147–60.

Creighton, James L. 1981. *The Public Involvement Manual*. Cambridge, MA: Abt Books.

———. 1992. *Involving Citizens in Community Decision Making: A Guidebook*. Washington, DC: Program for Community Problem Solving.

———. 2005. *The Public Participation Handbook: Making Better Decisions through Citizen Involvement*. San Francisco: Jossey-Bass.

Cullen, Gordon. 1961. *Townscape*. London: Architectural Press.

Cullingworth, J. Barry. 1993. *The Political Culture of Planning: American Land Use Planning in Comparative Perspective*. New York: Routledge.

Cullingworth, Barry, and Roger W. Caves. 2003. *Planning in the USA: Policies, Issues, and Processes*. 3rd ed. New York: Routledge.

Cullingworth, Barry, and Vincent Nadin. 2006. *Town and Country Planning in the UK*. 14th ed. London: Routledge.

Cuthbert, Alexander R. 2007. "Urban Design: Requiem for an Era." *Urban Design International* 12: 177–223.

Day, A. Robert, and Barbara Gastel. 2006. *How to Write and Publish a Scientific Paper*. 6th ed. Cambridge: Cambridge University Press.

Davis, Martha. 2005. *Scientific Papers and Presentations*. 2nd ed. Burlington, MA: Academic Press.

DeGrove, John M., and Nancy E. Stroud. 1987. "State Land Planning and Regulation: Innovative Roles in the 1980s and Beyond." *Land Use Law and Zoning Digest* 39 (3): 3–8.

Delafons, John. 1962. *Land Use Controls in the United States*. Cambridge, MA: Joint Center for Urban Studies of the Massachusetts Institute of Technology and Harvard University.

Design Trust for Public Space and City of New York Parks & Recreation. 2010. *High Performance Landscape Guidelines: 21st Century Parks for NYC*. New York.

Diamond, Henry L., and Patrick F. Noonan. 1996. *Land Use in America: The Report of the Sustainable Use of Land Project*. Washington, DC: Island Press.

Dobbins, Michael. 2009. *Urban Design and People*. Hoboken, NJ: John Wiley & Sons.

Duany, Andrés, and Elizabeth Plater-Zyberk. 1997. "Il lessico del New Urbanism" [The lexicon of New Urbanism]. In Danilo Palazzo (ed.), "Orientamenti di pianificazione ambientale negli Stati Uniti" [Orientations of environmental planning in the United States], *Urbanistica* 108 (gennaio-giugno): 67–69.

Dublin Docklands Development Authority. 2008. *Dublin Docklands Area Master Plan 2008*. http://www.ddda.ie/index.jsp?p=123&n=484 (accessed February 14, 2011).

Duhl, Leonard J., and John Powell, eds. 1968. *The Urban Condition: People and Policy in the Metropolis*. New York: Basic Books.

Dutton, John A. 2000. *New American Urbanism. Re-forming the Suburban Metropolis*. Milan, Italy: Skira Editore.

Envision Central Texas (ECT). 2003a. "Bastrop, Proposed Urban Design Guidelines." http://www.envisioncentraltexas.org/resources/Bastrop_Guidelines.pdf (accessed July 21, 2011).

———. 2003b. "Bastrop, Test Site Concept Plan." http://www.envisioncentraltexas.org/resources/Bastrop_Summary.pdf (accessed July 21, 2011).

———. 2003c. "Downtown Lockhart, Proposed Urban Design Guidelines." http://www.envisioncentraltexas.org/resources/Lockhart_Guidelines.pdf (accessed July 21, 2011).

———. 2003d. "Downtown Lockhart, Test Site Concept Plan." http://www.envisioncentraltexas.org/resources/Lockhart_Summary.pdf (accessed July 21, 2011).

———. 2003e. "Downtown Pflugerville, Proposed Urban Design Guidelines." http://www.envisioncentraltexas.org/resources/Pflugerville_Guidelines.pdf (accessed July 21, 2011).

———. 2003f. "Downtown Pflugerville, Test Site Concept Plan." http://www.envisioncentraltexas.org/resources/Pflugerville_Summary.pdf (accessed July 21, 2011).

———. 2003g. "East Austin Rail Corridor Featherlite Tract, Proposed Urban Design Guidelines." http://www.envisioncentraltexas.org/resources/EastAustin_Guidelines.pdf (accessed July 21, 2011).

———. 2003h. "East Austin Rail Corridor Featherlite Tract, Test Site Concept Plan." http://www.envisioncentraltexas.org/resources/EastAustin_Summary.pdf (accessed July 21, 2011).

———. 2003i. "ECT Scenarios Summaries." http://envisioncentraltexas.org/resources/3_Scenario_Summaries_v2.pdf (accessed July 21, 2011).

———. 2003j. "Executive Summary." http://www.envisioncentraltexas.org/resources/1_Exec_Summary.pdf (accessed July 21, 2011).

———. 2003l. "McNeil Junction, Proposed Urban Design Guidelines." http://envisioncentraltexas.org/resources/McNeil_guidelines.pdf (accessed July 21, 2011).

———. 2003l. "McNeil Junction, Test Site Concept Plan." http://www.envisioncentraltexas.org/resources/McNeil_Summary.pdf (accessed July 21, 2011).

———. 2003m. "Resources: Scenario Briefing Packet." http://www.envisioncentraltexas.org/resources.php (accessed July 21, 2011).

———. 2004. "A Vision for Central Texas." http://www.envisioncentraltexas.org/resources/ECT_visiondoc.pdf (accessed July 21, 2011).

Faga, Barbara. 2006. *Designing Public Consensus: The Civic Theater of Community Participation for Architects, Landscape Architects, Planners, and Urban Designers*. Hoboken, NJ: John Wiley & Sons.

Fisher-Gewirtzman, Dafna, Dalit Shach Pinsly, Israel A. Wagner, and Michael Burt. 2005. "View-Oriented Three-Dimensional Visual Analysis Models for the Urban Environment." *Urban Design International* 10: 23–37.

Flint, Anthony. 2009. *Wrestling with Moses: How Jane Jacobs Took on New York's Builder and Transformed the American City*. New York: Random House.

Fossa, Giovanna, Robert Lane, Danilo Palazzo, and Robert Pirani. 2002. *Trasformare i luoghi della produzione/Transforming the Places of Production*. Milan, Italy: Edizioni Olivares.

Francis, Mark. 2001. "A Case Study Method for Landscape Architecture." *Landscape Journal* 20: 15–29.

———. 2003a. *Urban Space: Designing for User Needs*. Washington, DC: Island Press.

———. 2003b. *Village Homes: A Community by Design*. Washington, DC: Island Press.

Fregonese Calthorpe Associates. 2003. "Survey Results." http://www.envisioncentraltexas.org/resources/SummaryofResults.pdf (accessed July 21, 2011).

Gaskins, Robert. 2007. "PowerPoint at 20: Back to Basics." *Communications of the ACM* 50 (12): 15–17.

Gastil, Raymond W., and Zoë Ryan. 2004. "Introduction." In *Open: New Design for Public Space*, edited by Raymond W. Gastil and Zoë Ryan, 8–9. New York: Van Alen Institute.

Gehl, Jan. 1987. *Life between Buildings: Using Public Space*. New York: Van Nostrand Reinhold. First published in 1971 as *Livet mellem fusene*. Copenhagen: Arkitektens Forlag.

———. 2010. *City and Town Life*. Washington, DC: Island Press.

Gehl, Jan, and Lars Gemzoe. 1996. *Public Spaces–Public Life*. Copenhagen: Danish Architectural Press.

———. 2000. *New City Spaces*. Copenhagen: Danish Architectural Press.

Gil, Efraim, and Enid Lucchesi. 1979. "Citizen Participation in Planning." In *The Practice of Local Government Planning*, edited by Frank So, Israel Stollman, Frank Beal, and David S. Arnold, 552–75. Washington, DC: International City Management Association.

Girling, Cynthia, and Ronald Kellett. 2005. *Skinny Streets and Green Neighborhoods: Design for Environment and Community*. Washington, DC: Island Press.

Givoni, Baruch. 1998. *Climate Consideration in Building and Urban Design*. New York: John Wiley & Sons.

Goldberger, Paul. 2004. *Up from Zero: Politics, Architecture, and the Rebuilding of New York*. New York: Random House.

Goodman, Robert. 1971. *After the Planners*. New York: Simon & Schuster.

Gore, Al. 2009. *Our Choice: A Plan to Solve the Climate Crisis*. Emmaus, PA: Rodale.

Grant, Jill. 2006. *Planning the Good Community: New Urbanism in Theory and Practice*. New York: Routledge.

Gustavii, Björn. 2003. *How to Write and Illustrate a Scientific Paper*. Cambridge: Cambridge University Press.

HafenCity, Hamburg, Germany. 1999. *Master Plan Concept for the HafenCity* (March). http://www.hafencity.com/en/overview.html (accessed February 14, 2011).

Hall, Kenneth B., and Gerald A. Porterfield. 2001. *Community by Design: New Urbanism for Suburbs and Small Communities*. New York: McGraw-Hill.

Hall, Peter. 1982. *Great Planning Disasters*. Berkeley: University of California Press.

———. 1995. "Bringing Abercrombie out of the Shades." *Town Planning Review* 66 (3): 227–41.

———. 2002. *Cities of Tomorrow*. 3rd ed. Oxford: Blackwell Publishing.

Hammer, Stephen, and Adam Hinge. 2009. *Battery Park City Green Building Guidelines*. New York: Center for Energy, Marine Transportation and Public Policy, Columbia University.

Handy, Susan. 1992. *Regional Versus Local Accessibility: Variations in Suburban Form and the Effects on Non-work Travel*. PhD diss., Department of City and Regional Planning, University of California at Berkeley.

Handy, Susan L., and Debbie A. Niemeier. 1997. "Measuring Accessibility: An Exploration of Issues and Alternatives." *Environment and Planning A* 29: 1175–94.

Hargreaves Associates, The University Architect. 1995. *University of Cincinnati: The Master Plan Update I*. Cincinnati, Ohio: University of Cincinnati.

———. 2000. *University of Cincinnati: The Master Plan Update II*. Cincinnati, Ohio: University of Cincinnati.

Hawkes, Peter, Sheila Cooper, Vincent Nadin, David Shaw, and Tim Westlake, eds. 1996. *The EU Compendium of Spatial Planning Systems and Policies*. Brussels, Belgium: European Union Commission, Directorate General for Policy and Cohesion.

Hillier, Bill, and Julienne Hanson. 1984. *The Social Logic of Space*. Cambridge: Cambridge University Press.

Hopper, Leonard J., ed. 2006. *Landscape Architecture Graphic Standards*. Hoboken, NJ: John Wiley & Sons.

Hou, Jeffrey, Julie M. Johnson, and Laura J. Lawson. 2009. *Greening Cities, Growing Communities: Urban Community Gardens the Seattle Way*. Seattle: University of Washington Press.

Hwang, Jie-Eun, and Kimberlie Koile. 2005. "Heuristic Nolli Map: Representing the Public Domain in Urban Space." *Proceedings of CUPUM05* 1 (July): 16. http://publications.csail.mit.edu/abstracts/abstracts05/hwang-koile/hwang-koile.html (accessed July 28, 2011).

Institute for Participatory Management and Planning. 1978. *Citizen Participation Handbook*. Laramie, WY: Institute for Participatory Management and Planning.

International Association for Public Participation (IAP2). 2007. "IAP2 Spectrum of Public Participation." http://www.iap2.org/associations/4748/files/IAP2%20Spectrum_vertical.pdf (accessed July 17, 2011).

Involve. 2005. *People and Participation: How to Put Citizens at the Heart of Decision-Making*. London: Involve. http://www.involve.org.uk (accessed July 2, 2010).

Irace, Fulvio (a cura di). 2007. *Renzo Piano. Le città visibili* [Renzo Piano. The visible cities]. Milan, Italy: Triennale Electa.

Jacobs, Jane. 1961. *The Death and Life of Great American Cities*. New York: Random House.

Jenks, Mike, and Colin Jones. 2010. *Dimensions of the Sustainable City: Future City 2*. London: Springer.

Jones, Allan M. 2003. "The Use and Abuse of PowerPoint in Teaching and Learning in the Life Sciences: A Personal View." *BEE-j* 2 (November) (electronic journal). http://bio.ltsn.ac.uk/journal/vol2/beej-2-3.pdf (accessed June 16, 2010).

Katz, Peter. 1994. *The New Urbanism: Toward an Architecture of Community*. New York: McGraw-Hill.

Kayden, Jerold S., Department of City Planning of the City of New York, and Municipal Art Society of New York. 2000. *Privately Owned Public Space: The New York City Experience*. New York: John Wiley & Sons.

Kolson, Kenneth. 2001. *Big Plans: The Allure and Folly of Urban Design*. Baltimore, MD: Johns Hopkins University Press.

Lancaster, Roger A. 1983. *Recreation, Park and Open Space Standards and Guidelines*. Alexandria, VA: National Recreation and Park Association.

———, ed. 1990. *Recreation, Park, and Open Space Standards and Guidelines*. Ashburn, VA: National Recreation and Park Association.

Lane, Robert, and Robert Pirani. 2003. "Sacred and Profane—Remaking Lower Manhattan." Slideshow presentation at a seminar organized by Danilo Palazzo and Giovanna Fossa, held at the Centro di Cinematografia Scientifica, Milan Polytechnic, February 5, 2003.

Lang, Jon. 1994. *Urban Design: The American Experience*. New York: John Wiley & Sons.

———. 2005. *Urban Design: A Typology of Procedures and Products*. Amsterdam: Architectural Press/Elsevier.

Leach, John Craig. 1992. *Planners and the Public: A Communication Gap*. Master of Environmental Planning thesis, School of Planning and Landscape Architecture, Arizona State University, Tempe.

Leone, Nicola Giuliano. 2004. *Elementi della città e dell'urbanistica* [Components of the city and urbanism]. Palermo, Italy: Palumbo.

Leupen, Bernard, Christoph Grafe, Nicola Körnig, Marc Lampe, and Peter de Zeeuw. 1997. *Design and Analysis*. Rotterdam: 010 Publishers.

Liddell, Henry George, and Robert Scott. 1940. *A Greek-English Lexicon* (revised and augmented throughout by Sir Henry Stuart Jones with the assistance of Roderick McKenzie). Oxford: Clarendon Press. http://www.perseus.tufts.edu (accessed August 22, 2010).

Lloyd Jones, Tony. 2001. "The Design Process." In *Approaching Urban Design: The Design Process*, edited by Marion Roberts and Clara Greed, 51–56. Harlow, United Kingdom: Pearson Education Limited.

Local Government Commission. 1991. *The Ahwahnee Principles*. Sacramento, CA: Local Government Commission.

Low, Nicholas, Brendan Gleeson, Ray Green, and Darko Radovic. 2005. *The Green City: Sustainable Homes Sustainable Suburbs*. Sydney: University of South Wales Press.

Luccarelli, Mark. 1995. *Lewis Mumford and the Ecological Region: The Politics of Planning*. New York: Guilford.

Lynch, Kevin. 1958. "Environmental Adaptability." *Journal of the American Institute of Planners* 24 (1): 16–24. Reprinted in Tridib Banerjee and Michael Southworth, eds., *City Sense and City Design: Writings and Projects of Kevin Lynch* (Cambridge, MA: MIT Press, 1990), 379–97.

———. 1960. *The Image of the City*. Cambridge, MA: MIT Press.

———. 1976. *Managing the Sense of a Region*. Cambridge, MA: MIT Press.

———. 1984. *Good City Form*. Cambridge, MA: MIT Press.

———. 1990. "The Travel Journal (1952–53)." In *City Sense and City Design: Writings and Projects of Kevin Lynch*, edited by Tridib Banerjee and Michael Southworth, 103–34. Cambridge, MA: MIT Press.

Lynch, Kevin, and Gary Hack. 1984. *Site Planning*. 3rd ed. Cambridge, MA: MIT Press.

MacKaye, Benton. 1940. "Regional Planning and Ecology." *Ecological Monographs* 10 (3): 349–53.

Madanipour, Ali. 1996. *Design of Urban Space: An Inquiry into a Socio-spatial Process*. New York: John Wiley & Sons.

———. 2006. "Roles and Challenges of Urban Design." *Journal of Urban Design* 11 (2): 173–93.

Malfroy, Sylvain. 2001. "Urban Morphology and Project Consulting: A Berlin Experience." *Urban Morphology* 5 (2): 63–80.

Mandoli, Dina F. 2007. "How to Make a Great Poster." http://www.aspb.org (accessed June 16, 2010).

Marsh, Chris. 2001. "Urban Design and Development Economics." In *Approaching Urban Design: The Design Process*, edited by Marion Roberts and Clara Greed, 105–17. Harlow, Essex, United Kingdom: Pearson Education Limited.

Marsh, George Perkins. 1864. *Man and Nature*. New York: Charles Scribner.

McGrath, Brian. 1994. *Transparent Cities*. New York: Sites Books.

McHarg, Ian. 1963. "Man and Environment." In *The Urban Condition: People and Policy in the Metropolis*, edited by Leonard J. Duhl and John Powell, 44–58. New York: Basic Books. Reprinted in Frederick R. Steiner, ed., *The Essential Ian McHarg: Writings on Design and Nature* (Washington, DC: Island Press, 2006), 1–14.

———. 1966. "Ecological Determinism." In *Future Environments of North America*, edited by F. Fraser Darling and John P. Milton, 526–38. Garden City, NY: Natural History Press.

———. 1969. *Design with Nature*. New York: Natural History Press/Doubleday.

———. 1981. "Human Ecological Planning at Pennsylvania." *Landscape Planning* 8: 109–20.

———. 1997. "Ecology and Design." In *Ecological Design and Planning*, edited by George F. Thompson and Frederick Steiner, 321–32. New York: John Wiley & Sons.

McHarg, Ian L., and Frederick R. Steiner, eds. 1998. *To Heal the Earth: Selected Writings of Ian L. McHarg*. Washington, DC: Island Press.

McManus, Phil, and Graham Haughton. 2006. "Planning with Ecological Footprints: A Sympathetic Critique of Theory and Practice." *Environment and Urbanization* 18 (1): 113–27.

Meeda, Bally, Neil Parkyn, and David Stuart Walton. 2006. *Graphics for Urban Design*. London: Thomas Telford Limited.

Mertes, James D., and James R. Hall. 1996. *Park, Recreation, Open Space and Greenway Guidelines*. Ashburn, VA: National Recreation and Park Association.

Meyer, Elizabeth K. 1997. "The Expanded Field of Landscape Architecture." In *Ecological Design and Planning*, edited by George F. Thompson and Frederick R. Steiner, 45–79. New York: John Wiley & Sons.

Morris, Smith Eleanor. 1997. *British Town Planning and Urban Design: Principles and Policies*. Harlow, Essex, United Kingdom: Addison Wesley Longman Limited.

Mostafavi, Mohsen, ed., with Gareth Doherty. 2010. *Ecological Urbanism*. Baden, Switzerland: Lars Müller Publishers.

Moudon, Anne Vernez. 1997. "Urban Morphology as an Emerging Interdisciplinary Field." *Urban Morphology* 1 (1): 3–10.

Moughtin, Cliff, Rafael Cuesta, Christine Sarris, and Paola Signoretta. 2004. *Urban Design: Method and Techniques*. 2nd ed. Amsterdam: Architectural Press/Elsevier.

Mumford, Lewis. 1938. *The Culture of Cities*. New York: Harcourt, Brace and Company.

Municipal Research and Services Center of Washington. 1994. *Level of Service Standards Measures for Maintaining the Quality of Community Life*. Report no. 31. Pp. 1–127. http://www.mrsc.org/Publications/levelservstandard.pdf#Page=20 (accessed July 28, 2011).

National Charrette Institute. 2007. "Charrettes." In *Planning and Urban Design Standards*, edited by Frederick Steiner and Kent Butler, 41–42. Hoboken, NJ: John Wiley & Sons.

Ndubisi, Foster. 2002. *Ecological Planning: A Historical and Comparative Synthesis*. Baltimore, MD: Johns Hopkins University Press.

Neuhart, John, Marilyn Neuhart, and Ray Eames. 1989. *Eames Design: The Work of the Office of Charles and Ray Eames*. New York: Harry N. Abrams.

New London Architecture. 2006. *Turning the Tide: Regenerating London's Thames Gateway*. http://www.rudi.net (accessed June 16, 2010).

Newman, Peter, Timothy Beatley, and Heather Boyer. 2009. *Resilient Cities: Responding to Peak Oil and Climate Change*. Washington, DC: Island Press.

New York New Visions (NYNV). 2002a. *Possible Futures: Draft for Discussion*. http://nynv.aiga.org/pdfs/Possible_Futures_LO.pdf (accessed September 5, 2010).

———. 2002b. *Principles for the Rebuilding of Lower Manhattan*. http://nynv.aiga.org/nynv_book.pdf (accessed September 5, 2010).

New Zealand Ministry for the Environment. 2009. *Urban Design Toolkit*. 3rd ed. http://www.mfe.govt.nz/publications/urban/urban-toolkit-2009/ (accessed July 17, 2011).

Niemeier, Debbie A. 1996. "Accessibility: An Evaluation Using Consumer Welfare." *Transportation* 24 (4): 377–96.

Nobel, Philip. 2005. *Sixteen Acres: Architecture and the Outrageous Struggle for the Future of Ground Zero*. New York: Metropolitan Books.

Nolen, John. 1927. *New Town for Old: Achievements in Civic Improvement in Some American Small Towns and Neighborhoods*. Boston: Marshall Jones.

Norberg-Shulz, Christian. 1980. *Genius Loci: Towards a Phenomenology of Architecture*. New York: Rizzoli.

Nordenson, Guy, Catherine Seavitt, and Adam Yarinsky. 2010. *On the Water/Palisade Bay*. New York: Museum of Modern Art.

North Ireland Planning Service. 2004. *Open Space, Sport and Outdoor Recreation*. http://www.planningni.gov.uk/index/policy/policy_publications/planning_statements/pps08.htm (accessed July 17, 2011).

———. 2005. *Parking Standards*. http://www.planningni.gov.uk (accessed May 5, 2010).

Oliveira, Vitor, and Paulo Pinho. 2006. "Study of Urban Form in Portugal: A Comparative Analysis of the Cities of Lisbon and Oporto." *Urban Design International* 11: 187–201.

Olmsted, Frederick Law, and Calvert Vaux. 1868. *Preliminary Report upon the Proposed Suburban Village at Riverside, near Chicago*. New York: Sutton, Bowne & Company. Reprinted in 1982 by the Wicklander Printing Corporation, Chicago, Illinois.

Owen, David. 2009. *Green Metropolis: Why Living Smaller, Closer, and Driving Less Are Keys to Sustainability*. New York: Riverhead Books.

Palazzo, Danilo. 1993. *Piani paesistici in Italia e pianificazione ambientale in Nordamerica. Un confronto per una riflessione sui rapporti tra discipline nella pianificazione* [Landscape plans in Italy and ecological planning in North America. A comparison to reflect on the relationship between disciplines in planning]. PhD diss., Venice Instituto Universitario di Architettura, Milan Polytechnic, Turin Polytechnic.

———. 1997. *Sulle spalle di giganti. Le matrici della pianificazione ambientale negli Stati Uniti* [On the shoulders of giants. The roots of ecological planning in the United States]. Milan, Italy: Franco Angeli.

———. 2002. *Master Plan dell'area dell'ex-macello a Monza*. Report. Milan, Italy: Department of Architecture and Planning, Milan Polytechnic.

———. 2011. "Pedagogical Traditions." In *Companion to Urban Design*, edited by Tridib Banerjee and Anastasia Loukaitou-Sideris, 41–52. New York: Routledge.

Panerai, Philippe, Jean Castex, Jean-Charles Depaule, and Ivor Samuels. 2004. *Urban Forms: The Death and Life of the Urban Blocks*. Oxford: Architectural Press.

Pennsylvania Housing Research Center, Pennsylvania State University. 2007. *Pennsylvania Standards for Residential Site Development*. University Park, PA: Author. http://www.engr.psu.edu/phrc/WhatWeDo/LD/download_publication.aspx (accessed July 28, 2011).

Platt, Rutherford H. 1991. *Land Use Control: Geography, Law, and Public Policy*. Englewood Cliffs, NJ: Prentice-Hall.

Popper, Karl. 1959. *The Logic of Scientific Discovery*. New York: Basic Books.

Porta, Sergio, Vito Latora, and Paolo Crucitti. 2006. "Centrality Measures in Spatial Networks of Urban Streets." *Physical Review E* 73: 036125-1–036125-5.

President's Council on Sustainable Development. 1996. *Sustainable America: A New Consensus*. Washington, DC: U.S. Government Printing Office.

Project for Public Spaces (PPS). 1984. *Managing Downtown Public Spaces*. Chicago: Planners Press, American Planning Association.

Regional Center Partnership of Somerset County, Regional Plan Association, and Lincoln Institute of Land Policy. 1999. *Somerset County Regional Center Vision Initiative*. Draft for discussion. http://www.rpa.org/1999/11/somerset-regional-county-cente.html (accessed July 17, 2011).

Regional Plan Association. 1998. *A New Life for Governors Island*. Draft for discussion.

Register, Richard. 2006. *Ecocities. Rebuilding Cities in Balance with Nature*. Gabriola Island, British Columbia: New Society Publisher.

Reilly, William K. 1973. *The Use of Land: A Citizens' Policy Guide to Urban Growth*. New York: Crowell.

Renzo Piano Building Workshop (RPBW). 2010. "London Bridge Tower. Project Description." http://rpbw.r.ui-pro.com (accessed May 7, 2010).

Resource for Urban Design Information (RUDI). 2009a. *A List of Courses in Urban Design and Related Subjects Overseas*. http://www.rudi.net (accessed June 25, 2009).

———. 2009b. *University Courses in Urban Design and Related Subjects in the United Kingdom*. http://www.rudi.net (accessed June 25, 2009).

Reykjavíkurborg. 2007. *Vatnsmýri, Reykjavík: A Call for Ideas*. http://www.vatnsmyri.is (accessed July 2, 2010).

Reynolds, Keith, Jennifer Bjork, Rachel Riemann Hershey, Dan Schmoldt, John Payne, Susan King, Lee DeCola, Mark Twery, and Pat Cunningham. 1999. "Decision Support for Ecosystem Management." In *Ecological Stewardship: A Common Reference for Ecosystem Management*, vol. 3, edited by William T. Sexton, Andrew J. Malk, Robert C. Szaro, and Nels C. Johnson, 687–721. Oxford: Elsevier Science.

Roberts, Marion, and Clara Greed, eds. 2001. *Approaching Urban Design: The Design Process*. Harlow, Essex, United Kingdom: Pearson Education Limited.

Rocci, Lorenzo. 1968. *Vocabolario Greco-Italiano*. 21st ed. Città di Castello: Società editrice Dante Alighieri.

Rodiek, Jon. 2005. "Human Habitats: A Focus for Design Education in the 21st Century." *Landscape and Urban Planning* 73 (2/3): 81–85.

Rodin, Judith. 2007. *The University and Urban Renewal: Out of the Ivory Tower and into the Streets*. Philadelphia: University of Pennsylvania Press.

Rogers, Millard F., Jr. 2001. *John Nolen and Mariemont: Building a New Town in Ohio*. Baltimore, MD: Johns Hopkins University Press.

Rogers, Richards. 2010. "Foreword." In Jan Gehl, *City and Town Life*. Washington, DC: Island Press.

Royal Institute of British Architects (RIBA). 1980. *Handbook of Architectural Practice and Management*. 4th ed. London: RIBA.

Royal Town Planning Institute (RTPI). 2008. *RTPI Accredited Degree Programmes 2008–2009 Academic Year*. http://www.rtpi.org.uk (accessed June 25, 2009).

Rydin, Yvonne. 2003. *Urban and Environmental Planning in the UK*. 2nd ed. New York: Palgrave McMillan.

Safe City Committee of the City of Toronto. 1992. *A Working Guide for Planning and Designing Safer Urban Environments*. Toronto: Planning and Development Department, City of Toronto.

Sale, Kirkpatrick. 1993. *The Green Revolution: The American Environmental Movement 1962–1992*. Ann Arbor: University of Michigan Press.

Salheen, Mohamed, and Leslie Forsyth. 2001. "Addressing Distance in the Space Syntax Syntactical Model." *Urban Design International* 6: 93–110.

Saliba, Robert. 1997. "The Prince of Wales' Urban Design Task Force in Lebanon: The Difficult Reconciliation of Western Concepts and Local Urban Politics." *Urban Design International* 2 (3): 155–68.

Samuels, Ivor. 2004. "Introduction to the First English-Language Edition." In *Urban Forms. The Death and Life of the Urban Blocks*, edited by Philippe Panerai, Jean Castex, Jean-Charles Depaule, and Ivor Samuels, vi–viii. Oxford: Architectural Press.

Sanderson, Eric W. 2009. *Mannahatta: A Natural History of New York City*. New York: Abrams.

Schneider, Kenneth R. 2003. *On the Nature of Cities: Toward Enduring and Creative Urban Environments*. Lincoln, Nebraska: iUniverse. (First edition, 1979.)

Schneider, Krista L. 2003. *The Paris-Lexington Road: Community-Based Planning and Context Sensitive Highway Design*. Washington, DC: Island Press.

Schwalbach, Gerrit. 2009. *Basic Urban Analysis*. Basel: Birkhäuser.

Scottish Executive. 2003. *Scottish Planning Policy Addendum to NPPG 17 Transport and Planning Maximum Parking Standards*. http://www.scotland.gov.uk/Publications/2003/03/16663/19411 (accessed July 17, 2011).

———. 2005. *Minimum Standards for Open Space*. http://www.scotland.gov.uk/Publications/2005/07/18104215/42175 (accessed July 17, 2011).

Sexton, William T., Andrew J. Malk, Robert C. Szaro, and Nels C. Johnson, eds. 1999. *Ecological Stewardship: A Common Reference for Ecosystem Management*. Oxford: Elsevier Science.

Shabecoff, Philip. 2003. *A Fierce Green Fire: The American Environmental Movement*. Washington, DC: Island Press.

Shirvani, Hamid. 2001. *The Urban Design Process*. New York: Van Nostrand Reinhold.

Shwom, Barbara L., and Karl P. Keller. 2003. "The Great Man Has Spoken. Now What Do I Do? A Response to Edward R. Tufte's *The Cognitive Style of PowerPoint*." *Communication Insight* 1 (1): 2–16.

Sides, H. Charles. 1999. *How to Write and Present Technical Information*. Cambridge: Cambridge University Press.

Simon, Herbert. 1969. *The Sciences of the Artificial*. Cambridge, MA: MIT Press.

Smith, Mary S. 2005. *Shared Parking*. Washington, DC: Urban Land Institute.

Sorrel, John. 2006. "Foreword." In Sarah Gaventa, *New Public Spaces*, 7. London: Mitchell Beazley, Octopus Publishing Group.

Spirn, Anne Whiston. 1984. *The Granite Garden: Urban Nature and Human Design*. New York: Basic Books.

———. 1998. *The Language of Landscape*. New Haven, CT: Yale University Press.

———. 2000. "Reclaiming Common Ground: Water, Neighborhoods, and Public Spaces." In *The American Planning Tradition: Culture and Policy*, edited by Robert Fishman, 297–314. Baltimore, MD: Johns Hopkins University Press.

———. 2011. "Ecological Urbanism." In *Companion to Urban Design*, edited by Tridib Banerjee and Anastasia Loukaitou-Sideris, 600–610. New York: Routledge.

Steiner, Frederick. 1991. *The Living Landscape: An Ecological Approach to Landscape Planning*. New York: McGraw-Hill.

———, ed. 2006. *The Essential Ian McHarg: Writings on Design and Nature*. Washington, DC: Island Press.

———. 2008. *The Living Landscape: An Ecological Approach to Landscape Planning* (paperback edition). Washington, DC: Island Press.

———. 2011. *Design for a Vulnerable Planet*. Austin: University of Texas Press.

Steiner, Frederick, and Dean Almy. 2010. "Conservation as Catalyst: Lady Bird's Urbanism." *Topos* 71: 74–79.

Steiner, Frederick, and Kent Butler, eds. 2007. *Planning and Urban Design Standards* (student edition). Hoboken, NJ: John Wiley & Sons.

Steiner, Frederick, David Pijawka, and Bill Kasson. 1998. *Sustainable Neighborhood Design for the Desert Southwest* (final report for the U.S. Environmental Protection Agency). Tempe: School of Planning and Landscape Architecture, Arizona State University.

Steiner, Frederick, Steven Windhager, Mark T. Simmons, Danielle Pieranunzi, and Allan Shearer. 2010. "The Salubrity of Sites." *Journal of Chinese Landscape Architecture* 26 (6): 13–18. (In Chinese.)

Steinitz, Carl. 2009. "Sketches from the Road." *Landscape Architecture* 99 (6): 78–83.

Strong, Ann L. 1990. "G. Holmes Perkins: Architect of the School's Renaissance." In *The Book of the School, 100 Years*, edited by Ann L. Strong and George E. Thomas, 131–49. Philadelphia: Graduate School of Fine Arts of the University of Pennsylvania.

Strunk, William Jr., and Elwin B. White. 1999. *The Elements of Style*. 4th ed. Boston: Allyn and Bacon.

Susskind, Lawrence, and Jeffrey Cruikshank. 2001. *Breaking the Impasse*. 13th ed. New York: Basic Books.

Sustainable Sites Initiative (SITES). 2009. *The Case for Sustainable Landscapes*. Austin: Lady Bird Johnson Wildflower Center, University of Texas at Austin. http://www.sustainablesites.org/report (accessed July 19, 2010).

Sydney Airport, Sydney, Australia. 2009. *Sydney Airport Master Plan 2009*. http://www.sydneyairport.com.au/SACL/Master-Plan.html (accessed February 14, 2011).

Syrinx. N.d. "Point Fraser Development." http://www.syrinx.net.au/product/key-projects/01-RE-point-fraser-development.html (accessed July 17, 2011).

Tadi, Massimo. 2007. *Timişoara 2020 Overall Vision: A Case Study*. Firenze: Alinea Editrice.

Talen, Emily. 2005. *New Urbanism and American Planning*. New York: Routledge.

———. 2009. *Urban Design Reclaimed: Tools, Techniques, and Strategies for Planners*. Chicago: Planners Press.

Tibbalds, Francis. 1988. "Mind the Gap! A Personal View of the Value of Urban Design in the Late Twentieth Century." *The Planner* 74 (3): 11–15.

Till, Jeremy. 2009. *Architecture Depends*. Cambridge, MA: MIT Press.

Trancik, Roger. 1986. *Finding Lost Space: Theories of Urban Design*. New York: John Wiley & Sons.

Treu, Maria Cristina (team leader). 1999. *Piano Particolareggiato per l'Area di Fiera Catena a Mantova* [Detailed plan for the Fiera Catena area in Mantova]. Milan, Italy: Department of Regional Science, Milan Polytechnic.

——— (team leader). 2001. *Documento Direttore per il Comune di Mantova* [Strategic plan of Mantua]. Milan, Italy: Department of Architecture and Planning, Milan Polytechnic.

———. 2004. "Un approccio ambientale alla pianificazione" [An environmental approach to planning]. In Frederick Steiner, *Costruire il paesaggio. Un approccio ecologico alla pianificazione*,

2nd ed., edited and translated by Maria Cristina Treu and Danilo Palazzo. Milan, Italy: McGraw-Hill Italia. First published as *The Living Landscape: An Ecological Approach to Landscape Planning* (New York: McGraw-Hill, 2000).

Tufte, Edward R. 2003. *The Cognitive Style of PowerPoint*. Cheshire, CT: Graphics Press.

Udall, Stewart L. 1988. *The Quiet Crisis and the Next Generation*. Layton, UT: Gibbs Smith.

UK Government. 2002a. *Assessing Needs and Opportunities: A Companion Guide to PPG17*. http://www.communities.gov.uk (accessed May 5, 2010).

———. 2002b. *Planning Policy Guidance 17: Planning for Open Space, Sport and Recreation*. http://www.communities.gov.uk (accessed May 5, 2010).

UK Government, Department for Transport. 2007. *Guidance on Transport Assessment*. http://www.dft.gov.uk/pgr/regional/transportassessments/guidanceonta (accessed August 30, 2010).

UK Government, Department for Transport, Local Government and the Regions. 2001. *Planning: Delivering a Fundamental Change*. London: UK Department for Communities and Local Government, London. http://www.communities.gov.uk (accessed June 16, 2010).

UK Government, Department of Environment. 1995. *RPG9a—The Thames Gateway Planning Framework*. http://www.communities.go\v.uk (accessed June 3, 2010).

United Nations. 2004. *World Urbanization Prospects: The 2003 Revision*. New York: United Nations.

University of Cincinnati. 1995/1999. *The Master Plan*. Update I: September 1995 and Update II: September 1999/2000.

———. 2003. *Signage Policy and Standards*. http://www.uc.edu/architect/documents/design/signage.pdf (accessed July 16, 2011).

University of South Florida Polytechnic, Lakeland, Florida, United States. 2009 (October). *2010–2020 Master Plan Update*. http://poly.usf.edu/Documents/CampusFacilities/I-4/Master-Plan/2010_MASTER_PLAN_UPDATE_091106.pdf (accessed July 16, 2011).

Urban Design Associates (UDA). 2003. *The Urban Design Handbook: Techniques and Working Methods*. New York: Norton.

Urban Task Force. 1999. *Toward an Urban Renaissance*. London: E & FN Spon.

———. 2005. *Towards a Strong Urban Renaissance*. http://www.urbantaskforce.org/UTF_final_report.pdf (accessed February 9, 2011).

U.S. Department of Transportation, Federal Highway Administration. 1983. *Calibrating and Testing a Gravity Model for Any Size Urban Area*. http://ntl.bts.gov/DOCS/CAT.html (accessed April 27, 2010).

Veal, A. J. Tony. 2008. "Open Place Planning Standards in Australia: In Search of Origins." School of Leisure, Sport and Tourism Working Paper 5. Lindfield, New South Wales: University of Technology, Sydney. http://www.business.uts.edu.au (accessed June 16, 2010).

Venturi, Robert, Denise Scott Brown, and Steven Izenour. 1972. *Learning from Las Vegas*. Cambridge, MA: MIT Press.

Wackernagel, Mathis, and William Rees. 1996. *Our Ecological Footprint: Reducing Human Impact on Earth*. Gabriola Island, British Columbia: New Society Publishers.

Waldheim, Charles, ed. 2006. *The Landscape Urbanism Reader*. New York: Princeton Architectural Press.

Wall, Ed, and Tim Waterman. 2009. *Basics Landscape Architecture: Urban Design*. Lausanne, Switzerland: AVA Publishing SA.

Wallace, David. 2004. *Urban Planning/My Way*. Chicago: Planners Press.

Walters, David. 2007. *Designing Community: Charrettes, Master Plans and Form-Based Code*. Oxford: Architectural Press.

Weller, Richard. 2009. *Boom Town 2050: Scenarios for a Rapidly Growing City*. Crawley, Western Australia: University of Western Australia Publishing.

Wilkinson, Paul F. 1985. "The Golden Fleece: The Search for Standards." *Leisure Studies* 4 (2): 189–204.

Yang, Pei-Ju Perry, Simon Yanuar Putra, and Meutia Chaerani. 2007. "Computing the Sense of Time in Urban Physical Environment." *Urban Design International* 12: 115–29.

Yeang, Ken. 1995. *Designing with Nature: The Ecological Basis for Architectural Design*. New York: McGraw-Hill.

———. 2006. *Ecodesign: A Manual for Ecological Design*. London: Wiley Academy.

Yin, Robert K. 2003. *Case Study Research: Design and Methods*. 2nd ed. Thousand Oaks, CA: Sage Publications.

———. 2009. *Case Study Research: Design and Methods*. 4th ed. Thousand Oaks, CA: Sage Publications.

Index

Figures/photos/illustrations are indicated by a " f " and tables by a " t ." The color plates are indicated by "p."